Warwickshire County Council

KCS 10/16			
2 3 JUN 2017			
Wigam 17			
Harrison 8			
21 AUG 19			

I0334862

This item is to be returned or renewed before the latest date above. It may be borrowed for a further period if not in demand. **To renew your books:**

- **Phone the 24/7 Renewal Line 01926 499273 or**
- **Visit www.warwickshire.gov.uk/libraries**

Discover • Imagine • Learn • *with libraries*

Warwickshire
County Council

Working for Warwickshire

0141436775

LOVE OF COUNTRY

Also by Madeleine Bunting

The Model Occupation:
The Channel Islands under German Rule 1940–45

Willing Slaves:
How the Overwork Culture is Ruling Our Lives

The Plot: A Biography of an English Acre

LOVE OF COUNTRY

A Hebridean Journey

MADELEINE BUNTING

GRANTA

Granta Publications, 12 Addison Avenue, London W11 4QR

First published in Great Britain by Granta Books, 2016

Copyright © Madeleine Bunting, 2016
Maps copyright © Emily Faccini, 2016

The permissions and illustration credits on pp. 337–339
constitute an extension of this copyright page.

Madeleine Bunting has asserted her moral right
under the Copyright, Designs and Patents Act, 1988,
to be identified as the author of this work.

All rights reserved.
This book is copyright material and must not be copied,
reproduced, transferred, distributed, leased, licensed or publicly
performed or used in any way except as specifically permitted in writing
by the publisher, as allowed under the terms and conditions under
which it was purchased or as strictly permitted by applicable
copyright law. Any unauthorized distribution or use of
this text may be a direct infringement of the author's
and publisher's rights, and those responsible
may be liable in law accordingly.

A CIP catalogue record for this book
is available from the British Library.

1 3 5 7 9 10 8 6 4 2

ISBN 978 1 84708 517 7
eISBN 978 1 78378 186 7

Typeset by M Rules

Printed and bound in Great Britain by T J International, Padstow

*Riches are what we find
in what is transient, perilous and oblique,
the random glitter of the sun and wind.*

IAIN CRICHTON SMITH, 'ABERDEEN',
NEW COLLECTED POEMS

Dedicated to the memory of three young men who fought in the First World War: my great-uncles Norman Kohnstamm (1897–1918) and Jack Kohnstamm (1898–1916), and their friend, my grandfather Maurice Farquharson (1899–1993).

Contents

JURA

Coire Bhreacain

Barnhill

Sound of Jura

THE PAPS

Feolin Ferry

Craighouse

ISLAY

Port Askaig

5 miles

ST KILDA

Stac an Armin

Stac Lee

BORARAIGH

2 miles

SOAIGH

Mullach Mòr

HIORT

Village Bay

DÙN

Stac Levinish

LEWIS/HARRIS

Butt of Lewis

LEWIS

Siabost

Barabhas Moor

Calanais

Timsgearraidh

Uig

Mangursta

Stornoway

Mealasta

Pàirc

HARRIS

Loch Seaforth

Rèinigeadal

Horgabost

Tarbert

Leverburgh

15 miles

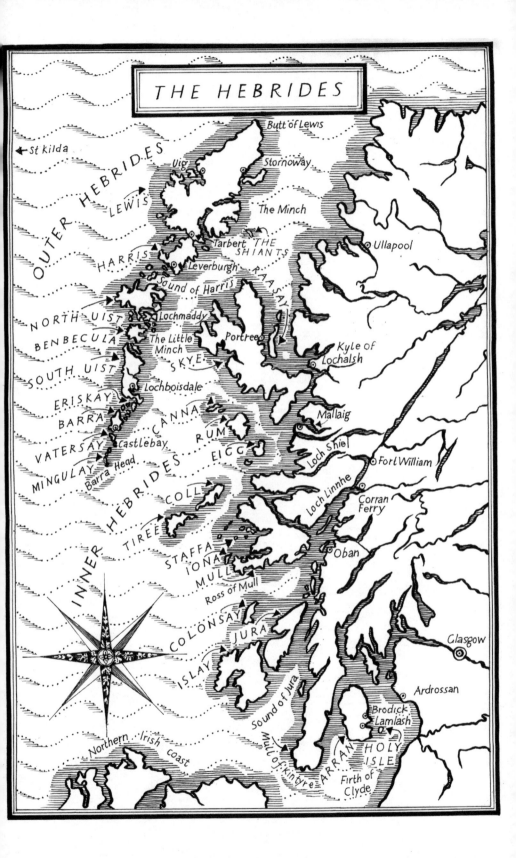

Illustrations

LOVE OF
COUNTRY

I

Taking Bearings

Tell all the truth but tell it slant
Success in Circuit Lies

EMILY DICKINSON, *POEMS*

I

At my writing desk in east London I look out over a series of back gardens, each separated by high walls. Beyond them lies the back of the parallel terraced street, and in a gap between, I glimpse the tall blocks of the new high-rise developments which have filled these old Victorian streets with newcomers. The neighbours' sycamore trees, heavy with ivy, crowd the sky into a small fragment. Accompanying the intermittent cry of the seagulls is the persistent hum of London's hungry heart, the roar of busyness, the diurnal tragedy of sirens, each a tiny jolt of anxiety. Down below in the house the washing machine whirrs on its frequent family cycles and the dog barks, waiting impatiently for a walk. Next to the kettle sit the insistent lists of shopping, of errands, of doctors to call, letters to schools, appointments: the management of family life.

In this crowded life, I plotted an escape. Beside the writing desk I wallpapered a big map so that my eye could slide from terraced brick to the wide spaces of north-western Scotland. I could trace the intricacies of its coastline, the long slivers of sea which cut into the land mass and, in return, the delicate peninsulas which stretch out into the blue. There were no smooth southern coastlines here of shelving shore and clean chalk cliff. This was hundreds of miles of dramatic volcanic convulsions, a history of forceful geology. My eye could wander over the hundreds of islands which speckled the blue spaces, the offcuts of rock left behind by this violence. Each offers its own character, its distinctive contour: the rounded diamond of Rum, Jura as pendant, odd-shaped Skye like a hand which has been run over, the fat lump of Mull with its long crooked finger pointing at tiny Iona. Beyond the Minch, the sea which separates the Outer Hebrides, this crazy geography of shapes becomes dizzying in a Long Island made up of dozens of islands and hundreds of skerries, where the land is as much of water, speckled with thousands of lochans. When my eye stretched to Harris and Lewis, it already seemed far from home, but there was more. Tiny specks far to the west, the last volcanic remnant before we tip off the continental shelf, leave Europe and head out into open ocean for the Americas. Here my mind landed, on a mark in the blue, and tried to imagine how it might feel to stand there and face out to the ocean, to be on that edge of home.

As I wandered back and forth across my map, skidding from island to island into bays and round headlands, I conceived a journey, or rather a series of journeys, which over several years could link together like worry beads on a thread, and which could carry me right out to the speck in the ocean. Intrigued by these islands and their extraordinary geography, fascinated by their separateness, each a world unto itself, I plotted the sequence of islands I would visit, a zigzag north-west through the Hebrides out into that blue space on the map. Out to the edge.

Many people travel in search of the exotic and the unfamiliar. I was travelling in search of home, in the hope of knowing and understanding where I could call home. Some look for novelty on their travels but I was looking for intimacy. Some look for the distance and space of other continents but I suspected there was plenty of complexity and astonishment under my feet in the damp Atlantic archipelago of the British Isles. This is my home country and it seemed to offer worlds far bigger than one lifetime could ever discover, but I wanted to try to know a few of them.

As I contemplated my map, and plotted my forays to the north-west, squeezed into school holidays, with children or friends cajoled into accompanying me, my personal pilgrimage to know home was overtaken by history, a nice irony for someone who has spent so much time studying the subject. It was no longer clear that I could call this north-west part of home at all. I could be a visitor but no more, I was told by the vibrant Scottish nationalist movement. I had stumbled into an old political quest on these islands to define home and where its boundaries lie. My route followed where my fancy took me and with this idiosyncratic approach I hoped to find an understanding of some of the certainties crowding the debate. I was in company with millions of others who were also – in their different ways – trying to know and understand home. I would listen to their journeys and hope they could help me on mine.

Home has been the most political of ideas: it has unleashed ferocious wars and terrible suffering, yet it is also the most intimate, a place where we find refuge and rest. No part of politics twists its way so deeply into our bone marrow. Everyone brings their own biography to the question of home. To understand why the map inspired my journeys and why these questions of home took me north-west to one particular frontier, the Hebrides, there are a few things in need of explanation, so that it is clear *where I am coming from*. A phrase which nicely captures how much geography shapes us.

Deep in the Highlands, twenty miles from the nearest town at Tain and sixty miles north of Inverness, two small rivers meet and there is a scattering of crofts. It is called Amatnatua, a Norse word for confluence, *Àmait na Tuath* in Gaelic, or Amat as it is commonly known. The Carron is a glamorous salmon river which forces its way through slabs of rock, plunging down waterfalls into dark pools flecked with cream foam and with glints of gold in its depths. Its roar reverberates around the valley. The Blackwater in contrast is dark treacle as the peat water meanders quietly between grassy verges.

At this confluence the dramatic contours of the north-west Highlands soften, opening out to the gentle undulations of Scotland's east coast. Here is the borderland between the two. The strath runs from east to west and the vegetation shifts in imperceptible degrees from luxuriant arable fecundity – wheat fields brimming in midsummer, verges thick with hogweed, willow bay and foxgloves – towards the rough harshness of the land in the west. Amat is a confluence of ecologies as well as rivers. Sheep graze in the green fields of the strath. Trees border the river Carron and cluster round the big houses on the shooting estates. But above the fields bracken and reeds take over, and up on the hills, bare of trees, rough boulders of ancient stone erupt from the heather. All the while the eye is drawn further west along the valley's single-track road towards the hills which rise in the distance. Every mile west takes you deeper into an emptied wilderness of ancient forest, a landscape of heather dotted by fir and birch where the timber of old trees has been whitened by sun and rain.

A compass is a tool used for navigation, but it is also much used for metaphor. Each point of the compass accumulates a weight of meanings, both cultural and personal. As a country, we attach significance to certain compass points: the south-west, the south-east, the north-east, the north-west. A compass point has even defined a political entity, in Northern Ireland. They can exert a compelling magnetism, so that one direction draws us back, again and again. They can become projects which we – sometimes unwittingly – pursue, and which can arrange our lives. From my father I inherited a legacy of the mid-twentieth century, when the North took a particular hold on the British imagination: W. H. Auden, Stephen Spender, Cecil Day-Lewis and George Orwell all headed north. J. R. R. Tolkien was reviving the study of the northern mythological sagas in Oxford, and published *The Hobbit*, perhaps the most famous export of Britain's fascination with the North. The writer John Buchan, author of *The Thirty-Nine Steps*, perceptively commented on the vogue: 'The North was where a man can make his soul or where the man who knows too many secrets can make his escape.' An apt assessment of a generation, burdened by the trauma of their fathers' war. Auden, who travelled in northern England and then further north to Iceland in the 1930s, wrote, 'One must have a proper moral sense about the points of the compass; North must seem the "good" direction, the way towards heroic adventures, South the way to ignoble ease and decadence. My feelings have been oriented by the compass as far back as I can remember. Norse mythology has always appealed to me infinitely more than Greek.'

On another occasion, the poet, raised in Birmingham, returned to the theme: 'Years before I ever went there, the North of England was the Never-Never Land of my dreams. Nor did these feelings disappear when I finally did; to this day Crewe Junction marks the wildly exciting frontier where the alien South ends and the North, my world, begins.'

In my family – and this personal geography sets in early – we also went north. Both born in London, my parents set up home in northern England, in Yorkshire, and every summer holidays we headed further north, as far north as my father could get. That still was not enough; once at Amat, there was another point further on, beyond our reach: the north-west, which lay beyond those hills on the horizon at the end of Amat's strath. This was where the road became a track and then dwindled to a path, which, with the aid of a compass and good map, took you thirty or so miles over the watershed to the west coast. Beyond that lay the Outer Hebrides, the furthest point of Britain's north-west. It seemed impossibly distant, and after I had discovered a tattered paperback of James Hilton's novel *Lost Horizon* in my early teens, his strange concoction of myth and fantasy transferred in my imagination onto those mysterious islands beyond the west coast. This became, in Auden's phrase, my 'Never-Never Land'.

Hilton had a shrewd insight into the emotional power of geography, how isolation has a dangerous romantic appeal, how horizons – which by definition we can never reach – both inspire and become the object of our most intense and unrealizable longings, whether for immortality, utopia or refuge from the world. Ridiculed as a deluded search for perfection, the prevalence of references to Shangri La in pop songs, hotels and tourist branding speak to the accuracy of Hilton's insight: that the twentieth century bred an intense but wildly ungrounded desire to find escape.

Every year the family van was loaded with a fortnight's worth of food and we drove through the night to get to Amat. My mother made beds for us five children in the back, and we slept as my father drove. We woke as the dawn broke over the Scottish Lowlands, and nothing else matched this intense childhood excitement of going north, certainly not Christmas or birthdays. We were heading to the Promised Land.

The experience of knowing a place as a child on holiday confers an astonishing power, quite disproportionate to the amount of time spent there. Our annual visit to Amat over the best part of ten years ensured it had a place in our family history as significant as our family home. We spilled out of the tiny two-up two-down croft. Five children ran barefoot across the fields and over the heather moors. Every day we swam in the icy-cold river Carron, gasping and shrieking in its small waterfalls and stumbling over the rocky boulders of the riverbed. The brave would dive and jump from the rocks. We knew the shape of that thirty-metre stretch of river intimately: every rock and patch of bank, the small island and the swinging suspension footbridge furred with pale-green lichen.

Some of the greatest pleasures to be had were visiting Willie and his sister Mary, who lived on the neighbouring croft. Neither had married, and we loved them for their gentle kindness and warmth. Willie had devoted accomplices on all the crofting tasks for the duration of our stay. We were there for milking in the early morning, fascinated by the rhythmic sound of the jet of milk hitting the pail and the slow accumulation of the steaming frothy milk. It looked so easy and yet when our fingers found the rubbery teats, our foreheads pressed on the cow's warm side, the jet of milk became no more than an intermittent dribble. We rode behind Willie on the tractor to turn the hay and then helped load the sweet-smelling bales onto the truck. It was unlikely that we younger ones were much help, but Willie seemed to enjoy our company, and we loved his. We would collect milk from Mary; she would take down the big jug from a shelf, remove the beaded lace covering which protected it from flies, and fill our jug. Later at home we would drink the strange-tasting unpasteurized milk, rich and creamy.

Every year Mary would invite us for tea and we sat in their sitting room – it was where I first learnt the word 'antimacassar' – in front of the lightest sponge cake I had ever tasted, hoping for a second slice. The highlight of the holiday was when Willie took out his fiddle for the ceilidh in the barn and we danced and sang with more enthusiasm than expertise. I went back in my early twenties when Mary had long since died and Willie was ageing. He no longer grew many crops, and most of his fields were turned over to sheep, but he was as warm-hearted as ever. When he saw me out walking in the early morning, he insisted on tumblers of whisky for breakfast. The ceilidh had become a regular occurrence and the family at the big house now came down to hear Willie's playing.

Even as a ten-year-old child, I sensed the tragedy of the history which lay around us. We scrambled over the ruins of old crofts, and could see how the presence of community on this land was retreating. Willie and Mary were the last heirs of an old tradition, since neither had children to pass it on to. A few miles from our croft was the church of Croick. We often ended up there on our rambles. I loved the smell of wood polish and I was fascinated by the collection plate, full of coins, which sat in the unlocked church waiting for donations. 'The Scottish are very honest,' my mother said to me in a voice of deep admiration. An empty strath, a large, empty church and a collection plate full of money; to a child this was deeply confusing.

Croick's handsome church told an old story eloquently. Built to a design of the great engineer Thomas Telford in 1827, it was a gesture of appreciation for the military service of the strath's many sons in the defeat of Napoleon. A large building with big windows looking over the valley, the long pews could seat a hundred people. Today there is one croft nearby and the old manse has been turned into a shooting lodge. Croick became famous in 1845, when the people of this area of Glencalvie were evicted to make way for sheep farms, less than twenty years after the church had been built for them by a grateful nation. A group took shelter in the churchyard and, to bear witness to their plight, they scratched their names and dates in the diamond panes of window glass. A reporter from *The Times* was with them and their story was carried in newspaper reports across the country.

Towards the end of my research for this book and the many journeys to the Hebrides it entailed, I took a detour and returned to Amat. I wanted to arrive where I had started all those years before. Memory proved a fickle friend. The hills had shrunk and the paths had disappeared. The single-track roads were better maintained, but the footbridges were ageing, long beards of lichen hung from their rusty wires. I was with my daughter, who was much older than I had been on those family holidays. We floundered through bracken and across sphagnum moss, brilliantly coloured blood red and lemon yellow. The light rain and summer warmth unleashed clouds of soft, vicious midges. We sweltered on in search of burns where I had once swum and bridges I vaguely remembered, accompanied by crowns of flies circling round our heads. The breath of the land hung heavy on this July day, pungent with peat and the scent of sun-baked rocks. Lingering over it all was its distinctive smell of rushing water, powerfully familiar despite the decades of absence. It brought back the memory of other smells long since gone: the honeysuckle which used to hang over the croft's front door, the sweet exotic scent of lilies in the porch of the big estate house (the first I had ever seen), the rich milk, the dead salmon we once found in the river, the clover in the hay and the diesel in Willie's tractor.

Amat had planted a sense of home and, in doing so, it satisfied the family desire to be north and held out a further dream of the west: it set the course. It was a meeting point of rivers and landscapes, a borderland where farmland met open moorland. It was not uncomplicated – what home is? It appeared to be a Promised Land, and yet was mute with trauma. It was riddled with contradictions I did not understand.

As an adult, holidays repeatedly took me to the north-west coast of Scotland to find that familiar unfamiliarity, feeling again and again the pull of this compass point. To Ardnamurchan when my children were small, and we sat with a new generation in another tiny croft, perched on the rocks on the most westerly point of the British mainland. From here, through binoculars, we contemplated the forms of Eigg, Rum, Muck and Canna and occasionally spotted the tantalizing outline of Barra far off beyond the Minch. I was passing on the tradition to my children, and I was still dreaming of journeys to this further horizon in the north-west.

II

Another aspect of the geography I learnt young has played its part. While the north-west called to the restlessness in me, a fragment of geological knowledge had left me unsteady. At about nine or ten, I overhead adults talking about how the mainland of Britain was tipping up. The north was rising and the south was falling. It was a tiny movement of a centimetre a year, but this did not register with me so much as the idea of the land in the north rearing up out of the sea, while the southern coast plunged beneath the waves. (I later learned that this glacial isostatic adjustment is the aftermath of the last Ice Age as the British land mass adjusts to the lightening of the load of glaciers now long since melted. It could last another 10,000 years.) At night this apocalyptic scenario played through my head; the ground under my feet was unsteady.

I tried to reassure myself that as Britain tipped up, Yorkshire would remain largely in place. The land mass of Great Britain was like a see-saw, and in Yorkshire we were at the pivot. After I followed the slide south as a teenager, York lost its centrality and I realized that, in terms of distance, the centre of Britain on the north-south axis is in the Borders. The Midlands are the middle of England and the term reveals the Anglocentricity of the national geography.

In my childhood nightmare I envisaged how the country's inhabitants might slide down the uptipped island to the south, and be left clinging precariously to the last chalky outcrops of the southern coastline, fearful of falling into the sea. This image has taken on a form of political and economic reality in recent years. London and the south-east greedily suck in people from the north and every other point of the compass; its appetite for their labour, talents and spending power is insatiable. The south-east of England is one of the most densely populated areas in Europe, well above countries with a long history of population density such as the Netherlands and Belgium. England has a density twice that of Germany, nearly four times that of France, and well over four times that of Scotland.

'The clue to many contrasts in British geography,' wrote the geographer Halford Mackinder in 1902, 'is to be found in the opposition of the south-eastern and north-western – the inner and the outer faces of the land. Eastward and southward, between the islands and the continent, are the waters known to history as the Narrow Seas; northward and westward is the Ocean.' The happy conclusion he drew from this is that Britain has the best of both: 'as liberty is the native privilege of an island people, so wealth of initiative is characteristic of a divided people'.

Tradition divides Britain diagonally, demarcating the south/east from the north/west, and imputes great significance to the contrast between these regions in the composition of British identity. For some, the tension between the two is creative, and Britain's ingenuity benefits from facing both the Atlantic and Europe. Celtic was the term coined in the eighteenth century for the Atlantic-facing arc of Scots, Welsh, Manx and Irish; the identity of the 'Celtic fringe' was repeatedly mythologized by, amongst others, the Victorian English and celebrated by the Irish poet W. B. Yeats in *The Celtic Twilight*. The Celt was defined as imaginative, dynamic and idealistic, while the Anglo-Saxon was reserved, pragmatic, cautious and industrious. With such distinctions has come condescension and, on occasion, racism. Twentieth-century critics have argued that the term Celtic fringe was pejorative, a description of where things frayed and thinned out. It was 'imprecise', writes Scottish historian Murray Pittock; 'the importance of cultural boundaries and identities are in inverse proportion to their distance from London'. Gaelic historian Malcolm Chapman maintains that the notion of Celtic was 'a projection, a construct based on oppositions of wild/tame, savage/civilized, idealist/utilitarian'. Since 1821 the population of the Celtic arc of the north and west has declined as a proportion of the population of the United Kingdom, from 46 per cent in 1831, to 20 per cent in 1911, to 16 per cent in 2014, due to famine, independence and emigration. This is a configuration of the country which we have been losing for nearly two centuries.

In the run-up to the Scottish referendum of September 2014, the Scottish National Party campaign subjected Britain, and the relationship of Scotland to England, to its most testing scrutiny yet. Politicians and writers framed the debate around the idea of 'losing Britain' and the notion has lingered on. A Canadian commentator, Stephen Marche, concluded on the day of the referendum that 'Britishness – as an idea and a way of being – has died in the process of debating it'. For some that loss can bring a profound sense of dislocation, for others it offers an overdue opportunity to reinvent the nation. I felt caught between the two: bereft and yet at the same time sympathetic to the enthusiasm of the latter. Was my journey to be elegy or part of the process of reinvention, or some combination of the two?

On the journeys I plotted on the wall in London, I would be going against the flow, heading north-west. That had been identified as a political necessity in 1955 by the Scottish nationalist John MacCormick: 'The new and spurious and artificial nationalism of Greater London requires a counterpoise if what we all unconsciously recognize as British is to survive.' As the political events unfolded in 2014, the ground was shifting beneath me. My route became a way to reflect on what was being lost and what new possibilities lay ahead. In the run-up to the referendum, writers, photographers and film-makers set themselves journeys as a way to gauge Scotland's self-questioning and explore the relationship between England and Scotland. It felt as if getting on our feet, literally, was the only way to keep balance, and to make sense of the moment.

Pilgrimage has a long history on this north-west littoral, and the journeys I chose in this quest would acknowledge these well-known traditions. I was curious about what pilgrimage might have offered the restless soul in past centuries. But I saw a difference: my pilgrimage did not lead me to a sacred site for spiritual benefit. Rather it was closer to the Hindu understanding of pilgrimage as a process of acquiring knowledge, in the sense defined by the philosopher Friedrich Hegel: 'the aim of knowledge is to divest the objective world of its strangeness and to make us more at home in it'.

Knowing my home country is a personal quest as well as a political one, deeply interwoven in family history. My parents were intent on bringing up their children with a clear understanding of two identities. Firstly, we were Catholics, which meant we attended Catholic schools, said prayers every night and went to Mass every Sunday. With all three requirements firmly in place, faith became the backdrop for our lives, transmission was by lived experience. The second identity called for more engagement from my parents: we were British/English (the two words were used interchangeably). My mother explained a precise ethnic genealogy to me of which I was very proud: we were one quarter Jewish, one quarter Irish, one quarter Scottish and one quarter English. By Jewish law, we were Jewish; by Catholic teaching, our baptism made us Catholic. Each grandparent represented a different heritage – Kohnstamm, Farquharson, McElearney and Bunting. My Jewish grandmother's was the most exotic, with links to an extended Jewish family in the Dutch West Indies and the less-often-mentioned German roots and lost German Jewish relatives. I was told that my much-loved grandfather was Scottish; only later did I understand that he had been born and bred in Southampton, and that his father and mother – a Farquharson and a Gordon, indubitably Scottish names – were north London, Hornsey born and bred. No matter, he was Scottish in family tradition. Out of this multi-ethnic mix, it was very important that we understood ourselves to be English and British. My mother insisted that we stood when the national anthem was played on television.

When I was on a French exchange visit, aged thirteen, barely able to speak a word, mortified with shyness and sick for home, I consoled myself by reading *Lorna Doone*, with its vivid evocation of the Exmoor landscape, and stitching a sampler I had bought in a village jumble sale: 'I made this in 1978 to commemorate the coronation of our dear Queen Elizabeth II.' The border was made up of flowers symbolizing the countries of Great Britain: the daffodil for Wales, rose for England, thistle for Scotland and shamrock for Ireland. It took hours of embroidering, and within a year I was acutely

embarrassed by its old-fashioned patriotism. It disappeared into the bottom of a drawer as my strangely anachronistic childhood tastes – closer to one born in the 1920s than the 1960s – were superseded by the discovery of pop music, make-up and boys.

Looking back, I see how that odd, ugly sampler was the declaration of a vivid understanding of nation accumulated from my parents: my mother's evocative stories of the Second World War and her evacuation from London as a child, my father's love of Winston Churchill and his nostalgia for his National Service in the Royal Marines. They invested more directly in our national than our religious identity. The latter they could subcontract to our schools, but the former was too important to leave to chance, precisely because we were Catholics, and because both parents had immigrant histories.

I took from this background a sense that our Britishness was a hard-won achievement not a birthright, a multigenerational journey in which individuals from very different communities had made common cause, married and raised their children. I saw in my 'Scottish' grandfather old-fashioned ideals of honour, principle and public service and his profound faith in the benevolence of British institutions; I saw in my Jewish grandmother a cosmopolitan ambivalence about England. I saw in my Irish grandmother an intense desire to belong to the English middle class. My English grandfather I never knew. Needless to say, my two sets of grandparents had nothing in common apart from a polite disdain for each other.

'I never felt it necessary to sacrifice one identification for another,' writes the American writer Saul Bellow. 'I've never had to say that I was not a Canadian. I never had to say that I was not Jewish. I never had to say I was not an American. I took all of these things for granted and in me you see a sort of virtuoso act of integration of all these diverse elements and I feel no particular conflict. I never felt any special discomfort over any of these elements. I've taken them all for granted because they are part of my history. If that history is mixed, scrambled, anomalous, difficult for any outsider ... that's not my fault ... I was faithful to what I was.'

Bellow talks of a 'reverence for all the sources of one's being' and it seems good advice for the complex legacy of my family histories and how they fitted into Britain. But in the 2014 referendum, it became uncomfortably clear that if nations were 'imagined communities', according to the thinker Benedict Anderson, then Britain had been under-imagined. Its understanding of itself in story, culture and emotion was thin; without the state project of empire, Britain was limping beyond its sell-by date. Monarchy offered a focus for some, but the institutions of parliament, the NHS and army were battered in prestige and morale. Britain had no narrative of nation beyond weak words – such as 'fairness' – used by politicians for their outdated claims to national exceptionalism.

While these questions of nation intrigued me, they had made few demands of me. As Anderson points out, the extraordinary feature of nationalism in the twentieth century was how it inspired so many people to die for it. In the graveyards of the Somme in France, only a few miles apart, lie three great-uncles. Two of them, from different sides of my family – one German Jewish, the other English – both aged eighteen, died in the Somme in 1916, a few days apart, separated by ethnicity, class, rank and faith, united by nationality.

In the last few years a box of letters introduced me to my great-uncle Norman, who died for Britain in 1918 at the age of twenty-one, two years after his brother Jack. They told of a passionate desire for glory on the battlefield which, over

three years of fighting, evolved into bitter fatalism and a
longing for English (sic) revolution. His mother and father
were German Jews, he was made British by his education at
Westminster and Cambridge, and by his death, fighting his
German cousins. He died for love of country: nation had come
before family.

III

'Like Samuel Johnson?' people asked when I described my
plan. There was a parallel, I conceded, though we took different routes: a Londoner who set out for the north-west, to visit
the Western Isles at a pivotal moment of intense discussion
of national identity in British history. Johnson's account, *A
Journey to the Western Isles of Scotland* (1775), and that of his
Scottish travelling companion James Boswell, *The Journal of
a Tour to the Hebrides* (1785), are celebrated, iconic in Britain's
understanding of itself as a new nation after the Act of Union in
1707 united England and Scotland. Johnson and Boswell were
not the first to write about Scotland's north-west – they were
following in the footsteps of a Scot, Martin Martin from Skye,
and a Welshman, Thomas Pennant – but their journey together
and their mutual affection and companionship provided a
new template for England and Scotland's relationship, despite
Johnson's infamous condescension towards aspects of Gaelic
Scotland. When they set out in 1773, the short history of Britain
had been dogged by rebellion in Scotland and resentment in
London. Beneath that lay a mutual suspicion rooted in more
than half a millennium of rivalry and conflict; historian Linda
Colley points out that between 1040 and 1746 every English
monarch save three had faced Scottish invasion or invaded
Scotland, or both.

Boswell and Johnson's journey was born out of curiosity and exploration. It could be said to reflect the Anglo-Scottish imperial collaboration which was to underpin the union for more than two centuries. Such was their appetite for novelty and knowledge, they disregarded comfort, willingly undertaking deprivation, a radical innovation for their time and no small feat for Johnson, then aged sixty-three and with a history of ill health. Voltaire reacted to their plan 'as if I had been talking of visiting the North Pole', wrote Boswell. In many places the roads were non-existent or very bad; it took a month to get to Glasgow from London and twelve hours from Glasgow to Edinburgh, and beyond these cities Johnson and Boswell had to walk or ride bareback on rough horses. On some occasions they ended up sleeping in a barn on straw.

Boswell wrote that they were curious to 'contemplate a system of life almost totally different from what we had been accustomed to see; and, to find simplicity and wildness, and the circumstances of remote time or place, so near to our native great island'. They wanted to see for themselves the natural phenomena they had known only through books. Johnson argued that ideas based on description 'are always incomplete and that at least, till we have compared them with the realities, we do not know them to be just'. They set out – like countless travellers, academics and journalists since – to see for themselves. 'I have now the pleasure of going where nobody goes, and seeing what nobody sees,' Johnson wrote.

Their travels had a particular resonance. 'We came thither too late to see what we expected, a people of peculiar appearance and a system of antiquated life,' wrote Johnson. This is a trope of the Highlands and Islands of Scotland: every generation has lamented loss, and believed they are catching the last fragments of a disappearing way of life. Loss has played a complex role in Britishness because Britain has also been the agent of so much loss, dispossessing and dislocating cultures in its imperial expansion. It is itself a country made out of the lost independence of other countries (Scotland, Wales and, some would add, Cornwall), and has used them to provide a patina of antiquity, and to claim that these losses were *necessary*. Now, conversely, a sense of loss spurs on nationalism – the Scottish nationalist Tom Nairn has written of a 'hidden river of loss' in Scottish identity.

When people likened the travels I was planning to Johnson's, I heard an implicit warning. Boswell wrote that Johnson, 'like the ancient Greeks and Romans, allowed himself to look on all nations but his own as barbarians'. Johnson attributed the degree of civilization he found in Scotland to the civilizing influences of union with England; he had a deep sense of superiority. But alongside this, there was admiration for the Western Isles. He was very impressed by the islanders' courtesy and he recounted with delight their sophisticated tastes in books, fine linen, silver and convivial hospitality. The reassuring message to his British readers was that this hitherto little-known Gaelic Scotland was part of home. 'A longer journey than to the Highlands must be taken by him whose curiosity pants for savage virtues and barbarous grandeur.' The Western Isles were the faraway nearby, accessible but still 'other', with a foreign language and a distinctive culture on the point of disappearing. This was the past, still present.

There is another precedent for my journey. Nearly two hundred years after Johnson, in 1937, another British writer set out for the Western Isles from London: the Northern Irish poet Louis MacNeice. He knew the power of the compass, as he explained in his memoirs: '"The West of Ireland", a phrase which still stirs me, if not like a trumpet, like a fiddle half heard through a cattle fair. My parents came from that West or, more precisely, from Connemara, and it was obvious that both of them vastly preferred it to Ulster. The very name Connemara seemed too rich for any ordinary place ... for many years I lived on nostalgia for somewhere I had never been ...'

MacNeice was commissioned to write a travel book on the Western Isles, but his visit was to prove disappointing, as he confessed in *I Crossed the Minch*: 'I went to the Hebrides partly hoping to find that blood was thicker than ink – that the Celt in me would be drawn to the surface by the magnetism of his fellows. This was a sentimental and futile hope. Once sitting by a river drinking beer with some Lewismen, while one of them sang a love-song in Gaelic, I felt strongly that I belonged to these people and that, for all I cared, London could sink into the mud. But the conviction of alcohol does not last.'

MacNeice was a warning to me that while my travels to the Hebrides might have been inspired by a desire to define and find home, that was not what he had found. He was a reluctant visitor and his account, published in 1938, begins with an appalling admission of his own ignorance: 'I am very sorry that I know no Gaelic. Before visiting the Hebrides, I did not realise that nearly all the islanders speak Gaelic, and that their language is integral to their life. Owing to my ignorance of their language I was unable to become intimate with the lives of the people. This book consequently is a tripper's book written by someone who was disappointed and tantalized by the islands and seduced by them only to be reminded that on that soil he will always be an outsider. I doubt if I shall visit the Western Islands again.'

MacNeice acknowledged that he had been looking for an escape from the demands of the metropolis. 'I thought it would be a rather nice rest after London – where people keep asking for lifts to Finsbury Park or to dramatise *Wuthering Heights.* Where tall women like Amazons walk into one's flat and throw over the tea table.'

MacNeice's longing for the West had engendered a restlessness. He grew up with the memory of a lost, cherished country, and this persisted beneath an appearance of being at home instilled by his elite English education. This was a Britishness I recognized, in which we half belong in many places and at the same time do not wholly belong in any. There is a distinctively British uncertainty about belonging which, at its best, makes us curious, tolerant and familiar with multiple identities; at its worst, it is insecure and self-aggrandizing.

IV

There was a grinding of the engine pulling up the anchor, the clank of chains in the belly of the ferry. Ropes were slipped from bulwarks and pulled aboard. The ferry eased its bulk from the docks of Ardrossan in Ayrshire into the churning waters of the Firth of Clyde. We were pulling away from the coast, with its shoreline rim of resort towns and golf courses. A ferry departure brings its own frisson of anticipation – a sense of separation, leaving behind familiar preoccupations and heading into the unexpected. The boat was busy for the short ride to Brodick on Arran, already visible across the water. Day trippers from Glasgow and seasoned hands heading home to Arran sipped cups of hot tea in a chilly breeze. The boat's café served up portions of chips and the smell drifted across the deck from the ventilation shafts. Under the bows slipped the cold grey water of a river which has bound peoples and lands across the globe. There are volumes of history in these tides and their currents. Ships, trains and bridges, manufactured beside these waters, have crossed oceans and continents, but my journey on the Clyde was a short one. The engines were already grinding to a halt, the gangplanks were going down and the doors to the car deck rising. I pulled my pack onto my back.

For all the brevity of the journey, Brodick feels indefinably different from the mainland: an air of holiday contentment blows with the stiff breeze along the seafront, where shops sell souvenirs and ice creams. I did not pause here amongst the holidaymakers. I headed to the bus which would take me down the coast to Lamlash, in search of another island: Holy Isle, the tiny teardrop sheltering in Lamlash Bay which looks back across the firth to the mainland, to Troon and Prestwick.

Holy Isle in 2010 was the starting point for my journeys through the north-west. It is not part of the Hebrides, being designated an island of the Clyde, but, as with the Argyll coast, it shares much history with the Hebrides, and it offered me important insights into the history of this Atlantic coast. A decade earlier I had visited several times and it was here that the idea first came to me to write about a journey north-west – it was a long time before I started work and the book would take me six years to complete. Holy Isle was also the starting point for another important and very personal journey in my life.

The island is just under two miles long and half a mile wide, its contour like a beautiful Japanese print: a conical-shaped mountain over the water. From the picture windows and neat gardens of the seaside villas which line the Lamlash shore, it appears very close and yet far away. It is only a twenty-minute boat ride, but there is always uncertainty about whether the boat is going out or when it might come back. The result is often unexpected stays in Lamlash, gazing across the water, guessing at the weather. Islands insist on patience, I learnt.

The distance between Lamlash and Holy Isle is not just this narrow stretch of water, but a juxtaposition of cultures. Lamlash is respectable gentility, a Glaswegian hinterland, serving as a retirement and weekend retreat. Holy Isle, after an interval of more than half a millennium, has reverted to a place dedicated to spiritual practice. Where the sixth-century Christian monk St Molaise once prayed and preached, now lamas from Tibet take his place. Purchased by a Buddhist monastery in 1993, it attracts a richly eclectic mix of pilgrims, some seeking enlightenment, some in search of themselves. It is ironic that in the 1930s the Scottish nationalist poet Hugh MacDiarmid lambasted the 'Tibetisation' of Scotland's west coast in a furious charge against the Anglo-British mythologizing of the Gàidhealtachd, as the culture, people and lands of the Gaels are known in Gaelic; he could never have imagined his criticism becoming reality.

Landing on the jetty at Holy Isle is to arrive in another world, with its diverse community of visitors, school teachers, American entrepreneurs, gap-year kids, herbalists and, amongst them, the shaven-headed monks and nuns who garden and build stone walls in the rain and wind, and chant their puja services. The lighthouse storeroom is now a shrine room, painted in the brilliant yellows, turquoises and scarlets beloved by the Tibetans. On my visits, I stumbled into conversations and encounters which struck me as outlandish, and admired the place all the more for its generous spirit: the French monk who described his mystical visions on his last day before silent retreat; the English monk I found moulding tiny statues of butter in a bowl of ice cubes, later to be burnt in the shrine room according to a book of Tibetan instructions; and the time when I was ill and was offered dried pellets of yak shit blessed by a famous Tibetan teacher.

I took the coastal path along the island and turned off where

a path climbs up the hill between the tall bracken of summer
to the cave of St Molaise. This is where he is said to have lived
and prayed. It is more like a shallow recess in the rock face
than a cave, with a sloping roof and one side open to the wind
and rain. Ten years ago I sat here on the muddy floor, littered
with sheep droppings, and listened to the sound of the waves
breaking on the rocks below and the rustle of bracken in the
breeze, and the idea took shape of a book, a journey, a labour
of love.

Grief-stricken at the end of my marriage, I had come to visit
and it changed my life. On top of Holy Isle's Mullach Mòr, with
its magnificent views over Goat Fell on Arran towards the Mull
of Kintyre, and back to the mainland over the Clyde in the other
direction, my path briefly crossed that of another pilgrim. I had
to leave the island the following day, but we exchanged names,
and back on Arran in the gardens of Brodick Castle I sat in the

sunshine and knew I would marry him and I saw in vivid detail our life together.

The island had brought me a husband. It had also captured my imagination in the damp cave of St Molaise. The story of how the island had come to be a Tibetan Buddhist centre covered a large canvas of global history. The admired young Tibetan monk, Akong Rinpoche, who undertook a perilous journey across the Himalayas to India to escape Chinese occupation, was spotted in a refugee camp and sponsored to come to Britain in 1963. He worked as a hospital porter before founding Europe's first Tibetan Buddhist monastery in the Scottish Lowlands. Akong Rinpoche's community bought Holy Isle to be a place of retreat in 1993. The history was full of implausible leaps of chance – not unlike finding a husband on the top of a Scottish mountain – and I learnt something to take with me on my travels north-west: that history on this coastline is unruly, and does not fit into an orderly narrative in which events march in an inevitable procession towards the present. Here, history gets recycled and ideas, stories, beliefs are reworked into new forms in the present. Where once Celtic monks sat in silence and chanted prayers, now Buddhist monks and nuns do likewise. On Holy Isle I was struck by the peculiar nature of history on Scotland's west coast, by how the local has absorbed and reflected the global.

Echoes reverberate across centuries. The twentieth-century journey of Akong Rinpoche to Scotland was the reverse of a similarly remarkable journey made by a Scot to Tibet in the late eighteenth century. George Bogle, born just outside Glasgow, was the first European to establish diplomatic relations with Tibet, and the first to study Tibetan culture and language. He led the way for a succession of Scots prominent in the Great Game, the diplomatic manoeuvring for power in Tibet by

Russia, Britain and China over the next two centuries. His vivid journals were later published in 1876 and helped to mythologize Tibet, inspiring, amongst others, James Hilton. China still cites Bogle's mission as evidence of British recognition of Chinese sovereignty over Tibet. From the Clyde to Tibet, and from Tibet to the Clyde, two journeys two centuries apart. There is no such thing as provincial on Scotland's Atlantic coast; for centuries, it has been one of the most globalized regions of the world. Successive waves of expansion, conquest, infiltration, settlement and emigration have been carried by the tides. Holy Isle's lighthouse has guided the ships in and out of Glasgow, the empire's second city. Now, in the lighthouse's old storerooms, the butter lamps flicker, casting a glow over the coloured paintwork and the rows of golden Buddhas. In the distance I could hear the waves crashing onto the jetty where provisions for the keepers were once unloaded.

On Holy Isle I learnt to watch out for the history of this seaboard, how it returns and reworks old stories. These places exert their own pull, making history as much as being made by history. However sceptical some might be, Holy Isle had proved a place of revelation – something which St Molaise well understood in the sixth century.

V

Standing on top of Mullach Mòr, where I met my husband, I looked north-west past the long finger of Kintyre – is it pointing at or straining to rejoin Northern Ireland? – and tried to decipher Jura, the next island in my journey in this complex geography of island, isthmus, peninsula and sea. I watched the boats in the Clyde far below as they headed up the broad firth inland, towards Greenock. As I knew from maps, the firth,

Love of Country

with the deepest coastal waters in the British Isles, splinters in several directions. One arm pierces deep into the Trossachs almost as far as Loch Lomond, another swings round to the east before dipping south under the Erskine Bridge to slip through Glasgow. East of the city, near Hamilton, like a ribbon unspooling, it meanders south through the hills of the Lowlands to its source.

The Clyde has played its part in many of the histories I will encounter on my journey north-west. The Clyde's towns sucked many Hebridean migrants into its huge maw of industry, teeming tenements, vibrant churches and heaving football grounds. For thousands more, the Clyde carried them on the first part of their journey on the emigration ships across the Atlantic and round the globe to Australia and New Zealand. The river shaped the experiences of millions, those who lived and worked along its banks certainly, but also many more around the world whose lives were transformed through the goods it made and sold.

That included my family – a piece of the Clyde's history, a Singer sewing machine, was central to the lives of four generations of women and still kept a cherished place in my family. In its honour, I once took a bus from central Glasgow on a quixotic pilgrimage. I wanted to visit the place where the sewing machine had been made. Over a century ago, Glaswegians had assembled it and packed it in a handsome wooden box. My journey was an honouring of my forebears' hours of labour with the Singer, and in memory of those wet afternoons as a child when my mother was making our clothes and the sing-song rhythm of the machine was the sound of home.

Our Singer sewing machine sat on a low table in the corner of the sitting room by the stove, and in winter both were almost continuously in use. My mother, the odd pin between her compressed lips, fed the cloth under the needle, her hands moving swiftly to pin, tuck and fold it. The sewing machine had once belonged to my great-grandmother and as soon as I was old enough I was using it to repurpose old clothes and make new ones. The click of the presser foot as it went down on the fabric, the rhythmic beat of the shuttle as I turned the worn wooden handle. Now I write instead, but the metaphors of stitching, embroidery and patchwork and the intimacy with fabric and its weave serve my sense of craft.

Sewing was the one thing my female forebears on both sides of the family had in common: the German Jewish wife of a prosperous businessman in Hampstead and, on my father's side, the seamstress in Charing Cross who, abandoned by her husband, raised eight children, and carried on sewing in the attic of her successful son's house well into old age. My mother remembered her grandmother turning to work on the Singer in the Second World War with her house full of evacuated grandchildren and Jewish refugees.

I had arrived at Clydebank on a rainy Monday morning. Once one of the world's foremost shipyards, more than four decades after it closed the vast site was an empty space of concrete slabs. When Singer opened in Clydebank in 1885, it was the biggest factory in the world, with 25,000 employees in a large complex of buildings. None of it remains, and only a pub and a railway station still bear the famous name. My mother's machine, with a gilt floral motif on the black body, has outlasted the building where it was made. The end plate bore a rich pattern of flowers and leaves. The aesthetic was that of a jewellery box, and the result was a machine regarded as feminine enough for women to use. The sewing machines saved hours of human labour, and millions of eyes from speedy deterioration; they transformed women's lives.

In Clydebank's new gallery, I fell into conversation with a volunteer guide. He had grown up in the town when it was a prosperous, proud place, bustling with people, and he wanted to bear witness to that past, to tell the school children and visitors of the ships built here and about the factory. 'The Singer factory had its own electricity generator and the waste water ran into the Forth and Clyde Canal,' he told me. 'In the warmth of this water, there were goldfish. They must have come on a ship from tropical parts. People caught them and sold them, and my parents bought one in a jilly jar for their children.'

As I sat on Mullach Mòr his story came to mind, offering a striking image to accompany the journeys I was embarking on – the wild goldfish travelling the globe and ending up in the grey Scottish waters which stretched below as flat as beaten metal on this quiet day I lay back, looking up at the bright cloud drifting across the bowl of pale blue, and reflected on the migration of these small fish and their unlikely resilience. I could smell the sweetness of the earth, the rough grass beneath my head and felt a small insect crawl adventurously along my bare arm. Turning onto my side, I looked towards Ardrossan on the mainland, where I left the car loaded with tent, warm clothes and books. In a few hours I would be on the road to Jura.

PART I

Imagined Geographies

Stories are compasses and architecture, we navigate by them, we build our sanctuaries and our prisons out of them, and to be without a story is to be lost in the vastness of a world that spreads in all directions.

REBECCA SOLNIT, *THE FARAWAY NEARBY*

2

Jura

Aborigine and Torres Strait islanders used the word 'country' to describe their profound connection to place. Country embodies the spirit ancestors who made the land, sea and all living creatures as well as the knowledge, stories and responsibilities tied to those places.

INDIGENOUS AUSTRALIA, BRITISH
MUSEUM EXHIBITION, 2015

I

Forty-odd miles as the crow flies from Holy Isle lies Jura. It drifts off mainland Argyll in a sea littered with small islands and skerries. Its smooth-edged bulk is impressive on the map, almost severed in the middle, where a big indentation on its Atlantic coast pinches the island to a narrow waist of land. It contrasts with neighbouring Argyll, whose coastline is in tatters, a succession of long skinny peninsulas. From the sea, Jura is even more imposing, the cliffs rearing up like a fortress from rocky shores. Above rise the three distinctive hills of the Paps, those softly rounded breasts of pale scree which look so compelling from every vantage point.

As the ferry ploughed along the east coast of Jura, there were few houses or trees on this wind-cleaned island. I glimpsed the single-track road twisting its way along the island past the tiny hamlet of Craighouse to its dead end at Ardlussa. From the ferry, Jura appeared to be near empty; it is one of the least-populated islands on the west coast of Scotland. 'There is nothing' is how people describe the place – an expression of either appreciation or horror. The writer Kathleen Jamie called it 'fabulous nothing'. Only slightly smaller than the Isle of Wight, which has a population of 133,000, Jura has under 200 inhabitants.

The ferry slipped into the narrow channel between dark cliffs, Jura on one side and the steep shoulder of Islay on the other, where it docked at Port Askaig. There is no direct ferry to Jura, so I paused on Islay for a few days before heading on to my destination. I had arrived in the Hebrides: 270 named islands, of which only forty-one are permanently inhabited, stretching 241 miles from north to south, with 2,500 miles of coastline.

Islay is a bustling place. It makes a fortune from its water and peat, and the stories it tells the world about them; it has eleven distilleries and a major share of Scotland's £4 billion a year whisky industry. The wind sweeps in from the Atlantic and whips across its undulating dunes, peat bogs and farmland. My family had joined me and our tent was perched on a dune. We felt every salty gust as the wind forced its way under tent flaps and through vents. When we built a driftwood fire to warm ourselves, it brushed smoke and sand in our eyes. Trips into Port Askaig, hunkered down in the Sound of Islay, offered welcome relief, but the break from the wind brought a dense smog of midges. At the inn we retreated indoors from the wildly optimistic tables in the garden, and peered through the window across to Jura. A brief interlude of golden sunshine transformed the Paps into a glamorous burnt umber which glowed against a fragment of blue sky, while my doggedly determined son stood at the end of the harbour fishing in a suffocating midge hood. He caught us two mackerel and the next day we grilled them for our lunch, in a thick smirr on the vast sands of Loch Gruinart with only the company of birds.

We packed up the tent to head for Jura. We were joining a pilgrimage route. Beyond the pier at Feolin where the ferry docked was a twenty-five-mile drive to the road's end, and then a seven-mile walk on a rough track over the moors to George Orwell's former home at Barnhill, at the northern tip of the island. As we landed after the short ferry trip, there was a sudden, miraculous clearing of skies. It was as if cataracts had been ripped from our eyes and the colours of sea and shore glowed with a sharp brilliance as we followed Jura's one road north.

A few miles along the coast, a rickety sign announced the gardens of Jura House. We took the path which meandered through a copse of short trees. Sunlight fell through the brilliant green of the oak leaves and splashed onto the thick lichen, which dripped from branches and wrapped round the tree trunks. We came to a half-open door in a wall. There was no sign of anybody. We pushed through and stumbled into another world. The walls created a sun trap and the cool dampness of the copse gave way to a rich cocktail of warm scents, and bees hovered over the herbaceous borders brimming with plants. Swathes of geranium, heuchera and anemone were punctuated by the tall spires of foxgloves and echium. The small brilliant-purple flowers of verbena bonariensis hovered on their slim stems and bronze fennel swayed in a breeze that was finally gentle. Pathways criss-crossed the elaborate beds and we were led under stone arches, from garden room to garden room enclosed by hedges or walls. Someone loved this garden and kept its exuberance within careful but gentle constraints.

Mixed in with the familiar plants was something more exotic: flavours of New Zealand and Australia, brought back – as I later discovered – from a gardener's plant-hunting expedition by camper van to Australasia: tree ferns, cabbage palms, bottlebrush and corokia. We saw snatches of brilliant blue sea where the garden sloped down to trees along the shore. Beyond the strait lay the cliffs of north Islay, swimming in the light haze as the sun burned the moisture-laden air. The excited voices of children and the splashing of water drifted up. We sat in balmy sunshine and our battles with the wind in Islay, on beaches thick with mist, receded. Here, we could feast our eyes on the flowers' hot oranges, yellows and pinks. There was even a tent with cheerful signs offering teas – though there was no one to serve them. We found a money box on our way out and left an entrance fee. We hadn't seen a soul. We left, dazed and enchanted.

Jura House garden was closed in 2011. The 12,000-acre Ardfin estate, belonging to the same family since 1938, was sold in 2010 shortly after our visit; the buyer, Greg Coffey, was an elusive Australian hedge-fund manager, a multibillionaire. Islanders were told that the garden was shut for renovation. The estate farm was also closed down and the livestock sold off. A planning application was submitted for a private eighteen-hole golf course.

There is more to be found on the internet than on the island about this new laird. Such is his skill as a financier, he has been nicknamed the 'Wizard of Oz'. Breathless news stories told of his fame in the financial world after walking away from one employer despite the offer of a £150-million deal to stay; the reports described twenty-hour working days, and a habit of taking his trading terminals with him on holiday so that he could check on his positions while his children slept. He had homes in Sydney, Switzerland, London and the south-east of England. At one point he was said to be earning £1.7 million a day. If true, the Ardfin estate, at £3.5 million, cost the equivalent of a few days' work: spare change for a man who reputedly retired at forty-one with an alleged fortune of £430 million. This is the stuff of twenty-first-century legends.

Coffey is not the first to be seduced by an island home; he is not even the first millionaire to buy a chunk of Jura. The island has been associated for decades with the Astor family, scions of the fabulously wealthy American Waldorf dynasty, and in particular with the former *Observer* newspaper editor, David Astor. The Conservative prime minister David Cameron has married into the Astor family and visits his father-in-law's estate for family holidays, a reminder of the persistence of Anglo-Scottish privilege amongst the British elite. Islands are a symbol of luxury amongst the global super-rich and Jura offers plenty of privacy and abundant space – acres and acres of 'fabulous nothing'. For a century, Jura has been an odd anomaly: remote but, as the crow flies, well under a hundred miles from Glasgow and Edinburgh; sparsely populated and yet associated with periodic influxes of the powerful, wealthy and glamorous, in search of space and privacy. Appropriately, one of the most bizarre artistic statements about wealth was made in Jura in 1994, when two members of a music band, The KLF, filmed themselves burning £1 million in banknotes in a disused boathouse at Ardfin. Half-burnt £50 notes were washed up on the shore in the following weeks. A screening of the film at Jura's village hall caused outrage amongst islanders; they needed money for repairs to the roof of the hall.

The seventeenth-century predecessors of these wealthy and glamorous residents were a Gaelic population a thousand strong. Martin Martin, the famous chronicler of the Hebrides, described them in 1703 as living in 'perhaps the wholesomest plot of ground either in the isles or continent of Scotland'. It is not a description that many since have been able to recognize; the population was decimated by successive waves of emigration as islanders gave up the struggle of making Jura's harsh landscape productive (it is claimed that there were no forced evictions). Ever since, the wide tracts of moorland have been used for shooting and the lochs for fishing; much of the island is unreachable by road or track. Deer vastly outnumber human inhabitants. The Atlantic coast is uninhabited now – although the rich sprinkling of Gaelic names suggests this was not always the case.

Orwell heard of Jura from his editor, David Astor, who regaled him with stories of its beauty and fishing – irresistible to the enthusiastic angler. Orwell, chafing at the restrictions and privations of wartime London, wrote in his diary in 1940, 'thinking always of my island in the Hebrides'. He had to wait until 1946 to make the journey, and it turned out to be a melancholy pilgrimage in the aftermath of the deaths of his mother, wife and a sister within the space of three years. The laird's wife in north Jura remembered Orwell's arrival: a 'sad and lonely man', who 'looked as if he had been through a great deal'. For his part, Orwell was enraptured: 'these islands are one of the most beautiful parts of the British Isles and largely uninhabited'. He added, 'Of course it rains all the time but if one takes that for granted, it doesn't seem to matter.'

II

An Australian hedge-fund manager, a second-generation American immigrant millionaire and a penniless English writer have all been seduced by the bleak grandeur of Jura over the last century, and between these disparate characters we glimpse the multifaceted history of one of Britain's cherished beliefs about its geography. It considers itself an island and is fascinated by other islands. Jura and her colourful cast of owners and tenants illustrates how islands have been used as places of prestige and status, as well as of insight and creative solitude.

Britain's understanding of itself – its identity and its place in the world – is deeply rooted in being an island. From this islophile geography has flowed political principles, cultural preoccupations and economic and imperial strategies. But it is not strictly true: Great Britain is not an island; it is made up of at least five thousand islands, around 130 of which are inhabited. It includes several groups of islands, such as the Isles of Scilly, the Hebrides, Orkney and Shetland, and is part of an archipelago known as the British Isles. The political entity of the United Kingdom and Northern Ireland covers the biggest of these islands – Britain – and part of the second biggest – Ireland. But this geographical reality has often been ignored, because *island*, in the singular, brings with it the attractive characteristics of inviolability, steadfastness and detachment. As one clergyman put it in a sermon praising the Act of Union with Scotland of 1707, 'we are fenced in with a wall which knows no master but God only'. Even more erroneously, England is described as an island. Martin Amis wrote a television essay on England in 2014, and the voiceover began with images of waves pounding chalk cliffs and the quintessential English mistake: 'England is an island nation.' England in fact shares its island with other nations – Scotland and Wales – yet the language of sharing, of being part of an archipelago, has not featured in the English nation's self-image. The cherished trope of 'island nation' reveals how Britain slimmed down both its islands and its nations. *Our Island Story: A History of England for Boys and Girls* (published in 1905) was a popular children's history for several generations; the Conservative prime minister David Cameron, raised in the 1970s, cited it as his favourite childhood book. It inspired his riposte to an alleged put-down by the Russians in 2013 about the UK being a 'small island', when he launched into a stirring defence of Britain as an island of principle, invention and economic success. Cameron hastily remembered to clarify his theme by adding, 'For the people who live in Northern Ireland, I should say we are not just an island, we are a collection of islands. I don't want anyone in Shetland or Orkney to feel left out by this.' Such are the tangles of our history and geography that trap our politicians.

There is a long-standing tradition of loving islands in the cultures of these island nations. In *Utopia* the sixteenth-century philosopher and statesman Sir Thomas More wrote how King Utopos created an island from an isthmus by digging a channel fifteen miles wide. Britain's detachment from continental Europe brought a degree of protection from invasion, and it was seen as God's geographical blessing for a chosen, favoured people. William Shakespeare, a Midlander, bequeathed a trove of vivid images of England in John of Gaunt's speech in *Richard II*:

> *This fortress built by Nature for herself*
> *Against infection and the hand of war,*
> *This happy breed of men, this little world,*
> *This precious stone set in the silver sea,*
> *Which serves it in the office of a wall,*
> *Or as a moat defensive to a house,*
> *Against the envy of less happier lands,*
> *This blessed plot, this earth, this realm, this England.*

It was a dream of 'this little world', of the island set apart, which represented a happier order of society, a 'blessed plot'. But there has also been an English ambivalence about islands and how they can encourage introversion; in a comparably famous passage, the seventeenth-century poet John Donne warned of the dangers of separation when he used the metaphor of island in his *Meditation XVII*: 'No man is an island, entire of itself, every man is a piece of the continent, a part of the main.'

In the eighteenth century, after the 1707 Act of Union with Scotland, the island theme became a unionist project for reform and progress. Daniel Defoe, a unionist, entitled his book of journeys in 1724–7 *A Tour Thro' the Whole Island of Great Britain*, a title which made clear its political commitment to the island now made whole. In Defoe's descriptions, Britain was a place of energetic activity, reordered for building, farming and hunting; it was to be 'improved', a term which became deeply political in Scotland. He developed this theme in his novel *Robinson Crusoe*, in which the tropical island was 'virgin land' to be tamed and harnessed in order to make it productive. Crusoe made tools, farmed and built a fortified estate with a town house and a country retreat in a story of ceaseless industry. He also prayed and read his Bible. Crusoe established dominance over the island's one inhabitant, Man Friday, who became his servant. It was a manifesto for empire, and articulated a model of Protestant Christian piety which owed something to the New Testament teaching to be 'in the world but not of the world'. The island, set apart, both expressed and offered spiritual advantages. Literary critic Peter Conrad takes the significance of Defoe's Crusoe even further, arguing that this was where the modern idea of the self was first given shape. Crusoe was the template for individual agency and its capacity to order the world.

When Johnson and Boswell set off to discover Britain's unknown north in Scotland, they headed for its islands. Their choice of journey reflected this British fascination, and both journals describe the abundance of islands recently brought within reach by the advances of eighteenth-century road building. They were close enough to visit, far enough away to excite curiosity. Both Johnson and Boswell were intrigued by the distinctive character of the islands they visited. They indulged their Crusoe-style fantasies, as Boswell recounted when they passed Scalpay, off Skye: 'Dr Johnson proposed that he and I should buy it and found a good school, and an episcopal church, and have a printing press where he would print all the Erse [Gaelic] that could be found.'

Johnson was enchanted by the island of Raasay, east of Skye: 'without, is the rough ocean and the rocky land, the beating billows and the howling storm; within is plenty and elegance, beauty and gaiety, the song and the dance'. On another occasion, Johnson expanded on what he would do if he were given the island of Isa in Loch Dunvegan. 'Dr Johnson liked the idea and talked of how he would build a house there, how he would fortify it, how he would have cannon, how he would plant, how he would sally out and take the isle of Muck, and then he laughed with uncommon glee and could hardly leave off,' Boswell recounted.

But within a few pages such mirth and enthusiasm had given way to its opposite when bad weather delayed their journey. Dr Johnson complained to Boswell that 'it would require great resignation to live in one of these islands. If you were shut up here, your own thoughts would torment you.' Boswell agreed, describing how 'we were in a strange state of abstraction from the world'. Johnson wrote of the danger of brooding when stranded on an island: 'the phantoms which haunt a desert are want and misery and danger: the evils of dereliction rush upon the thoughts; man is made unwillingly acquainted with his own weakness'. At another point, Johnson irritably commented, 'I want to be on the mainland and go on with existence. This is a waste of life.' Islands can be places of delightful retreat and of maddening frustration; heaven or hell.

In British literature, islands emerge as places of particular power. They offer magic, intrigue and adventure as well as damnation. *Treasure Island, Peter Pan, Swallows and Amazons* and *Lord of the Flies* are all set on islands. It is significant that three of these authors – Robert Louis Stevenson, J. M. Barrie and Arthur Ransome – spent formative periods of time in the Hebrides. 'Islands we beheld in plenty but they were of "such stuff as dreams are made on" and vanished in a wink,' wrote Stevenson from the South Pacific, quoting *The Tempest*, but he could have been writing about his boyhood summers in the Hebrides. He based Treasure Island on the small island of Erraid off south-west Mull.

Islands have been central to the British imagination and it went beyond fiction. Islands proved to be the key to Charles Darwin's discovery of the scientific theory of evolution. His voyage in 1831 aboard the *Beagle* circled the globe by way of a sequence of archipelagos, including the Cape Verde islands, the Falklands and crucially the Galapagos, before crossing the Pacific via Tahiti to New Zealand, and then back home past the Cocos Islands and Mauritius. For a seafaring nation, islands are a welcome refuge, they have some familiarity, but they also threaten stagnation and stasis. The word *insular* is pejorative. The British did, after all, use islands for prisons. Napoleon was sent first to the Mediterranean island of Elba then to Saint Helena in the South Atlantic.

For the best part of three hundred years, islands were also an imperial strategy. From Malta, Cyprus and Manhattan, to Sri Lanka, Singapore, Hong Kong and the Solomon Islands, Britain built an empire out of islands. This imperial preoccupation lasted well into the twentieth century. The claiming of Rockall in 1955, an Atlantic stack more than two hundred miles off the Scottish coast, probably counts as one of the most quixotic land grabs (one still disputed by Ireland, Iceland and Denmark), not to mention the Falklands War in 1982.

Some island-lovers want to do more than visit; they want to live out their own Robinson Crusoe dream and create their own 'blessed plot'. The Astors and the Australian billionaire on Jura were the first intimation of this recurrent theme on my journey north-west through the Hebrides: flamboyant, sometimes eccentric islophiles went to extraordinary lengths, at huge cost, to create their 'little world' on remote islands. Throughout the nineteenth century, mansions and grand estates were built in the Hebrides. Perhaps one of the most remote and compelling is that of the Dundee linen manufacturer Erskine Beveridge, who sank a handsome portion of his family fortune into a house, long since a ruin, on the tidal island of Vallay off the coast of North Uist in the Outer Hebrides. The imposing baronial roofline looms over the mudflats; inside, the rich-coloured paintwork, panelled bay windows and tiled fireplaces still convey the glamour. For some of these ventures, no expense was spared; stone and soil were imported to build dreams on rocky outcrops in the Atlantic. Once the island estates were bought, the mansions built and the gardens laid out, these plutocrats then discovered that they had subjected themselves to the uncertainties of the west-coast climate; while they had mastered much of the natural world, they were still at the mercy of the winds and the tides when it came to getting or leaving home.

The unpredictable accessibility of islands was central to the plot of *I Know Where I'm Going!* (1945), one of the British film director Michael Powell's most famous films. The glamorous heroine, a Londoner, heads to a Hebridean island to be married to her fiancé, and ends up stranded on the mainland by heavy storms, where she falls in love with a penniless sailor. Islands

can throw you off course; they are places of the unexpected and
that is part of their appeal. It is particularly true of the Hebrides.
They disrupt the best-laid plans, sabotage the most cherished
fantasies and offer the most startling – and seductive – surprises.
They demand pragmatism and cheerful adaptability of their
inhabitants. Islands don't lend themselves to grand plans and
big theories – the weather is too fickle.

Islands can provoke a volatile emotional intensity, even, as we
have seen, in rationalists such as Samuel Johnson. This was the
subject of a haunting novella by D. H. Lawrence, *The Man Who
Loved Islands*, said to have been inspired by the writer Compton
Mackenzie, an islophile and Scottish nationalist. Mackenzie
lived on a succession of islands – Capri, Herm and Jethou in
the Channel Islands – before moving to Barra in 1928, where
he lived for nearly twenty years. Lawrence's novella, set in the
damp mists and gales of unspecified islands, is a cautionary
tale of the seductive dangers of islomania. Over the course of
adventures on three islands, the hero invests – and loses – a fortune in creating his 'little world', and then becomes increasingly
unstable before he finally loses his mind and retreats alone to a
rocky outcrop. Islands proved the ruin of him.

Mackenzie triggered Orwell's interest in the Hebrides before
Astor encouraged him to choose to go to Jura. Along with close
associates such as Hugh MacDiarmid, Mackenzie helped establish the Hebrides as a place of refuge, solace, even salvation, for
a civilization in crisis in the middle of the twentieth century.
During these decades of war and depression, fault lines were
emerging in Britain's identity – as a 'blessed plot' and as an
empire in decline – which became central to Orwell's writing.
The Hebrides offered an artist a vantage point, suggested
Mackenzie. It was near enough to still feel part of home, but far
enough away to salvage some perspective – the only consolation

available – in a terrible half-century of violence. The islophile fascination for the Hebrides shifted in the twentieth century beyond the preserve of wealthy plutocrats and became an absorbing passion for a succession of writers and, as the publishers spotted, their readers.

Mackenzie was part of an exodus of writers from England as restlessness scattered creative talent from London in the 1920s. Lawrence Durrell went to Corfu; D. H. Lawrence to Mexico and Italy; Basil Bunting went to Tenerife; Aldous Huxley to California. Such was the exodus that in 1936 Durrell wrote home asking, 'IS THERE NO ONE WRITING AT ALL IN ENGLAND NOW?' There were some practical reasons for writers to flee the metropolis, looking for cheap rents on ramshackle but spacious houses. The discomfort of leaking roofs, draughty cottages and having to gather one's own fuel and water became an accepted part of the creative experience. Orwell rented Barnhill on Jura in 1946 and described putting it to rights in letters to friends. Avril Blair, Orwell's sister, referred to it as her brother's Robinson Crusoe streak. A couple of years later, the writer Gavin Maxwell was doing likewise at Sandaig, further up the west coast overlooking Skye. Beachcombing for fish boxes with which to furnish his croft forms the opening chapter of Maxwell's bestseller, *Ring of Bright Water*, published in 1960.

Another lure, as both Mackenzie and Orwell discovered, was that the Hebrides offered these English eccentrics an unusual degree of personal freedom from convention and class. While Hebridean communities had their own powerful mores of respectability, these incomers were regarded as 'gentlemen' and treated with hospitable courtesy, their foibles tolerated. (There were limits to this tolerance. Louis MacNeice reportedly caused offence on his Hebridean journey by sharing a bedroom with his then girlfriend, a married woman.)

Many of these writers in the mid-twentieth century shared a sense of crisis and decline. This prompted their urge to escape, either to salvage the means for their own survival, or in search of inspiration for the process of renewal. Orwell's friend Cyril Connolly wrote in 1929: 'I am tired of this country. I do feel it is a dying civilization – decadent but in such a dull way – going stuffy and comatose instead of collapsing beautifully like France.' Orwell was sympathetic to these ideas. His novels of the 1930s, such as *Coming Up for Air*, conveyed his distaste for a changing country: he depicted in grim detail the banal conformity of urban life, the mediocrity of cheap consumerism, the pettiness of the class system and its minutely graduated snobbery. His loathing of twentieth-century, urban, industrial Britain was the vivid setting for his dystopian portrayal of state authoritarianism in *Nineteen Eighty-Four*, the novel he wrote in Barnhill. A keen and knowledgeable naturalist, on Jura Orwell was surrounded by the natural world, and he plunged into the demanding physical exertions of crofting, hunting and fishing. He set up his typewriter in front of the window overlooking the sea, and with that vista in front of him, he infused the novel with a pervasive horror of the dirty, urban tedium of its setting.

It was not just Orwell who developed a fascination for the Hebrides. The islands inspired a wealth of books during the 1930s and 1940s, with readers hungry to hear more of their beauty, distinctive culture and echoes of a peasant life now long lost further south. The books were sometimes sentimental, sometimes purple in their prose, but they fed the British imagination. Many of them were on my father's bookshelves as I grew up, and survived his ruthless regular culling into his old age. One of the best of the crop was the breathless *Island Going*, by an Oxford student, Robert Atkinson, with its exuberant tales of derring-do and ornithology on far-flung Hebridean islands, such as the rat-infested Shiants, a group of islands off the east coast of Lewis, and the gentler occupation of Rona, forty-four miles north of Lewis, by Leach's petrels. This romantic escapism to north-west Scotland contrasted sharply with the Scots' own deep sense of gloom over the state of their nation, captured by Edwin Muir in *Scottish Journey* in 1935; he talked of a 'silent clearance' in which 'Scotland is gradually being emptied of its population, its spirit, its wealth, industry, art, intellect and innate character'. The country was in deep economic crisis, but this did not seem to impinge on many of the writers who headed north in search of the solace of the natural world.

In *The Islands of Scotland*, published in 1939, on the eve of the Second World War, Hugh MacDiarmid, who was born in the Scottish Borders, lamented that the 'fake glamour of the Hebrides has become a weariness to the flesh and a real obstacle to their true apprehension', but with that caveat he issued a trenchant call: 'it is impossible to write about the Scottish islands today without recognizing civilization's urgent need to refresh and replenish itself at its original sources'. His book was a manifesto for moral and political renewal tucked into a supposed travel book. He pointed out that several of Scotland's leading writers had retreated to islands, such as John Lorne Campbell on Canna and Compton Mackenzie on Barra: 'All that is still greatest in literature and art and philosophy was created not in the great cities . . . but under conditions destitute of all these modern blessings and, for the most part, in places as lonely and bare as these islands are. In short megalopolitan cultures can ill afford to affect superiority to these little poorly inhabited places; they have contributed far more to the spiritual wealth of mankind than the great cities have done or seem at all likely to do.'

A comparable moral project was threaded through the books of the English ecologist Frank Fraser Darling. He recounted his extraordinary feats of endurance on the island of Rona and later on the island he bought in 1937, Tanera Mòr in the Summer Isles. His two books, *Island Years* and *Island Farm*, published in 1940 and 1943, had a passionate ambition to reconnect urban industrial Britain with the natural world. He scorned the comforts of modernity to demonstrate a visceral engagement with nature and its elements – the rain, storms and wild tides – and celebrated the dirt and sweat of his smallholding and husbandry. There are few descriptions of Hebridean incomer life more daunting than his account of the backbreaking rebuilding of the small jetty on Tanera Mòr, as he and his wife dragged rocks into place. They spent several years with their small child, building their 'little world' of house, garden and jetty. A deeply knowledgeable naturalist, Fraser Darling tracked deer and birds with assiduous patience and attentiveness. For city-dwelling readers in the midst of a terrible world war, it was a brilliantly conceived reminder of the natural world, as well as a form of escapism: a glimpse of a world long lost in England, the absorbing physical struggle with the elements offering some distraction from the anxiety and violence of war. This muscular environmentalism had a pioneering message which gathered increasing numbers of adherents and advocates throughout the second half of the twentieth century. Fraser Darling went on to become one of the founders of the World Wildlife Fund. He epitomized the phenomenon in this period described by the literary critic Sam Hynes: 'writers turned their travels into interior journeys and parables of their times, making landscape and incident the factual materials of reportage – do the work of symbol and myth – and form the materials of fable'.

When Maxwell came to write the bestselling *Ring of Bright Water*, he picked up the same themes, using the coastline of north-west Scotland as part of his manifesto: 'these places are symbols of freedom whether it be from the prison of over dense communities and the close confines of human relationships, or from the less complex incarceration of office walls and hours. Man has suffered in his separation from the soil and from other living creatures of the world.'

However, unlike Fraser Darling, Maxwell had little interest in crofting and used his home at Sandaig as a place of retreat: a 'fortress from which to essay, raid and foray, an embattled position behind whose walls one may retire to lick one's wounds and plan fresh journeys to further horizons'. His record as an environmentalist was ambiguous at best. He may have written lovingly about otters, but one of his earlier books was a brutal account of his attempts to set up a basking-shark fishery in the Hebrides. But no matter, with *Ring of Bright Water*, the Scottish west-coast island dream came of age, and it made his book an international bestseller. Its sales were ranked third after the

Bible and Churchill's memoirs in the post-war period in the English-speaking world. It made Maxwell, an unlikely candidate, a world-famous prophet of conservationism. He received over 14,000 fan letters. 'I have two copies of the book, and I keep one in my office drawer; it sets the mind free even in the city,' ran one, 'a breath of fresh air through the stale channels of an age of false values.'

This was the high-water mark of a twentieth-century love affair with the Hebrides. It inspired a generation of smallholders and artists, who moved onto islands such as Skye, Mull, Eigg and North Uist, following in the steps of Fraser Darling, Orwell and Maxwell. They turned to the writings of Gaelic enthusiasts such as John Lorne Campbell for a better knowledge of the islands' culture. But for the reading public, the appeal of damp crofts on inaccessible islands waned, and was replaced by sagas of farmhouse renovations in Provence, Alicante and Tuscany, or exotic travels to the likes of Patagonia or Siberia. Taste shifted away from Buchan's fascination with the North and 'making the soul', towards the exotic, the distant and the unfamiliar. Scotland's west coast had been domesticated; it was no longer perceived as a wild frontier.

A new generation of writers have drifted back to the Hebrides in the early decades of the twenty-first century, though this time they come as passing visitors; not for them the hardship of experiments in self-sufficiency. Several have found their way to Jura, inspired by Orwell. The opportunities for perspective are still compelling. Novelist Will Self describes how either at the outset or towards the completion of a book he retreats somewhere distant, often by the sea, often in Scotland: 'I like islands . . . because they're discrete and legible, just like stories.' In another article Self reflected that 'there remains a part of me – the ultimately sceptical, anthropological observer of it all – that

is for ever marooned in the North Atlantic, peering curiously
at this unhappy antheap of mass human society'. For Kathleen
Jamie and Robert Macfarlane, the appeal of islands lies not so
much in their vantage point for a critique of urban Britain as in
a delicate, insistent evangelizing project, urging readers to pay
attention to the fragile natural world and the language we use
to imagine it.

Tucked in the middle of this century-long history of writers and their love affairs with the Hebrides is Orwell, its most
celebrated exponent. On north Jura, Orwell found the clarity
of vision for a piece of fiction which shaped the politics of the
post-war world. From there he had the critical distance not just
to see his own times clearly, but to divine in them the threat
they posed to human freedom. So sharply prescient was his
distinctive vision that his surname became an adjective. He
imagined a way of framing a question which can be asked of
any age: what freedoms are hard or impossible to imagine in this
moment in history?

It was a perspective only possible from an island, only imaginable in such remote isolation. Jura was everything that was
threatened in *Nineteen Eighty-Four*; it offered an abundance of
wild natural beauty, and required a visceral physicality of its
inhabitants. Orwell understood these qualities to be among the
precious constituents of human freedom. Only in their midst
could he imagine with such grim vividness the oppression which
he portrayed in *Nineteen Eighty-Four*.

III

After the gardens of Jura House, we followed the single-track
road which twists and turns, heading north for twenty-five
miles. We sped past glowing white beaches while our teenagers

vehemently protested. We glimpsed a luxurious shooting lodge with its elegant inhabitants sitting on a terrace, the view looking over a swathe of green lawn to the brilliant blue sea, the perfect image of landed entitlement. We whisked past a charming cottage where honeysuckle clambered over the front door, fuchsia splashed delicate scarlet flowers, and a couple were sitting out to bask in the rare sunshine. The road came to an end abruptly in the middle of a moor. Signs instructed us not to drive any further. The journey to Barnhill was not going to be easy. We hoisted packs with water and our picnic onto our backs and set off with the three children, still protesting at the beaches we had left behind and the eight miles round trip of track across open moorland that lay ahead. We walked for several hours in the stark, austere landscape of undulating moor under the clear blue sky. There was not a tree. We crossed a stream where the children paddled in sparkling water the colour of manuka honey. The only living creature we saw was a stag on a hillside half a mile away; he stood and watched us closely as we studied him through our binoculars, his head erect under the heavy weight of his branched antlers.

This was the track Orwell used on his decrepit motorcycle to ride down to the only stores on Jura, at Craighouse, to collect supplies and mail. We finally reach the crest of the hill above Barnhill on the northern tip of Jura; looking east, the blue sea is embroidered with the rocky promontories, inlets and islets of the Argyll coast. Beyond, the mainland was thick with mountain peaks and ridges which faded into blue shadows against the blue sky. It was a scape where land disintegrated into sea, where mountains merged with the sky. The blurring of elements – land, sea, air – and the huge scale of what lay before us was exhilarating.

Nestled in a dip below us was the lone house, with the dormer window of the attic room where Orwell wrote *Nineteen Eighty-Four*. This was where we stopped, deterred by another notice asking Orwell pilgrims not to intrude on those renting the house. We sat on a large flat rock to eat our picnic and contemplate the views, Orwell's three-year stay on Jura, and the longevity of the nightmare he dreamed and wrote here.

Barnhill both inspired and emotionally sustained him, but it also contributed to his death. We watched the figures of those staying in the house come and go; they were mending something, then mowing the grass in the garden. This was where Orwell had thrown himself into the renovation and gardening which accelerated the onset of tuberculosis and led to his death in 1950 at the age of forty-six. He dug the garden, planted fruit

trees and cut peat on the moor to supplement fuel rations. He repaired outhouses, kept a small amount of livestock, fished in the nearby lochs and at sea, and shot rabbits to feed the household – his sister Avril, his young son Richard and visiting friends. He kept meticulously detailed diaries, charting the fluctuations of weather, the temper of the sea, the work he was doing in the garden, and observations of the plant and animal life around him. 'Latterly the weather has been quite incredible … last week we went round in the boat and spent a couple of days on the completely uninhabited Atlantic side of the island in an empty shepherd's hut – no beds but otherwise quite comfortable. There are beautiful white beaches round that side. This last week we've all been breaking our backs helping to get the hay in, including Richard who likes to roll about in the hay stark naked.'

On another boat trip to the west side of Jura, Orwell misread the tide tables and was caught in the famous whirlpool of Coire Bhreacain. The boat capsized and Orwell had to rescue three-year-old Richard from the water; they swam to a small island and built a fire to attract the attention of a passing boat. Orwell admitted the accident 'was very unpleasant while it lasted' but the next day he was back on the water. He was a dedicated fisherman – going out in the boat every night at one period to fish and gather lobsters, despite it being 'very dangerous'. He enjoyed the sharp, brutal edges of rural life, the bloodied rabbits which he carried back from the moors – or gave to Richard to carry – the live snake that he once skinned in front of startled companions. He had great respect for the precision required to complete these routine tasks of country life. He recorded in detail how to set, sharpen and maintain the scythe, which he carried on the back of his motorcycle to cut the rushes which grew on the track.

There was no daily postal service, no telephone and no electricity at Barnhill. The nearest shop was a twenty-five-mile round trip, the nearest doctor was on Islay. Orwell was delighted: the place was 'extremely unget-at-able' he declared. He had fled the telephone, the requests for journalism and the busy chatter of London life, he explained in letters. His recurrent fear of assassination since his time in Barcelona in 1936–7 abated, although he still kept a gun at hand. But he wanted his friends to visit and gave detailed instructions for the forty-eight-hour journey from London, with train and ferry times. What resulted were some very tense ménages with assorted friends and relatives, which Avril was left to deal with when Orwell retreated to his room and his typewriter. One visitor, a young student, David Holbrook, reminisced, 'I wanted to talk to him about life, about politics, Spain and that sort of thing, but he was wheezing away about an Arctic tern.'

Orwell's letters portray Barnhill as a powerful emotional counterbalance to his pervasive pessimism in those years. After an autumn spent in bed in the damp house in 1947, he was taken to a Lanarkshire sanatorium for treatment and he wrote to a friend, 'Not much use worrying about Palestine or anything else. This stupid war is coming off in about 10–20 years and this country will be blown off the map whatever else happens. The only hope is to have a home with a few animals in some place not worth a bomb. If the show does start and is as bad as one fears, it could be fairly easy to be self-supporting on the island provided one wasn't looted.' His comments owed much to that mid-twentieth-century British conception of islands, and the Hebrides in particular, as salvific, the last refuge. 'When one considers how things have gone since 1930 or thereabouts, it is not easy to believe in the survival of civilization,' he wrote.

The first title he had considered for *Nineteen Eighty-Four* was *The Last Man in Europe*. On stormy nights in Barnhill, his sense of foreboding may have led him to think he was writing about himself.

When he was discharged from the Lanarkshire sanatorium in 1948, he insisted on returning to Barnhill, a decision from which his sister Avril regretted not dissuading him. But he took great pleasure in the cherry blossom, the tulips and violets in his garden. It was the effort of living in Barnhill which badly affected his health, although no doubt the damp climate also contributed: the round of physically demanding chores – fishing, peat cutting, digging the garden and hunting – took their toll. He could not be persuaded to relinquish them and in due course he relapsed. He had to leave Jura for treatment again and this time there was no going back. But Barnhill was still on his mind. His letters from the sanatorium repeatedly returned to the place and his plans for the garden and how to arrange the management of the farm, and above all to his deep pleasure in providing this environment for Richard. 'I think Jura is doing Richard good ... he is most enterprising and full of energy and is out working on the farm all day long. It's nice to be able to let him roam about with no traffic to be afraid of,' wrote Orwell from Lanarkshire in January 1948.

Barnhill and Richard were interlinked, and he rarely mentioned one without the other; both were projects which gave him hope and a future which he could contemplate with pleasure, in contrast to the fear of more war, totalitarianism and the threat they posed to human freedom and decency. Even when he was very ill, and unlikely to recover fully, he was planning Barnhill as a summer home, and proposing schemes for looking after the livestock.

Jura's remoteness was Orwell's only explanation for his decision to move there. But given his deep love of the English countryside, it was an intriguing choice. There were plenty of remote houses in England where the farming and gardening might have been more productive. Jura was a landscape quite unlike any other he had lived in, and it enabled him to produce a novel which was quite unlike anything else he had ever written, and at a speed, despite his illness, which he had never managed before.

Barnhill gave him the vantage point from which to create its opposite in *Nineteen Eighty-Four*. The character Julia offers the one glimmer of hope in the book; her unabashed love of sex was 'above all what he [Winston] wanted to hear' because it was 'not merely the love of one person but the animal instinct'. Living at Barnhill gave Orwell an experience akin to Julia's 'animal instinct', of a deeply experiential, instinctive world away from abstractions.

In *Nineteen Eighty-Four* Orwell describes people who can no longer understand freedom or truth because history has been corrupted, repeatedly rewritten in the 'Records Department', and in the process their identity and that of England has been erased. Freedom is no longer imaginable because there is no language to describe it; as the state functionary Syme says, 'Don't you see that the whole aim of Newspeak is to narrow the range of thought? In the end we shall make thoughtcrime literally impossible, because there will be no words in which to express it.' At one point, Orwell's character Winston Smith can no longer remember his parents. He asks himself, 'Did his parents live in England? England was its name, he thought, or Britain.'

Orwell was writing these lines when living amongst a Gaelic community; the neighbouring crofters with whom he shared the tasks of harvesting would never have been allowed to forget their parents, nor where they had lived, given the Gaelic emphasis on genealogy and place. Did Jura and its losses – of language and of history – creep into the background texture of *Nineteen Eighty-Four*, providing small details in the vision of how identity – and thus freedom – were lost? Literary critics of Orwell's work have tended to regard Jura as incidental, no more than a backdrop, and their focus has been on Orwell, the man. Their references to Jura have often been simply comments on its remoteness. But Orwell had an acute sense of place; he understood how it expressed history and generated identity. He used vivid evocations of both city and countryside to express his most important political ideas in books such as *Keep the Aspidistra Flying, Coming Up for Air* and *Down and Out in Paris and London*. This Atlantic edge of Britain has been a battleground for different interpretations of freedom, and how history and identity create the conditions for them, as I was to discover several times on my journeys. What Orwell found on Jura were reminders of those freedoms which had been lost in urban Britain, and which sustained and inspired him.

Half a century later, when Simon Schama came to make his television history of Britain, he and his film crews chose to film a sequence on Jura in the episode on the twentieth century. It was a conscious echo of an earlier, comparably ambitious television series by Kenneth Clark, *Civilisation*, which had used the neighbouring island of Iona for a similarly redemptive role. Schama's was the secular version. He argued that two Winstons – the main protagonist of *Nineteen Eighty-Four* and Churchill – were the most memorable representations of resistance to totalitarianism in the mid-twentieth century. Jura had played a role in defining freedom in the twentieth century.

Prophecy, vision and salvation – the Hebrides have been rich in their practices, a millennium before Orwell ever arrived, ill and sad. Jura offered the exhilarating autumn adventure of his last years and stimulated a remarkable creativity and also, against all the odds, happiness.

IV

From Barnhill it is only a few miles out to sea to the Coire Bhreacain whirlpool, but it was several years later before I managed a return visit, on the full-moon spring tide at the equinox during Easter, one of the best times of the year to experience the whirlpool which had nearly drowned Orwell. My son Matt and I had rifled through pictures on the internet; the grey seas were not of much interest to him, but the ribs used to ride the whirlpool were, and we booked seats and crossed our fingers for a fair wind. The night before our trip we stayed in a pub nearby on the Argyll mainland. There were only one or two customers all evening in the bar, and when the fire alarm went off in the middle of the night, we discovered the place was deserted – we were the only people stumbling around the hamlet in our pyjamas in search of help. I finally fell back into a fitful sleep, only to be woken by a full moon, its light pouring through the small window. The brilliance was caught on ragged cloud, showering sparks on the sea, and stroked the edge of the hills. The moon was still bright when we got up before 6 a.m. to get to the harbour. Only on the spring tides is it possible to see the full force of the Coire Bhreacain, when the moon exerts its greatest gravitational pull on the ocean and there is the biggest tidal range. The whirlpool lies just to the north of Jura, where narrow straits separate the tip of the island from its neighbour, Scarba. Here, the full force of the Atlantic breaks through the long string of land formed by the islands of Jura and Islay into the narrow Sound of Jura. Coire Bhreacain is one of the biggest whirlpools in the world.

When we arrived at the little port of Ellenabeich on the island of Seil, the night was thinning to the grey light of dawn, and a few people were beginning to gather. Some had driven from Fort William, sixty miles away, in the early hours; one man had brought his father from Belfast on a long-planned trip. Sleepy, nervous or shy, there was not much talking as we put on oilskins and life jackets. The sky was heavy low cloud, and the cliffs above the old slate-mining port were sombre. About fifteen of us boarded the rib in the small harbour, each perched astride stools, as if riding a horse. I could barely move for my layers of warm clothing, waterproofs and life jacket.

As we made our way out of the harbour, the cliffs of the south coast of Mull were just visible, breaking through the mist, while to our immediate left was the island of Luing, with its low-lying fields and farmhouses. Ahead was the island of Lunga, and between it and the steep hill of Scarba was Bealach a' Choin Ghlais, the Grey Dogs. A rush of wild white water poured through the gap between the two islands. The skipper turned the engine off, and in the eerie quiet of this running water, he said the boat was moving at eleven knots an hour.

We sailed on round Scarba, its rugged slopes looming over us. A sea eagle was perched on a pine tree, and on the shore a pair of stags were grazing. A jetty and a track disappeared into the bracken, leading towards a lone white house, perched higher on the hillside. As we came round Scarba, with the dark mountains of Jura ahead, the horizon opened out in the narrow gap between the islands, and beyond an unbroken surface of beaten grey stretched across the Atlantic. These islands are the first landfall after thousands of miles of ocean, and their rocky shorelines have been exposed to its force for thousands of years.

We hugged the shore of Scarba as we approached Coire Bhreacain itself. Atlantic water rushed through the narrow gap between the two islands. The anticipation was sharp. Waves puckered the sea's surface: thousands of small pyramids of water springing up with a jerky movement, the wind whipping the white spray from their peaks. They offered some warning of what was to come. As the boat plunged into the rough water, I felt rather than saw Coire Bhreacain. Like the rider on a bucking horse or bull might sense the beast beneath them, the whirlpool's force travelled up my spine, reverberating in my thighs and calves and through the rest of my body. The powerful sensation brought with it an appreciation of the smallness and fragility of thin bones, of muscle pumping warm blood. We were separated from Coire Bhreacain's overwhelming strength only by this fragile rib, made of plastic, rubber and boards. We were skimming its surface while the huge waters swirled and collided beneath us.

From a distance, there is little to see apart from a ruffling of the sea's surface; it is only in the physical experience, being in a boat moving over this strange patterning of the water, that one can appreciate the extraordinary phenomenon. Coire Bhreacain exposes the shortcomings of our language for water and its qualities. We have become land creatures and our relationship is with solid matter. When water moves, we are tongue-tied, searching for metaphors. How to describe the slabs of water as they rush towards each other? Or the glassy stretches of smooth water and how they crumple, bubble and blister and then re-form? They boil into creases and then subside back into smoothness. These patches of smooth water in the whirlpool, sometimes dozens of metres wide, are called 'plates'. It is an oddly domestic term for something so disruptive, just as it jars as a term for the enormous formations of the earth's crust.

These plates were strangely unnerving. The deceiving calm. Every now and then, there was a sudden pothole in the turbulence, a standing wave, as if of polished marble, and a hollow in the water before the surface re-formed. Swirling currents appeared suddenly beneath the prow, choking with white water, only to melt into the rush and re-form elsewhere. Coire Bhreacain is not one, but dozens of whirlpools, forming and re-forming across a wide area. The poet Robin Robertson uses the metaphor of the water feeding on itself in his poem 'Corryvreckan'. It was not until I rode this furious boiling of the ocean that I too could imagine how water could eat itself. In Gaelic, Coire Bhreacain means 'cauldron of the speckled sea'. The name speaks of a safe distance, since the whirlpool only looks speckled from neighbouring cliffs. According to Gaelic myth, the goddess of winter, Cailleach Bheur, washed her great plaid in the whirlpool as autumn became winter; once washed, the plaid was pure white and she laid it over the land. By conceiving of the whirlpool as a laundry tub, Gaelic domesticated its wildness as part of the gods' care of the earth.

The English poet Arthur Clough described Coire Bhreacain in his poem on Scotland, radicalism and emigration, *Bothie of Toper-na-Fuosich* (1849):

> *Sets in amain, in the open space between Mull and*
> *   Scarfa,*
> *Heaving, swelling, spreading the might of the mighty*
> *   Atlantic:*
> *There into cranny and slit of the rocky, cavernous bottom*
> *Settles down, and with dimples huge, the smooth*
> *   sea-surface*
> *Eddies, coils and whirls.*

In the midst of the chaotic swirl of water I looked up at Scarba's cliffs on one side and the mountains of Jura on the other, and their forms seemed to echo the water. Twisting masses of disrupted layers of rock, a history of movement as chaotic and forceful as that of the water below. Fluid and solid seemed to collapse into each other, and language was upended by Coire Bhreacain's frenzied turmoil into a jumble of colliding metaphors. The lumps and slabs of water slid beneath the boat and broke up into bubbles; the layers of rock twisted in the cliffs above.

The seabed beneath Coire Bhreacain is dramatic. There is a ridge of rock just twenty-nine metres below the surface of the water before it plunges down to a trough 219 metres deep. At high tide, the Atlantic pours up the long Sound of Jura from Islay, squeezing between islands and islets up into the inlets of Loch Melfort and Seil Sound, a distance of over fifty miles. In the narrowing funnel, its height rises higher than that in more open water to the west. The narrow gaps between the line of islands at the Bealach a' Choin Ghlais and Coire Bhreacain act as pressure valves. Fifteen minutes after the high tide, as the water recedes down the Sound of Jura, it sucks in water from the west, drawing it through the gaps. As it does so, the water is forced to rise over the ridge of rock in the seabed. The bathymetric survey reveals a seabed of deep fissures and swollen outcrops, so the water passing over it is bullied and twisted every which way. When the wind is from the west, the waves can reach over four metres. Even on a calm day, it creates a wall of water, and when we smashed into it, the salt spray hit us in the face like a bucket of cold water.

The skipper lamented that the wind was 'flattening' the waves, so the whirlpools lacked depth. He talked of other occasions when the whirlpools were as big as swimming pools, nearly two metres deep, and the boat could slide into their centre. He turned off the engines. A whirlpool spun us slowly around and the sound of rushing water was everywhere. These whirlpools do not suck; they are not like the plughole of a bath. Yet the spinning alone was enough to capsize and almost drown Orwell.

Back in the harbour at Ellenabeich, I talked to Jess, who 'runs' the ribs over Coire Bhreacain together with her husband. 'My son can drive the boat round the whirlpool like a bicycle in a velodrome,' she explained. 'Most of the time, in slack water, you can cross Coire Bhreacain on a lilo and you can even swim across it. George Orwell just got his timings wrong. But there are parts of Coire Bhreacain we don't go near. A massive standing wave can be over three metres high, like a wall across the front of Coire Bhreacain. A big boat can push right through it, but any other boat can't cross. It's all to do with the moon as it pulls on the oceans, creating the tides,' she added. 'The moon pulls the water table up and down in the land as well. I tried lunar planting my garden but I was hopeless.' Jess sounded remarkably grounded for someone whose business was moving water.

After we staggered off the boat as if drunk, all day the world was less steady. The moon and its pull, tugging at the waters of the oceans, of the land and of our own bodies, had left me giddy. We wandered along the shore back on the mainland, and listened to the calm water lapping at the seaweed-coated rocks, a distant reverberation of the turbulence out to sea.

3

Iona

A thin place – only a tissue paper separating earth from heaven.

GEORGE MACLEOD

I

A boat could take you across the Firth of Lorn from the churning grey waters of Coire Bhreacain in a few hours to my next stopping point, Iona. The direct route by sea from Jura would take you north-west towards the steep grey cliffs of south Mull, past Carsaig, where on one holiday my then eight-year-old daughter raced into the chilly sea to swim with dolphins she had spotted. Then west along the Ross of Mull to where Iona sits on its tip, like a ball about to be kicked out into the Atlantic. But without access to a boat or the skills to sail it, my route was more prosaic: a ferry from the harbour at Oban to Mull and then a drive across Mull to catch another ferry to Iona: the Hebrides' most famous island, inspiring many narratives of faith and nation in the British Isles.

For much of the history of this archipelago, the sea has been the means of transport, carrying people, ideas and materials. Iona sits squarely at what was a central point on one of the main searoads, within easy reach of the coast of Ireland to the south and beyond to Wales, Cornwall and across the Channel to Brittany and, even further south, across the Bay of Biscay to Galicia. To the north, routes stretched to Cape Wrath and the northern shores of Scotland before splitting: one led east across the North Sea towards Denmark and Germany, another headed south down Britain's east coast.

Along these routes Irish monks travelled to found small communities and live as hermits, building small stone cells, or using caves for shelter. On many islands on this north-western seaboard, there is the presence of these men and the ruins of their chapels, a visible reminder of the extraordinary story of their faith. The Iona monks spread into almost every part of the British archipelago, connecting, educating and evangelizing its many peoples. Of all the ambitious bids to shape and exert dominance over the isles' complex geography, the Iona monks were the first and, in curious ways which they could never have possibly imagined, the most persistent, reaching down the centuries, into the heart of twentieth-century British politics.

The searoad brought the warrior aristocrat saint Colum Cille (also known as Columba) from Ireland in 563. He landed first on Kintyre, a peninsula off south-west Scotland. The cave where he found shelter was almost hidden in deep bracken when I visited it several years before, following a trail of tattered faded ribbons and votive offerings of trinkets and pebbles from the nearby beach. Legend has it that he moved further north to Iona so that he could no longer see the coastline of his Irish homeland. From Iona, the searoad carried the Iona monks around northern

Scotland and down to the Northumbrian island of Lindisfarne. I grew up in a small village in North Yorkshire called Oswaldkirk; it was named after the Northumbrian prince, Oswald, who fled to Iona after his father was killed in battle, and lived in exile on the island, before returning to retake his kingdom. He had become a Christian on Iona and he later invited the Iona monks to evangelize the tribes of Northumbria. I loved the awkward syllables of Oswaldkirk; the name faithfully remembered the old history of how Britain became Christian.

In the seventh century two monks, brothers, trained in the Iona tradition, reached even further south, St Chad to Bradwell-on-Sea on the Essex coast, where the church he founded sat out on the marshes facing the grey waters and mud flats. One chilly Boxing Day many years ago, I visited the simple reconstructed stone church. The salty wind whipped across the North Sea; inside the church, the chill ate into my bones. This was the wet wildness with which these monks lived, perched on their exposed coasts. Even further south, St Cedd founded a community in 654 CE on a slight promontory by a crossing in the Thames at East Tilbury. The estuary of sandbanks and marshes could be forded here at low tide and the place was an important point of exchange, trade and travel from the south Essex coast to north Kent. This church was not intended as a retreat from the world but as an assertion of the sacred, right at its centre. The church of St Catherine (the current structure dates back to the twelfth century, when the history of the Celtic monks was already old) stands at the end of a small road just off the web of motorways and dual carriageways which have succeeded the sea and carry the tide of traffic. East Tilbury now is a place on the way to nowhere, bypassed for many centuries; an area of small farms, gravel pits and with a large yard of spare car doors stacked up in piles.

A short journey from my home in east London, I found St Catherine's ancient British history still vibrant on the Sunday I visited. The service was finishing and the congregation dispersing; someone offered coffee, and the vicar, his face bright with enthusiasm, explained St Cedd's model of evangelism as described in a book by a Victorian scholar. As we talked, children played in the aisle and neighbours chatted; the parish was preparing for the celebrations of the imminent 1,350th anniversary of St Cedd's death. Afterwards, I walked along the dyke which prevents the Thames flooding the low-lying fields; on the horizon were the tall metal frames of the petrochemical works on Canvey Island. Boats had to steer carefully here, keeping to the deepest channel, around the sharp curve in the river. Flocks of plover rose over the marshes and turned in the sky above. I spotted a seal on a mudbank and watched as it rolled into the Thames and swam off. Not far to the west, the Dartford Crossing and the M25 quietly hummed.

We landlubbers find it hard to see how places as disparate as Iona, Lindisfarne, Oswaldkirk, Bradwell and Tilbury were once linked by the sea. Britain's sense of space has moved onto land since the eighteenth century's innovations in road building. This explains why Iona's history can be easily misunderstood. For the last three centuries, anyone writing about Iona has mentioned its remoteness, and huge romantic weight has been added to this word, but when it was founded and flourished as a monastic centre, it was well connected. Colum Cille was a diplomat and a kingmaker, forging alliances and building institutions. None of these extraordinary achievements would have been possible if Iona had been remote. The small island was busy with diplomats, students and delegations from royal courts in Ireland and Scotland. Significantly, Colum Cille regularly went on retreat from Iona to an island called

Hinba. Monasteries such as that of Iona were not places of retreat from the world, but were amongst the most powerful institutions of their time.

Throughout the journey from Coire Bhreacain to Iona, I had to keep reminding myself of this history. Without it, I was in danger of lapsing into the seductive mythology of remote Iona. After our giddy adventure over the whirlpool, my son and I had left the slate-mining port of Ellenabeich to head up to Oban, and the journey seemed easy enough as we lined up to wait for the short ferry crossing to Mull. But the wind had picked up from the south-west and all crossings were cancelled. Only the shorter crossing between Lochaline and Fishnish in the Sound of Mull was unaffected. To get from Oban to Lochaline involved a drive up Loch Linnhe, a short crossing at the Corran ferry and then the long route over the hills of the Morvern peninsula down to Lochaline; it would add another two and half hours to our journey. The decision was easy: it was bright spring sunshine, and the open road was more appealing than sitting on Oban's docks.

Snow was scattered like icing sugar on Ben Nevis above Fort William as we looked back from the single-track road which took us over the Morvern hills. We bowled along near-empty roads across moorland interrupted only by the occasional farm. Ahead, across the narrow sea channel, Mull's Beinn Mhòr rose high against the pale blue sky. At the end of the road in Lochaline at a hut by the jetty, rock cakes and scalding tea were on sale for waiting passengers. As the small ferry pulled away, the sea was sparkling in the late-afternoon sunshine. The gloom and foreboding of the grey seas of the day before were already a distant memory; good weather in the Hebrides has a disconcerting habit of swiftly establishing itself as normal. It was too windy to be warm but this high blue sky lifted our spirits.

On Mull we followed the twisting, single-track road over the hills and down the south-west peninsula towards Iona. By now I was worried about catching the last ferry (our third of the day) as the road wound round the intricate bays and small villages along the rocky coast of the Ross of Mull. At the dock, the ferry was waiting; parking, we crammed our last things into bags and backpacks to run to the boat, dog on lead. We had made it. Iona lay a short distance across the water, the pale grey form of the abbey just distinguishable against the light of the setting sun dipping towards the sea beyond the island.

The journey had taken us most of the day; two centuries ago it would have taken several. For Johnson and Boswell, the journey was only possible by horseback, and it was not one they enjoyed. Mull was 'black and barren', complained Johnson, commenting on 'this gloom of desolation'. After these exertions, Johnson must have felt that he had arrived at the end of the world. He noted that only one house on Iona had a chimney and it was not used; the more common practice throughout the Hebrides until well into the nineteenth century was to light a fire in the middle of the small house, the smoke escaping where it could through the thatched roof, giving rise to the term 'blackhouse'. He added sarcastically that, even with a chimney, the house 'rejoiced like the neighbours in the comforts of smoke'. He concluded sadly that 'the island which was once the metropolis of learning and piety has now no school for education, nor temple for worship, only two inhabitants that can speak English and not one that can write or read'. (It did not seem to occur to him that Gaelic would have been the language of this metropolis of learning.) He went on to muse, 'perhaps in the revolutions of the world, Iona may be sometime again the instructress of the western regions'. Several have sought to fulfil his prophecy.

II

Scientists have described the Hebrides as a biological frontier between continent and ocean, between two great ecosystems of opposite character; to the east, Eurasia's land mass stretches six thousand miles to Kamchatka and the shores of the Bering Sea, and to the west lie the marine pastures which were historically prolific with vast stocks of fin fish and shellfish. The temperatures are relatively mild, but Iona's position on the rim of one of the world's great oceans exposes it to the full force of the storm belts of the North Atlantic. The Hebrides is one of the windiest places in Europe, with gales gathering enormous fetch across the ocean, arriving on the islands laden with sea salt. On an average of five days in every month, the winds reach gale force, and in the winter, it can be twelve days a month. The hydrography of the Hebrides is complex, with currents, waves and tides which can make the sea treacherous. The strong winds and heavy rain slow down plant growth on these islands, making agriculture on the poor acidic soils difficult. They also subject the human body to a damp chill whose cooling effect is much greater than the average temperature suggests. Life here for Colum Cille and the monks was very hard; it was cold and usually wet. The crops could be wiped out by flood, heavy rain or wind, and famine and malnutrition were not unknown. The sea journeys from island to island were fraught with risk. This edge of the known world was a place of danger. Yet despite its vulnerability to the Atlantic's weather systems, Iona became a centre of learning, power and wealth.

The Atlantic had been richly mythologized in Europe long before the small coracles of the Irish monks spread out from Ireland to explore the islands along this frontier. The Atlantic was named after the Greek god Atlas, who bore his heavy burden, holding the sky and heavens on his shoulders to keep them apart from the earth in the extreme far west, where the sun set. Here, heaven and earth were close to meeting. It was the dwelling place of the three Hesperides, daughters of Atlas and goddesses of the evening, bathed in the golden light of sunset, which had been a gift to celebrate the marriage of Zeus and Hera. There, they tended the trees of golden apples which gave immortality.

After a dull day of rain, there were moments on my travels when the clouds cracked open, and Zeus' bridal gift blazed a brief, brilliant light from a place far away in the west. Every one of those moments brought the suggestion of elusive splendour, a glorious realm beyond the horizon, tantalizingly just beyond human reach. It provoked a stab of intense yearning for a place which was richly wondrous, where all tedium, banality and suffering were banished. In Greek myth, one of Hercules' twelve labours was to fetch the golden apples of the Hesperides. According to the poet Hesiod, 'the islands of the blest by the deep eddying Ocean' were where the glorious dead 'untroubled in spirit dwell' and 'for whom the grain-giving fields bear rich honey-sweet fruit three times a year'.

There is a recurrent mythical theme of lands lost in the Atlantic. One lost island was known as Hy Brazil or Brazil Rock, and was only taken off maps of the west of Ireland in 1865. Atlantis was a lost continent, the preserve of Poseidon, where the people became wealthy and corrupt and sought to conquer the world. It was swallowed up by the sea after incurring the wrath of Zeus. The twelfth-century Arab geographer Al Idrisi referred to 30,000 islands in the Atlantic, but he warned that passage to the riches of these fabled lands was full of danger in the 'sea of perpetual gloom'. The Atlantic struck terror into Europeans over the course of centuries. The Greeks also referred to the Atlantic as Oceanus, a sea which they believed encircled the the known world. In the fifth century BCE Pindar warned that 'what lies beyond cannot be trodden by the wise or the unwise ... one cannot cross from Gadir (Cadiz) towards the dark west. Turn again the sails towards the dry land of Europe.' The ocean held terrifying monsters and demons, and huge tangles of seaweed which could entrap and devour the vessels which dared to sail out of sight of land. A hungry place, it consumed the lives of sailors. Pythagoras suspected that the earth might be round and that it might be possible to sail from Spain to India, but such theories were impossible to test because of the barrier of the ocean and its 'destitution and loneliness'. The emptiness of the ocean was the cause of terror as much as the physical danger. Archaeologist Barry Cunliffe in *Facing the Ocean*, his magisterial overview of the prehistory of the Atlantic coastline, writes: 'The domains of land and sea were conceived as separate systems subject to their own very different supernatural powers, the interface between them was a liminal place and as such, was dangerous.'

The Christian monks arrived on Iona steeped in the theological traditions of the early Christian ascetics of Europe and the Near East; in particular they were inspired by the Desert Fathers of Egypt. They saw this coast as their 'green desert,' a place of 'revelation' and 'science' (in the sense of knowledge). In the twelfth-century Irish text the *Book of Leinster*, a young man 'heard a sound in the wave, to wit, a chant of wailing and sadness'. He cast a spell on the wave 'that it might reveal to him what the matter was'. For the Christian monks on the islands scattered along the Hebrides and west Ireland, the ocean was a theatre of the cosmic struggle between the Creator God and evil. Removed from the distractions of a corrupted world, a monk could take his part in that battle for his own salvation.

Psalm 107 told the monks that 'those who go down to the sea in ships, and have business in its many waters, see the works of the Lord and his great deeds in the deep'. The seventh-century hermit on Rum, Beccán mac Luigdech, wrote a poem which vividly captures the wildness of the seas the monks lived with: 'the wave-strewn wild region, foam-flecked, seal-filled/Savage bounding, seething, white-tipped' runs the translation from the Gaelic. Natural phenomena such as thunderstorms and lightning inspired utter terror, and there were monsters and dangers at every turn. Beyond brief, fragile human life lay the horrors of judgement and eternal hellfire. Few would be saved, Christian preachers warned. God was above all to be feared by the pious in a chaotic world full of evil. This was a place in which to recognize and confront fear, and to throw oneself, utterly dependent, upon the mercy of God.

Such profound pessimism elicited intense piety, with acts of constant supplication and propitiation. Colum Cille's biographer, Adomnán, recounted how the saint slept on bare rock, and stood exposed to the winds in the freezing sea of early morning to recite the psalms, his form so thin that his ribs could be seen. The monks saw themselves as *peregrinati*, and their concept of pilgrimage was a form of martyrdom in which they removed themselves from all that they loved, all that was *familiar*, from the family and community they knew, the rituals and traditions of their homeland, for the sake of God. Liberated from the requirements of family and tribe, and in particular from expectations to fight as warriors, these monks begged for God's mercy, poured forth their praise and confessed their sins of gluttony, lust and avarice. Their pilgrimage was to seek salvation. They had gone into exile for God and they were searching 'for the place of one's resurrection'.

This bleak picture is a far cry from Iona's pilgrimage

industry of the last two centuries. On the short ferry trip across the Sound of Iona, we were surrounded by the crowds arriving for Easter celebrations. A young American talked volubly about meeting his beautiful Spanish girlfriend on Ibiza and how he 'practised healing' on her until he discovered that he was falling in love. Many were carrying musical instruments and backpacks, and were swathed in colourful scarves. Amongst the heterogeneous passengers, the conversation was animated; some sought company, music and relaxation; some were seeking salvation. On arriving at the jetty, their backpacks and guitars were loaded onto vans and they peeled off in groups to walk the final mile to their hostels, laughing and talking. The next morning, the ferries disgorged contingents of day trippers at frequent intervals, who filled the pubs, restaurants and tea shops. The hotels were teeming with guests; the shops were doing a brisk business in Celtic memorabilia, bookmarks, jewellery, music and books. The distinctive knotwork and interlacing of Celtic design has found its way into thousands of homes and churches across the British Isles embellishing furniture, church vessels and jewellery. The islanders might be a bit bemused by the pilgrims' enthusiasm ('They're a few feet off the ground,' was the wry comment of one), but it gives them a living.

The candles flickered on the ancient stones of the abbey late into the evening during Good Friday's vigil. It felt cool, the walls impregnated with the winter's storms, and in the sombre silence people sat for five minutes, an hour or longer. Two days later the first service on Easter Sunday was at dawn. It was still dark when I got up in the quiet bed and breakfast, sitting with a cup of tea to watch light break over Beinn Mhòr on Mull across the Sound as the stars slowly faded. Leaving my son sleeping, I slipped out to head to the abbey. The sky was stained a soft

pink and over the island of Erraid to the south hung a pale
yellow full moon, its light gently glittering on the calm sea. At
this early hour of 5 a.m., the air vibrated with the magnificent
sound of thousands of birds singing; amid the larksong erupted
intermittently the distinctive sound of the corncrake, a harsh
rasp echoing from the field. It was just as the Iona boatman had
described the day before, like a finger dragged along a comb.
A soft wind blew and I heard the murmur of millions of small
movements of water against the rocks of the Sound, the tiny
slaps and gurgles of a sea breathing quietly. 'The sigh of all
the seas breaking in measure round the isles soothed them;
the night wrapped them; nothing broke their sleep, until the
birds beginning and the dawn weaving their thin voices into its
whiteness,' wrote Virginia Woolf in *To the Lighthouse*, set on the
Hebridean island of Skye.

As I neared the abbey, I saw other figures hunched over in
the cold, hurrying in the same direction, silhouetted against the
lightening sky. Around a hundred of us gathered in the dark
outside the small tenth-century St Oran's chapel in the abbey
grounds. The women were closest to the door, the men were
asked to hang back as a reminder that after his resurrection
Christ revealed himself first to two women. A young woman
began to sing, her clear voice rising into the twilit sky overhead.
Tapers were passed around as women whispered with excitement, 'Jesus has risen, Jesus has risen. The Light of the World.'
Tears came to my eyes and I could feel intense sensations passing along my spine. For a moment, it was possible to glimpse the
salvation dreamt of by those Irish *peregrinati* in their lonely vigils
on remote headlands all those centuries before, inspired by the
idea of an extraordinary event in which a man rose from the
dead, a man who declared himself the Son of God and offered
salvation. Something stirred deeply in me.

'The man is little to be envied whose piety would not grow warmer among the ruins of Iona,' declared Johnson after his visit, a comment which, for its time, was a remarkable acknowledgement of Britain's Catholic past. The intense moment I had experienced faded, but it left an uncomfortable reminder of lost faith, that reserve of belief and meaning beyond reach. As the sun rose above Beinn Mhòr and splashed bright sunshine on the daffodils, I walked back up the road to breakfast, listening to the larks and corncrakes in full voice.

Much of Iona's power lies in the place. Like Holy Isle off Arran, it is a small island off an island, and the ritual of departure and arrival is played out twice. We were removed from the world twice over, and even Oban, with its supermarkets, car parks and traffic lights, seemed very distant. Iona felt like the last outpost, a lighthouse without the elevation: a scrap of low-lying land in the ocean which could be swallowed up like one of those mythological islands if a fierce Atlantic storm unleashed a monstrous wave. Only three miles long by one and half miles wide, it can be walked in a few hours; it has beaches, a small hill, rocky foreshore and the distinctive machair of these Hebridean islands, the thin layer of cropped green turf over white shell sand which sustains a brilliant embroidery of flowers. With so little on the island, the eye is repeatedly drawn to the horizon. From the west shore the Atlantic spreads out, unbroken by land for thousands of miles until it reaches Newfoundland. From the long beaches at the northern tip I looked across the sea towards the string of the Treshnish Isles and the island known as Bac Mòr, or the Dutchman's Cap. Back on the busy east side in the grounds of the grey stone abbey, the coastline of Mull lies across the narrow Sound. The shoreline of Ardmeanach on Mull is made up of steep grey cliffs with wide rugged skirts of scree and no trace of crofts or trees. Closer to, the Ross of Mull offers a contour of low rounded granite outcrops whose masses seem to be crouching as if in fear of the sea. Boulders are scattered along its coastline, creating inlets and islets. The little ferry port of Fionnphort has the boldness to insist on street lamps, but they were an incongruous intrusion at night when they light up the dark sky, matched only by the blazing lights of the cruise ships which anchor in the Sound. Along the coast I can pick out a single-track road leading down to a cluster of houses perched uncertainly amongst the bare, scored rocks. Iona's abbey is built of this rock, dragged and heaved into boats, sailed across the Sound and carried up from the shore. In later centuries, the rock was blasted out of the hillsides and loaded onto ships to be transported first round the north of Scotland to Aberdeen for polishing, before circumnavigating the world. This rock was used to build the world's cities: Glasgow, Liverpool, Manchester and London. It built bridges, including Jamaica Bridge and Kirklees Bridge in Glasgow, and Blackfriars Bridge, Holborn Viaduct and Westminster Bridge in London. It has travelled as far as New Zealand, and blocks as big as five metres high made their way to America. Its popularity was due to its exceptional durability and its beauty. A pale reddish brown, the coarse-grained crystals are a riot of matter, caught colliding millions of years ago.

From Iona, my eye frequently landed on Mull and its ungiving character. It contrasts with the rolling green fields which surround Iona's abbey, the harbour's lanes and the cottage gardens, and the brave stunted trees which have survived the Atlantic storms. Easter was late this year, and unexpectedly warm. Lambs tottered onto their unsteady legs or lay comatose, stoned by the warmth, on the turf. The sheep-cropped machair was already green after the salty winds of winter, and as absurdly neat as an Oxbridge lawn, edging the beaches of brilliant white sand, which shot the sea with an implausible Caribbean turquoise. There was a softness and clarity in the air as leaves unfurled from sticky pink buds before our eyes, and daffodils lazily nodded their heads in the flower beds. Robert Louis Stevenson, who spent time as a boy on the neighbouring island of Erraid, wrote of 'the inimitable seaside brightness of the air'.

At such a time of year, the miracles attributed to Colum Cille on Iona by Adomnán appeared entirely credible; the place was indeed magical. 'By divine grace he had several times experienced a miraculous enlarging of the grasp of the mind so that he seemed to look at the whole world caught in one ray of sunlight,' wrote Adomnán of Colum Cille. When the saint prayed in his retreat hut on the island of Hinba, 'rays of brilliant light could be seen at night, escaping through the chinks of the doors and through the keyholes'. In particular, Adomnán wrote of Colum Cille's voice and how his fellow monks remembered its power resonating in their chapel or singing the psalms on the shore. He added that the Loch Ness monster only had to hear it to recoil in fear.

Colum Cille found his vocation at the age of forty-one, then regarded as late middle age, when he set sail from Ireland with twelve companions for Scotland. The hagiographies and mythologies which have accumulated around him make it hard to discern the historical record, but it is known that he was a scholar, a man who left the security of tribe and home in pursuit of learning; he was a poet and he illuminated manuscripts. He is also known for his kindly attentiveness to the problems of all those who came to him for advice. The monastery he founded on Iona was a centre of learning, a centre on Britain's furthest edge. Its monks travelled round the British Isles and to Europe, founding monasteries as far away as Belgium and Switzerland. In their coracles, they travelled deep into the continent, along rivers such as the Seine, Somme and Loire. Iona produced two of the leading cosmographers of their age: in 742 Fergil went to Austria, where, known as Virgil of Salzburg, he advanced the argument that there could be life on the other side of the world. He was threatened with excommunication for his novel ideas, and his writings were destroyed in mysterious circumstances. Later that century another monk, Dicuil, wrote a geography book, *De mensura Orbis terrae* (*On Measurement of the Earth*),which attempted to measure the surface of the earth, detailing the then-known world of Europe, Asia and Africa. He incorporated accounts of travellers to the Faroe Islands and Iceland, and produced a list of what was believed to be the world's five great rivers and six highest mountains. His grasp of distant geography was remarkable; he included the then canal between the Nile and the Red Sea.

The most powerful evidence of the scholarship on Iona lies in the illuminated manuscripts, of which the *Book of Kells*, now housed in Trinity College, Dublin, is the most astonishing. It is one of the greatest artworks ever accomplished in the British Isles and there has been much scholarly debate about how and where it came to be written. The consensus has settled on Iona. The illuminations are overpowering in their intense, complex patterning and vivid, riotous imagery of animals, saints and scenes from the life of Christ. In borders and around capital letters, animals chase and devour each other: cats and mice, an otter and a fish, a moth with a chrysalis, snakes, peacocks and lions. Its pages are a rich and faithful interpretation of the mythologies of the eastern Mediterranean, that confluence of classical civilizations, the Middle East and Africa out of which had emerged Christianity. Aspects of the design have been linked to places as various as Rome, Carolingian Europe, Byzantium and Armenia, but even life-long scholars admit to finding its range of pattern and image bewildering in its profusion and variety. Mathematicians and engineers have studied its complex geometry, marvelling at its exactitude. One scholar,

Margaret Stokes, commented in 1869 on 'the intense concentration of mind necessary for the accomplishment of work so minute where the power of the brain would seem, as it were, drawn to a needle's point to fulfil its purpose'. Some of the spirals are on such a minute scale, only 0.1 mm wide, that it has proved impossible to copy them, even with modern compasses.

This vivid imagery is not just decorative, it is part of the communication of the text. The pictures of animals are a form of commentary. In his definitive study, Bernard Meehan shows how the imagery flows in tandem with the text, anticipating or underlining points. The patterns are symbolic: one of the most common abstract elements is the lozenge representing Logos, the Word of God. Its four corners represent the cosmos, the quadripartite world in which four angels stood at the four corners of the earth, holding the four winds; the four seasons; the four elements of earth, air, water, fire; the four properties of heat, cold, moisture and dryness; the four humours of the body. The lozenge was an imagined geography, an orderly representation of the unruly world the Iona monks experienced on this edge of the Atlantic. Logos, the Word, was the central symbol of their faith, and had a sacred power. Throughout the *Book of Kells* there are allusions to speaking and hearing; figures gesture to their mouths or ears, tongues are often extended or bear fruit. Words, spoken or written, were cherished for their transformational power. Blessings, incantations, recitation and curses, all carried the authority of an omnipotent God.

The sheer sophistication and scale of the achievement represented by the *Book of Kells* is remarkable. Its production required a well-organized community of craftsmen: cattle farmers, tanners to prepare the calf skin, traders to bring the rare and brilliant powdered colours, metalsmiths to make the sharp knives, not to mention farmers to cultivate the hard soil to ensure there was food

for this community of skilled craftsmen. Above all, it required a
huge body of knowledge from across the known world – from
civilizations and cultures as diverse as central Asia, the Near East,
the Mediterranean and Celtic Ireland – to be assembled on this
Hebridean island, and with it the skill and flamboyant courage to
illuminate the Word, God's revealed truth for the world.

III

Colum Cille's memory was already several centuries old when
monks returned after the devastation of the Viking raids in
794 – when the monks had fled and taken the precious manuscripts to the safety of Ireland. A new monastery was built and
it thrived through the Middle Ages from its association with
the saintly Colum Cille. Significantly the kings of three countries, Scotland, Norway and Ireland, chose Iona for their tombs,
marking their burial site with the knotwork carvings and crosses
which impress visitors.

These ruins were already well known when Johnson visited,
and he helped propel their fame. Within a few decades of his
visit in 1773, the remains of the medieval monastery were an
obligatory stop on the route of travellers up the west coast.
Colum Cille and his monks have cast a long shadow, capturing
the imaginations of all four nations of these islands – Scotland,
Ireland, England and Wales. The Irish monastic diaspora of the
fifth to the eighth centuries was 'a remarkable phenomenon, an
explosive energy generated by an insular faith', concluded Barry
Cunliffe. Their history was extraordinary on many counts: as
navigators, as geographers, as poets, as illuminators, as scholars,
as diplomats and as believers. They have been seized upon
as a symbol of faith and of nation over the last three hundred
years: a dedicated and disciplined community who ensured that

a tradition of scholarship and learning survived in a dark age. Kenneth Clark's television series *Civilisation* featured Iona as the emblematic symbol of the precarious survival of civilization clinging to its westernmost edge. The series was hugely successful in both Britain and the US, tapping into Cold War anxieties of a nuclear holocaust. For Clark, a Catholic, Iona was a metaphor for the fragility of belief, now threatened, he believed, by a new barbarian dark age.

Successive generations of all four nations have claimed Iona as part of their past – and not without some rivalrous jostling as to who is the rightful heir: Ireland, Scotland, Wales, England or Britain? Ireland and Scotland have energetically promoted their claims in recent years, while the claims of England have been fading as knowledge of church history is forgotten, apart from in places such as Lindisfarne, the Northumbrian monastery founded by Iona, or in unexpected pockets much further south such as St Catherine's in East Tilbury.

Iona's most powerful legacy has been its religious vision of a moral community, but it is contested; there are many different interpretations of Celtic Christianity. Some writers, drawing on Gaelic poems and prayers, see echoes of contemporary preoccupations such as environmentalism and the rejection of institutional religious hierarchies. Various books in the genre have become international bestsellers, offering a form of spirituality which is full of consolation and encouragement and diffused with a vague sense of the divine. This interpretation of Celtic Christianity has been sharply critiqued by scholars who argue that it bears little relationship to history; Iona had close links to the Catholic Church and its hierarchical structures, they maintain, and Celtic Christianity had a gloomy view of the savagery of nature and the sinfulness of the human soul. The quarrel has been passionate.

One of the most outspoken voices in the latter camp is that of the admired Gaelic scholar and theologian Donald Meek. He grew up on Iona's neighbouring island, Tiree. Part of his critique is directed at the way in which the culture and beliefs of this periphery have been appropriated and reinterpreted to fulfil the dominant culture's requirements: 'The romantic repossession of regions and cultures which have been abused by imperialism seems to be one of the ways by which the well-heeled, modern descendants of the conquerors come to terms with their own and their forefathers' misdeeds. Romanticism of this kind glamourizes the past, sanitizes the present, assuages guilt and compensates for the loss. More cynically, it is largely an aromatic salve which allows its partakers to enjoy and "preserve" (in their own terms) a certain part of minority culture while doing little to support what remains of the living reality.'

Meek points out that the enthusiasm for Celtic Christianity has entailed little interest in Gaelic (the language of many of the prayers and poems on which it was based) and even less interest in the faith of the modern-day descendants of this Gaelic faith tradition. He describes today's interpretations of Celtic Christianity as a form of Occidentalism, comparable to the Orientalism critiqued by the influential writer Edward Said, which allows metropolitan Western culture to mythologize and romanticize other cultures to serve its own ends, while retaining its own sense of superiority. In both Occidentalism and Orientalism, the object has been silenced, and the dominant culture defines itself against this silent other. 'Celtic natives have a long history of suffering in silence while an external view of themselves and their culture is promulgated by the "superior" power,' suggests Meek. There is a rich history of early Christianity in Ireland, Scotland and Wales, he maintains, and there has been no need to invent one. In his view, a process of cultural appropriation is repeatedly evident on Scotland's west coast; it underlines how some identities gain dominance and others are marginalized.

Later, towards the end of my journey, in part provoked by Meek's argument I attended a Free Presbyterian church one Sunday evening in Stornoway on Lewis in the Western Isles. Could I find some echo here of the faith of Colum Cille? The Free Presbyterians are occasionally pilloried in the national media as reactionary for their refusal to compromise with modernity. Their relations with Catholics, attitudes towards homosexuality, sabbatarianism, and their tendency to engage in bitter internal disputes all prompt controversy. Everyone was dressed in sober black, grey or navy and, as the only woman without a hat and the only person wearing jeans, I felt out of place. In the sparsely filled pews, there were no children. The congregation was small, but the vigorous a cappella chanting of the psalms filled the high-ceilinged church. A seventy-five-minute sermon was delivered on the judgement of God, how the chaff would be burnt in the unquenchable fire, and on the Prince of Darkness. The minister's sonorous voice was full of gloom and lamentation, rising to a crescendo as he declared the urgent need for repentance. He spoke of how Christ would bring rest, but he seemed exhausted by his own theology. After an hour of preaching, he raised the emotional temperature further, lowering his voice to ask with particular insistence, 'Whose heart is closed tonight?' When the service ended, the congregation quietly dispersed. Several turned to me, curious about who I was and where I came from. I noticed with a start how gentle their friendliness was, and how softly sad their kind faces. It seemed as if the relentless severity of the service had been cathartic, helping them to accept the harsh ways of the world. It was a world away from the exuberant pilgrims I had encountered on Iona. It's a measure of the power of Iona and Colum Cille's memory that both would claim to be heirs.

More than anyone, George MacLeod, the Church of Scotland minister, hoped to revive Iona as an 'instructress of the world'. He founded the Iona Community in 1938 and embarked on an ambitious project to rebuild the medieval ruins with teams of unemployed workmen. A First World War military hero and grandson of a distinguished minster, MacLeod had built up a reputation as a charismatic preacher and energetic minster in Govan, Glasgow, during the Depression. The project became a symbol of national renewal at a time of desperate economic uncertainty as first the depression and then the wartime bombing along the Clyde decimated Scotland's industries. He attracted volunteers from all over Scotland, Europe and America. The community he founded – pacifist, deeply engaged in the struggle against injustice and poverty – followed strict rules of modest living, prayer and service. It had an inspirational impact (well beyond its membership of several hundred) on Scottish Christianity, on Scottish Labour politicians and ultimately on British politics.

Some of the community live on Iona to run the retreat centres, where they welcome the pilgrims and visitors; others are scattered across Scotland and a few live in England. On Iona, 'answering the same questions every week with newcomers is hard work', admitted the community's director, Joanna Anderson. We sat on a bench in the abbey grounds on Easter Sunday to talk. She was a brisk corrective to Iona romanticism.

'Do you like the place?' I asked.

There was a long pause and she conceded she liked the view of Mull across the water. She had no time for the dewy-eyed interpretations of Celtic Christianity which she saw as often coming from America. 'Who knows what it was about,' was her comment. But for one thing, she continued, it was not an early form of environmentalism. Colum Cille and his monks were terrified of nature – its thunder, lightning and violent storms – and felt intensely vulnerable in the face of their complete dependence on the sea for transport. She had felt this keenly over the last winter as storm after storm hit the island, cutting them off from Mull.

'People go on about how special Iona is. Day trippers say they can feel the peace, but I have never felt that. This is a place where I have always worked and it's incredibly hard. I came here because no one else was prepared to. I can't be doing with the romanticism. For me this place is about building a community with people as they are. Helping people to accept each other. Strangers become friends and those friendships can last a long time. That doesn't fit with romanticism for me.'

Iona is not about retreat, she continued, but engaging with people from all over the world and turning them towards the most marginalized, whether that is asylum seekers, immigrants or Palestine. Her own history with Iona began as a child. A small copy of one of the great Iona crosses, St Martin's, was in her family home in Liverpool, she remembered. On her first visit she hated it and swore she would never return. But she did, and she met her husband on the island, and for a while they brought up their children here. Now she was back for another stint, drawn by George MacLeod's vision. The weight of expectations arriving every day on the ferry was a heavy burden, and I sensed a woman holding a magnificent but fragile enterprise together.

Next morning I caught sight of her on the jetty, waving off the hundred or so pilgrims who had spent Easter on Iona. There were hugs and fond farewells as people on the ferry leant over the handrails to wave; it was oddly moving to witness these newly made friends saying goodbye before they scattered again across the globe.

Sometime later when I was passing through Glasgow I took a detour to visit a couple who were central to the Iona Community for several decades. John Harvey, a former leader of the Iona Community, and his wife Molly now live in Pollokshields, south Glasgow. They are still members of the community. On the wall of their hall hangs a set of black and white photos of the abbey, a token of the inspiration Iona has been in both their lives. The contrast between Iona and urban Glasgow could not be starker. They live in an area of the city which has been roughly treated; a short walk from their home is the motorway and a junction of major roads. Apart from the time they have spent on Iona, John and Molly have lived in some of the poorest parishes in Glasgow, a commitment which stretches back to radical experiments in the 1960s when they pooled their money with a group of other ministers and their wives. In comparison, the demands the Iona Community places on its many members have been relatively easy, they said: a tithing of all personal income (giving away a tenth), accounting every month to one's local fellow members, and once a year to the leader of the community, on how one has spent one's money and time.

'The accounting grew out of a conviction that the Christian community is not serious about community without being serious about how you share your cash. Resources are what make a community work, otherwise you're just talking hot air,' said John, who acknowledged that, as leader of the community, he had had to ask people to leave as well as accept resignations from those no longer able to bear this scrutiny of their lives.

'The problem back in the early years,' Molly interjected, 'was that it was the men making all the decisions. The women were in the kitchen while the men were in the sitting room deciding about the family money.'

'It's not so much the tithing that is difficult as the accounting. The fact that you are open with each other about money,' adds John. 'A community is not the same as a golf club.'

John remembered how, as a young man in 1958, Iona had been a revelation to him. A committed Presbyterian, his understanding of Christianity in Scotland had, until then, been almost entirely based on a history which began around 1560.

Iona revealed to him the previous millennium and the role of Celtic Christianity and Roman Catholicism in Scottish history. Inspired by Colum Cille's evangelizing of the Picts of mainland Scotland, John saw the modern-day equivalent in the then slums of Glasgow. He found compelling the community's vision of a Christianity which transcended denominational boundaries.

'Jesus didn't come to set up a church when he said, "Follow me." He didn't say, "Worship me." The point is that you're not supposed to stay in one place; you are on the move.'

A fortnight before, they had both been demonstrating at Faslane, the nuclear submarine base in the Clyde. Molly has been imprisoned for previous demonstrations. Iona has inspired a very demanding practice of community and political engagement in their lives; nor did it seem they were opting for quiet retirement.

'I used to take groups of families from Glasgow to stay in Iona (it was mostly mothers and children). They told me that it was an incredible experience: living with important people like teachers, doctors, being on first-name terms and doing basic chores together, like cleaning the loos,' said John.

'The professionals would say that it had been a privilege to meet and spend time with people with difficulties whom they only ever met as professionals, to get to know them as individuals. There are not many places where this happens, where the barriers come down,' he said.

'I remember one very tough group from a young offenders' institution. One night I heard a sobbing in the abbey and it was a young lad. He told me, "I never thought anyone in a church would want to shake my hand." That kind of thing happened every week on Iona and people left as high as kites, while the staff might be left in pieces after a difficult group. It was very hard work.'

*

Of the many legacies of this small rocky island, one has recently had national impact. In the graveyard next to the abbey I found unexpected and poignant signs of another pilgrimage route. Across the close-cropped turf, a narrow path had been worn by visitors to one particular gravestone. Such has been the traffic of feet, islanders have complained that the graves of their relatives are being disturbed. The grave has accumulated a few pebbles as offerings, rather like those at Colum Cille's first landing place, the cave on Kintyre. It is the gravestone of a politician, John Smith, the leader of the Labour Party who died suddenly of a heart attack in 1994, at the age of fifty-five. It has been more than twenty years since his death, and his two protégés, Tony Blair and Gordon Brown, have eclipsed his name, but the path worn in the grass is a tribute to a man who was loved and admired. A large part of that affection is due to his passionate commitment to a Scottish parliament, for which he campaigned from the 1970s; as leader, he ensured that Scottish devolution became Labour Party policy, along with a raft of measures on social justice, some of which were implemented after the 1997 victory. He was the Labour prime minister Britain never had, and he left his mark on a generation of political leaders. Many of the political ideas which he bequeathed to his protégés bear traces of his love of Iona and its long history of inspiring moral communities. After his sudden death, his wish to be buried in Iona was granted, unusually, by the islanders, and following a funeral attended by thousands in Edinburgh, his coffin, like those of the medieval kings buried on the island, was brought by boat.

Two years before, in 1992, Smith had become leader of the Labour party in the wake of a deeply demoralizing election defeat, the fourth in a row. Labour could have once again fragmented into bitter factions, but for Smith's steadying influence. However, that was not all. Smith's achievement was to lay the ground for the Labour victory of 1997, and one of the ways he did so was by drawing into British politics distinctive elements of the Scottish Christian tradition, including some derived from the example of the Iona Community. It represented a radical new departure for a Labour party which had adopted a secular political language of class, identity and human rights. Smith brought morality back into left-wing politics, openly acknowledging the importance of Christianity to him with his characteristic common sense and careful intelligence (for which he was often likened to a bank manager). Half of his Shadow Cabinet were Christian Socialists, and, significantly, he gave cover for an ambitious young Shadow Cabinet colleague, Tony Blair, to come into the open about his own religious faith.

In an important speech in Bloomsbury Baptist Church in March 1993, Smith laid out how his Christian beliefs underpinned his politics and, in doing so, he repositioned Labour in territory that Thatcher had seized in the 1980s: the freedom of the individual. 'The moral goal of our society is to extend and encourage individual freedom,' he declared, and explained that Labour stood between laissez-faire individualism on the one hand and Marxism on the other. This was the centre ground on which New Labour would be built, a triangulation between the aspirational individualism of Thatcherism and the collective traditions of the Labour party, both now wrapped by Smith in the language of morality. He even quoted the Scottish philosopher so admired by Thatcher, Adam Smith, to make his case. Smith argued that human freedom was best developed and expressed within the social structures of community, family and nation. The intrinsically social nature of human beings ensured that it was through relationships with others that individuals reached fulfilment. We are not obstacles to each other's freedom, but the means. It was relationships which 'crucially determined our capacity for personal freedom and spiritual fulfilment'. No politician since has dared to suggest that politics could play a part in spiritual fulfilment. It was a belief that Colum Cille, the diplomat-contemplative, would have recognized.

Iona has always been associated with a distinctive intertwining of the secular and the spiritual. Colum Cille may have devoted himself to ascetic practice, but he was also an aristocrat and deeply engaged in the structures of political power. The Iona Community has continued this tradition of political engagement. Smith took from this history a belief that the nation has to have a moral vision; political pragmatism is not enough. The nation has to stand for some larger purpose, which he framed in terms of enlarging individual freedom, and justice. 'Why would anyone bother going into politics unless it was to speak up for those who can't speak up for themselves?' he once said in a comment which revealed both his sense of moral responsibility as a politician and also a strong streak of paternalism. Smith's moral project for the nation, shaped by his Scottish Presbyterianism, was high-minded, principled and built on a Biblical model of patriarchal leadership. It was a tradition which had served empire, the centralized bureaucracies of the Second World War and the welfare state. Smith's contribution was to reinterpret that tradition for an age which privileged individualism and personal freedom. It set Blair on course to develop his Shadow Home Secretary brief to emphasize individual responsibility, summarized in his famous slogan, 'tough on crime, tough on the causes of crime'. Gordon Brown, son of a Presbyterian minister, also took up Smith's vision with enthusiasm as part of a generation of Scottish politicians who were to dominate the Labour governments of 1997–2010. At least four Cabinet ministers had close links to the Hebrides: Douglas Alexander was baptized on Iona, and his father was a minister and member of the Iona

Community; Alasdair Darling and Brian Wilson married women from Lewis and have homes there; and George Robertson came from Islay. Fragments of Gaelic communitarianism had arrived in Westminster, and for Blair they were reinforced by the thinking of another Scot – one whom Blair claimed to be his greatest intellectual inspiration – the Quaker philosopher John Macmurray (a friend and admirer of George MacLeod).

More than twenty years on, there has been a bitter and enduring debate about how much of this moral vision survived Labour's arrival in power; disillusioned critics argue that it was abandoned quickly once in office, that it was compromised by wars and crippled by embittered personal relationships. Accusations of opportunism have been rife and there have been complaints that this Scottish moral vision always inspired more rhetoric than achievement, and that it shaped an authoritarian style of leadership. But it still had purchase in 2014: when Gordon Brown gave his impassioned plea to 'save Britain' in the last days of the Scottish independence referendum, he used the language of solidarity and the nation as a moral community.

These ideas and ideals formed a strand of British politics which was profoundly Scottish in inspiration. England's pragmatism in politics has struggled ever to match the passion, the imagination and deep historical resonance provided by this Scottish moral tradition. At key moments in British history, politicians such as William Gladstone, Keir Hardie, Tom Johnston, to name some of the most prominent, have used the Scottish moral vision to reset the course of the nation with a higher purpose of social justice and mutual responsibility. It was a mark of John Smith's impact that subsequent party leaders, both Conservative and Labour, have attempted to set out their electoral stall as a moral project, with varying degrees of credibility and sincerity.

Smith needed a moral vision to inspire solidarity in a nation deeply divided by bitter political conflict during the 1980s; he and his protégés wooed the middle classes back to Labour. Just as John Harvey spoke to me of the bridges he witnessed being built in Iona between people from different social classes, with different life experiences, so Smith steered the Labour party away from a language of class war and laid the basis for a pragmatic coalition. Two decades on, politicians use the language of morality for the same purpose, bidding for an ever-more elusive sense of national solidarity in Britain. They want to describe a nation with a sense of meaning and purpose, to which people feel they belong and, crucially, for which they are prepared to make sacrifices, participate and contribute. In 2014 this Scottish tradition coalesced around a new nationalism: Scotland became the means to build this solidarity. In the fevered debates of September 2014 in Glasgow, I recognized the rhetoric, I heard the echoes of the Promised Land, but it was no longer about my country.

4

Staffa

*To the southern inhabitants of Scotland, the state
of the mountains and islands is equally well
known with that of Borneo and Sumatra; of both
they have heard a little and guess the rest.*

SAMUEL JOHNSON, *A JOURNEY TO THE
WESTERN ISLES*

I

The journey from Iona to neighbouring Staffa takes thirty-five
minutes in a day-trip boat. The weather was still brilliantly
clear spring sunshine, and as my son and I sailed between Iona
and Mull's west coast we could see in the distance the dramatic
outline of Rum, which would be my next island stop, forty miles
away. Three islands and three chapters on my journey were
simultaneously visible, relating to each other as physical entities
rather than the pale brown and green shapes on a map pasted
on my wall in London.

Beyond the bulge of northern Mull, Rum's mountains rose steeply, a pale blue shadow on the horizon, and beyond them I could make out the faint, jagged outline of Skye's Cuillins. These great bulks of ancient rock were hovering delicately in the bright light as if the next breeze might blow them away altogether. The boat skipper told us that on some days Barra could be seen beyond Coll across the Minch to the west, but that kind of clarity always presaged rain, he added, laughing – a particular feature of the Hebrides in which the heavy weight of water vapour lends luminosity to the light.

The skipper was in a buoyant mood as he worked his way round the boatload of day trippers, plunging enthusiastically into conversation with each group, discussing puffins, seals, sea eagles and anything else anyone wanted to talk about. With us, it was politics and religion. His boat was flying the Saltire flag, and he warmed to his theme of Scotland's independence, his eyes sparkling with amusement. He was a Yes voter, he declared; he had had enough of New Labour and wanted socialism. As for religion, he did not have much to do with the Iona Community; George MacLeod had never sought the islanders' opinions about the rebuilding of the monastery back in the 1930s. He chuckled at how one of his passengers, a minister, had once walked out of a service, horrified at its interpretation of Christianity, with its guitars and votive offerings. But, if Christianity had a future, the skipper continued, it was more likely to look like the Iona Community.

Packed onto our boat were tourists from Scotland, England, North America and Europe. As we sailed past a beach where seals were basking in the sunshine, cameras came out, their mechanisms clicking. The seals looked up, curious, their eyes rounded with apparent surprise. We passed swiftly and they lumped their ungainly bulk over the rocks to settle back down.

Their bodies blended with the rocks as the beach receded behind us.

Staffa has been a paradox for a long time. The small island – about half a mile long – rose to fame in the late eighteenth century; with its remarkable rock formations and cave it was billed as a marvel of nature, an opportunity to encounter the sublime in the wilderness of Britain's north-west. But the sublime required solitude, and as early as the 1800s visitors were already complaining of sharing their visit with a host of other fashionable savants in pursuit of wilderness, solitude and contemplation of a natural wonder. People were carving their initials in the rocks of Fingal's Cave. Even worse, the indignant cried, the experience was marred by those on neighbouring islands intent on making a living from the visitors.

Staffa attracted a succession of writers, poets, composers and artists in the early nineteenth century. Most famously Sir Walter Scott's poem *The Lord of the Isles* ensured that from the 1830s paddle steamers from the Clyde brought parties of tourists to visit Staffa on their routes round Mull, Skye and Iona. By the middle of the nineteenth century, railways and steamers meant that the west coast was within reach of Thomas Cook tours. Staffa had become a required destination for anyone with pretensions to a cultured sensibility. Wordsworth miserably concluded after his visit in 1833 that he had come too late:

> *We saw, but surely, in the motley crowd,*
> *Not One of us has felt the far-famed sight;*
> *How could we feel it? each the other's blight,*
> *Hurried and hurrying, volatile and loud.*

It became a measure of the visitor's discernment and good taste to complain about the quantity of visitors on Staffa. After a century of complaints, one might have imagined that visitors would have understood – even accepted – that Staffa was a convivial experience. But even in the mid-twentieth century, the Scottish mountaineer and writer W. H. Murray was insisting that 'to know Staffa one must go alone'. That privilege has been accorded only to those wealthy enough to have their own boat. Elitism and the sublime have long been intertwined – the true experience of the latter has always required education and/or wealth.

The sea had been too rough for Samuel Johnson to land on Staffa. Even with a now sturdy jetty, our boat was rocked by the swell, and required careful manoeuvring between the famous hexagonal basalt columns. Swathes of them have been knocked over, like the crumbled filaments of a chocolate flake. They are tilted on their sides, stilled in a spectacular volcanic moment which leaves them stacked in sinuous forms echoing the shape of the waves. The sea surges through a channel between them, racing to crash against the rocks. This stubbled shoreline is no friend to boats or people. Old photos show ladies in their crino-lines, wide hats and heels, picking their way along the shoreline to Fingal's Cave. In time concrete steps and a path were built, and iron railings were bolted into the rock to help the steady stream of visitors.

We eyed the narrow path over the rocks to Fingal's Cave and sized up the cheerful boatload of disembarking visitors. The cave could wait, we decided, and headed in the opposite direc-tion, straight up a steep flight of steps to Staffa's summit, where we were greeted by a fresh wind sweeping across the island. Undulating rough grass, bleached by the winter winds, came to an abrupt halt at cliffs which dropped sheer to the pounding surf below. There was a small cairn, the rough markings of a small ruin, but no tree or even a stunted bush: it was as if the wind had scoured the place. We sat on the cliffs with the murmur of the surf below, eating lunch; it was like perching precariously on an earthenware platter sailing in the sea.

All around us were scattered islands. Some were easy to identify, such as the distinctive contours of the Treshnish Isles; others blurred into each other in the light haze. To the north-west, long low-lying Coll merged into Tiree. To the north-east, Ulva and Gometra were hard to distinguish from each other or from Mull. Due east lay the bleak island of Inch Kenneth, which Lord Redesdale, father of the six Mitford sisters, had bought for a refuge in 1938 as the Second World War threatened. The most controversial of his daughters, Unity, spent her last years there suffering from a failed suicide attempt which had left a bullet lodged in her brain. She surrounded herself with the memorabilia of her fascination with Hitler. Allegedly the house was festooned with swastikas and photographs of the Führer.

Closest to Staffa lies Little Colonsay. It seemed to have got lost, to have cast off its anchor many millions of years ago and drifted away from the island of Colonsay, which is well to the south, the other side of the Ross of Mull. This was island spotting at its best, more than a dozen to identify and name, their pale blue contours teased out from their neighbours. I raised a toast to them all, a nip of whisky from the flask. The blue sky arced over the level sea as the waves rode calmly to crash on the rocks below. The island did not feel steady and it wasn't the whisky; it was if some giant had flung it like a frisbee to skim low over this spread of water. It was exhilarating. In winter it would be terrifying; the last inhabitants left Staffa in the eighteenth century and one early traveller reported the verdict of one who had lived eight years on the island: 'that part of his existence [was] fraught with gloom and anxiety; stating that he and his companions were often involved in showers of spray when the whole island shook, and their ears were assailed with the incessant thundering of the waves as they rolled into the cavern'.

After an hour largely to ourselves, our fellow visitors began to emerge at the head of the steps and joined us on the empty slopes, following the paths which criss-cross the island from cliff to cliff. We packed up the remains of our sandwiches, descended the steps and took the concrete path over the basalt columns to the cave. Above our heads, the fluted pillars supported the bulky layer of rock. From the boat, these cliffs had reminded me of a bad 1980s haircut with frizzy curls on top. Now, as the grandeur of these astonishing rock formations closed in around us, such frivolous analogies seemed inappropriate. The columns' regularity has astonished countless visitors: there are thousands of pillars in the shape of regular hexagons, some several metres long, some less than a metre. The famous naturalist Sir Joseph Banks, who first brought the cave to national fame, wrote in his journal in 1772: 'Compared to this, what are the cathedrals or the palaces built by man? Mere models or play-things! Imitations as diminutive as his works will always be when compared to those of Nature! Where is now the boast of the architect? Regularity, the only part in which he fancied himself to exceed his mistress, Nature, is here found in her possession; and here it has been for ages uncounted ... How amply does Nature repay those who study her wonderful works.'

Sixty million years ago, the great volcanoes of north-west Scotland spewed huge lava flows which stretched down to north-west Ireland in the south and up to the islands of the Shiants off Lewis in the north. As the lava cooled from above and below, it contracted, and cracks opened up known as a fracture network. Such networks are familiar – watch a muddy puddle dry out – but what stunned Banks was the process by which the cooling lava contracted into a pattern of regular columns, most of which were hexagons. This pattern in nature has intrigued researchers, and years of study have been devoted to how materials such as mud, paint and glaze dry out and create fracture networks. The hexagon, which dominates cooling lava's fracture network, is the shape with the greatest number of sides that tessellate and thus is the most efficient way to split an area. A similar hexagonal structure is found in other natural forms such as beehives and cells.

Pillars of dark grey grainy rock frame the entrance to Fingal's Cave, seventy-five metres long and twenty metres high. The basalt pillars line the sides, stumps stepping down into the sea. In the clear water, more columns are visible. The colours of the rocks flow from grey to a deep green-black in the body of the cave, and in places the layer of rock beneath the basalt is exposed, washed by the sea to shell pink. The cave's roof is uneven where the pillars have been smashed by the sea, and is splashed with pale lichens. The sea heaves its weight, a brilliant green, along the cave's length, burrowing into the island until it smacks into the back, the dull, vibrating thud echoing in the space. The light gleams in the clear water and bounces off the dark rock.

II

Fingal's Cave had another name before Banks renamed it: An Uamh Bhin, the Melodious Cave, because of the sound the waves made as they beat on its walls. Banks was on a voyage of exploration to Iceland in August 1772 when he stopped to stay on the island of Mull. Intrigued by reports of a cave from his hosts, the Macleans, he was rowed over to camp on Staffa. He spent a day measuring and investigating. An Uamh Bhin was already well known in the Hebrides, but Banks' name has

stuck ever since he published his *Journal of a Voyage* in 1772, for
an audience eager to hear more of his remarkable explorations.
Having likened it to a cathedral, he drove the point home with
a series of superlatives: 'this piece of architecture, formed by
nature, far surpasses that of the Louvre, that of St. Peter at

Rome, all that remains of Palmyra and Paestum, and all that the genius, the taste and the luxury of the Greeks were capable of inventing'. Banks chose a name which ensured instant fame. He claimed the cave was associated with the Scottish legend of a king, Fingal, and his poet son, Ossian, the subject of a recently published cycle of epic poems by James Macpherson.

This publishing sensation had thrust Gaelic culture centre-stage in European cultural life. A new Homer had been discovered on the continent's north-west fringe, declared the rapturous critics of literary Europe. Macpherson, a Scottish schoolteacher, had travelled the Highlands gathering Gaelic folklore and in 1760 he published *Fragments of Ancient Poetry Collected in the Highlands of Scotland and Translated from the Gaelic or Erse Language*. The following year he published *Fingal, an Ancient Epic Poem in Six Books*, which tells the story of a king, Fingal, related to the Irish mythological character Fionn mac Cumhaill; written by his poet son Ossian, it recounts their great battles, lost loves and heroic deeds. In 1765 a collected edition, *The Works of Ossian*, was published. Macpherson's gatherings of Gaelic folklore entranced Napoleon, who was said to keep a copy close to hand, and were acclaimed by Goethe, Schiller, Diderot and Victor Hugo. They influenced the Romantic movement in Scotland and England and in due course they crossed the Atlantic to inspire writers such as James Fenimore Cooper, author of *Last of the Mohicans*, and, later, the poet Henry Wadsworth Longfellow and Henry Thoreau. In London, Macpherson's work provoked fierce controversy as the literary world struggled to grasp the concept of a sophisticated oral tradition from the northern shores of Britain. The question of what Macpherson had found and what he had written himself has dogged the work ever since. Johnson believed a language had to be written to achieve greatness and, overlooking the existence of Gaelic manuscripts several centuries old, declared with great authority that Macpherson's writing was a fraud. An arrogant scepticism (often on the part of English critics) has persisted, infuriating many Scots, who believe that the literary controversy has overshadowed the work and obscured the now substantial Gaelic scholarship which has established Macpherson's sources. The controversy's impact has been lasting and damaging, it is argued, bequeathing a nagging sense of uncertainty as to the authenticity of Gaelic culture. These arguments were at their peak in the latter part of the eighteenth century, when one American critic called the controversy a 'seismograph of the fragile unity within the restive diversity of imperial Great Britain'. It added to the allure and sense of mystery which provided Scotland with a role in the still-new nation of Britain. The naming of Fingal's Cave linked Staffa to this combination of myth, debate and nation-building. As in other emerging European nations at this time, a contested mythology became the way in which questions of authenticity – who had it and who did not – could be argued and used to assert cultural dominance.

Macpherson's tales were full of mist and gloom, an invigorating blend of tragedy and nostalgia for a lost age. Yet Macpherson was not specific about the places where the myths had taken place. Banks stepped into the gap and An Uamh Bhin became Fingal's Cave. A natural wonder and the myth have proved a potent blend in which both have shaped perceptions of the other.

The basalt columns may be much bigger on the Shiants, off the east coast of Lewis – at 106 metres they dwarf those on Staffa – and they may be more dramatic at the Giant's Causeway in Antrim, but Staffa has a cave. Caves have long been places of inspiration in European mythology. The gloom, dank chill and unfamiliar soundscape – the sensory deprivation of caves – have ensured that in classical times, and since, they are regarded as places of revelation.

In Celtic history, St Columba's first stopping point in Scotland on the Mull of Kintyre was a cave, and St Molaise lived in a cave on Holy Isle. In classical Greece, caves were places of pilgrimage where a pilgrim might commune with the gods through a priest or oracle; the most famous was Delphi, where petitioners could bring their questions and the oracle would emerge from the cave with answers and prophesies. Banks' choice of name nodded both to this classical tradition and to Macpherson's interpretation of the Gaelic tradition, and the stage was set for the place to transfix a procession of distinguished visitors over the following decades. Staffa became an icon of Britain's new national geography, a pilgrimage site for a nation searching for myths powerful and dramatic enough to sustain its rapidly swelling sense of self-importance and global mission.

The name was significant, but so also was the namer. Banks was a towering eighteenth-century figure, a pioneer of a grand new age of exploration and science. His fame derived from his groundbreaking travels in Newfoundland in 1766, and with James Cook to Brazil, Tahiti and Australia between 1768 and 1771. He documented countless plants and birds, and his penchant for naming ensured that no less than eighty plants bear his name. He became advisor to King George III on the building of the botanical gardens at Kew, and a long-serving president of the Royal Society. Banks' enthusiasm for Fingal's Cave pointed to marvels within Britain which he believed matched any he had found on his long voyages. This Scottish coastline had been regarded as an empty space in the British imagination, as Daniel Defoe admitted when he wrote *A Tour Thro' the Whole Island of Great Britain* in 1724: 'our geographers seem to be almost as much at a loss in the description of this north part of Scotland,

as the Romans were to conquer it; and they are obliged to fill
it up with hills and mountains, as they do the inner parts of
Africa with lions and elephants for want of knowing what else
to place there'. Defoe even confessed that he did not bother
to visit the Hebrides, and did not expect anyone else to do so,
given the hazards of getting there and that there was so little to
see. Banks turned these eighteenth-century prejudices upside
down; many of those who followed him to the Western Isles
could never have hoped to reach Tahiti, but Staffa was a worthy
alternative. The perception of exoticism lasted well into the
nineteenth century; as late as 1883 C. F. Gordon-Cumming, in
her whimsical memoir *In the Hebrides*, drew a comparison with
her travels in the Himalayas: 'my attention was forcibly arrested
by many very striking analogies between many of the customs
and legends of the Western Islanders and those of Eastern highlanders [Himalayan peoples]'.

For a nation whose horizons were expanding at dizzying
speeds – the new continent of Australasia, the vast ocean of the
Pacific and its chains of islands were all being charted in the last
quarter of the eighteenth century – there was a powerful new
impulse to know its own home. There was a surge in mapping
and surveying; improved roads and communications opened
up new regions such as Snowdonia, the Lake District and
the Highlands. This era of nation-building required domestic
exploration. The new national identity was restless, curious
and mobile; between Defoe's *A Tour Thro' The Whole Island* and
Johnson's *Journey* fifty years later there were plenty of accounts,
often illustrated, of this process of travelling to know home.
The nation was being reimagined as a set of experiences. Two
major cultural ideals made this home-making meaningful: the
picturesque provided an aesthetic with which to view these new
landscapes, and the sublime offered guidance as to the required

emotional experience. Regions which had been marginal were now drawn into the sphere of the nation, and assigned a role to delight, inspire and enthuse visitors with images of the antique and the authentic. The splendours of these new regions redounded to the glory of the new nation of Britain, demonstrating the variety and beauty of her great landscapes. Staffa had all the necessary features to provide the sublime – the awe-inspiring geology, the revelatory power of caves, the promise of solitude – in this new national geography.

The sublime was an experience of greatness beyond all possibility of calculation, measurement or imitation, declared Edmund Burke in *A Philosophical Enquiry into the Origin of Our Ideas of the Sublime and Beautiful* (1757). At a time when rationalism was leading to scientific and technological breakthroughs, Burke was clearing a cultural space for human experience of the opposite: the wild and spontaneous. Experience of the sublime overwhelmed the rational mind, scattering one's faculties. The language could be startlingly violent: the sublime 'commits a pleasing rape upon the very soul' wrote one contemporary commentator. The sublime needed to provoke dread; it intimidated and threatened with such force that all rational thought processes were stilled. Deprivation of some form was often entailed, whether of company, sound or light. Since many of those who pursued the sublime had the comfort and security provided by Britain's new wealth, this frisson of fear was experienced from a place of safety. The inhospitable fierceness of nature was now to be sought out; the travails of journeys in the Highlands and Islands, such as storms, terrible terrain and lack of physical comfort, were to be endured as part of the Romantic quest for the sublime.

Burke argued that there could be several simultaneous emotional responses and they could be contradictory: an experience could prompt both horror and delight. Burke's writings were based on empiricism, attending to and reporting his own psychological experience, and his insights became hugely influential. The individual's emotional response was privileged over accepted convention. Burke had laid the basis for modern tourism; only by visiting somewhere could one experience the full emotional response now considered of such importance.

In an age when the art of conversation was regarded as one of civilization's greatest benefits, the sublime was expected to overwhelm one's capacity to speak. While the picturesque could generate all manner of conversation around its finickety requirements – as Jane Austen elegantly satirized in *Persuasion* – the sublime should render the visitor speechless. It was oddly enfeebling, suggested cultural historian Malcolm Andrews, that if you had correctly experienced the sublime, you could not actually talk or write with any eloquence about it. In due course even the prolix Sir Walter Scott, along with John Keats and William Wordsworth, duly recorded himself speechless when he encountered Fingal's Cave. Scott wrote that it was 'one of the most extraordinary places I ever beheld. It exceeded, in my mind, every description I had heard of it ... composed entirely of basaltic pillars as high as the roof of a cathedral and running deep into the rock, eternally swept by a deep and swelling sea, and paved, as it were, with ruddy marbles, [it] baffles all description'. In the inn after a visit in 1814, he penned a few lines:

> *Cliffs of darkness, caves of wonder,*
> *Echoing the Atlantic thunder;*
> *Mountains which the grey mist covers*
> *Where the Chieftain spirit hovers.*

As visitors struggled to rally their senses, many followed Banks' lead. 'It was impossible to describe it,' wrote Keats in a letter to his brother Tom in July 1818, before resorting to the cathedral metaphor used by Banks, and complaining about the other visitors, who would 'unweave/ All the magic of the place'. He apologized for the poem he scribbled on his visit, adding 'it can't be helped':

This Cathedral of the Sea!
I have been the pontiff-priest
Where the waters never rest,
Where a fledgy sea-bird choir
Soars for ever; holy fire
I have hid from mortal man.

Perhaps the fact that over the previous two days Keats had walked thirty-seven miles in heavy rain across south Mull contributed to the overheated character of his lines. He was soaked, exhausted and had to sleep on the mud floors of kindly but impoverished islanders on his way to Staffa. It was a journey which biographer Andrew Motion believes led to his death, fatally weakening him before he nursed his brother dying of tuberculosis. But Keats considered the effort worthwhile: the 'solemnity and grandeur' of Fingal's Cave 'far surpassed the finest cathedral'. With a nod to how Romanticism was casting Scotland in a new role in the nation, Keats wrote that he hoped his Scottish tour would 'give me more experience, rub off more Prejudice, use me to more hardship, identify finer scenes, load me with greater mountains and strengthen more my reach in Poetry'. He drew on Fingal's Cave for the setting for the vast historical drama of his poem *Hyperion*, as he discussed at length in his letter to his brother immediately after visiting: 'Suppose now the Giants who rebelled against Jove had taken a whole mass of black columns and bound them together like bunches of matches – and then with immense Axes had made a cavern in the body of these columns ... About the island you might seat an army of Men each on a pillar.'

For Banks' contemporaries, this was a period of spectacular technological invention, and they saw Fingal's Cave as an important lesson in humility for any person tempted to pride. Banks' travelling companion, Bishop Linköping, wrote, 'here nature has shown that when she pleases she can set man at nought even in this respect and make him sensible of his own littleness'. The cave was a warning against triumphalist pride and hubris, not just of individuals but of nations, a reminder of the power of nature, and above that, the Divine Creator, God. But along with the humbling came inspiration and an 'enlargement of the mind'. Thomas Gray recommended an annual pilgrimage to the Highlands for poets, painters, gardeners and clergymen (in that order) and if they did not, 'their imagination can be made up of nothing but bowling greens, flowering shrubs, horse ponds, fleet ditches, shell grottoes and Chinee rails'. In late-eighteenth-century London, a lady commenting in a letter on the Ossianic controversy praised Macpherson, the new Homer: 'I honour him for carrying the Muses into the country and letting them step majestic over hills, mountains and rivers, instead of tamely walking in the Park or Piccadilly.' Both commentators revealed an insecurity that England's quiet landscape could not fire the imagination or inspire the required moral fibre. The softly rolling chalk downland of southern England or the mild undulations of the Midlands could not stimulate or uplift with the kind of epic drama now provided by Scottish landscape and poetry, thanks to Macpherson and Scott.

A great golden age of heroic virtue and antiquity was being projected onto the Hebridean archipelago, and imprecision was a part of it. This was the myth of antique origins that the new elites of the British Empire – industrialists, nabobs, empire-builders, bankers and adventurers – needed to bolster pride and purpose; theirs was an ancient, glorious nation with a geographical reach well beyond their small island. That these origins should lie on the edge of an ocean amongst a seafaring warrior people was only fitting for an assertive maritime power. As swathes of Britain were convulsed by industrialization and urbanization, the sacred and mythological needed to be distant and unchanged.

Britain was not alone in projecting onto the periphery the most intense imaginings of nation. It was a phenomenon evident at this time in other European powers. What many of them shared – Russia, Germany and Britain, for example – was a process of imaginative self-definition which took artists, poets and writers to their country's boundaries, to the edges where the accepted understanding of civilization and order gave out and encountered the 'other'. Russia looked to the Caucasus mountains, Germany to the Alps, its forests and coasts. Britain looked north and west to Iona and Staffa.

Ossianic myths bolstered Britain's new multinational elite as a martial people. They offered 'the most animating and lofty ideas, calculated to inspire the mind with heroic courage and virtue', wrote one traveller to Scotland who had the obligatory Macpherson tomes in their suitcase. They recast elite aspirations away from the historic cultural dominance of France in the aftermath of the Revolution, when aristocratic status could no longer safely define itself by conspicuous consumption. What emerged in the late eighteenth and early nineteenth centuries was a more martial, energetic masculinity. As Keats had acknowledged of his journey, hardship was part of the experience. In time, hunt-ing, shooting and fishing became the unifying rituals of the British upper classes. Ossianic warrior culture was no threat to the British constitution, because it lay in a far distant past, and could now be used to inspire military prowess. Gaelic warriors had been safely repurposed as a mythology to inspire young British gentlemen in public schools to fight for empire. Fingal's Cave proved an emblem of this pivotal moment in the late eighteenth century, as Britain and her elites appropriated Gaelic culture to reimagine themselves.

III

The artist who captured this maelstrom of nation-building, ambition and insecurity, and the role of Staffa, was a man from the Thames estuary, J. M. W. Turner. He travelled on the famil-iar pilgrimage to Staffa in 1831, compiling numerous sketches along the way as part of a project to illustrate Sir Walter Scott's *Poetical Works*. Scott had visited Staffa in 1810 and again in 1814, and he worked a description of Fingal's Cave into *The Lord of the Isles*, a poem which described Scotland's struggle for independ-ence from England up to the Scottish victory at Bannockburn in 1314. Turner's vignette of Fingal's Cave was chosen to illustrate the extract of the poem in the *Poetical Works*. For the engraving Turner had followed contemporary convention, positioning himself in the cave, and looking out towards a setting sun. A sketchbook of Turner's drawings of the cave testify to his fascination with the remarkable geology, but when he came to produce his painting of the place, he had an entirely different set of preoccupations.

On the day he visited in 1831, the weather was bad and Turner recounted in a letter that the passengers refused to continue on their planned tour to Iona so they circled Staffa three times. 'The sun getting towards the horizon burst through the rain cloud, angry, and for wind.' From this moment he composed *Staffa, Fingal's Cave*, one of his most famous paintings. It was exhibited in May 1832, and he added some lines of Scott's poem, as he often did with his paintings (he regarded poetry and painting as 'sister arts'):

> *Nor of a theme less solemn tells*
> *That mighty surge that ebbs and swells,*
> *And still, between each awful pause,*
> *From the high vault an answer draws.*

A week later, Mendelssohn's *Hebrides Overture* premiered in London. The German Romantic composer had visited in 1829 and had written to his family in Berlin with a fragment of the music he had allegedly heard in Fingal's Cave. 'In order to make you understand how extraordinarily the Hebrides affected me, I send you the following which came into my head there.' It developed into the *Overture*. Those weeks in May 1832 marked the high watermark of Staffa's iconic status. Two of the greatest artists of the age had put Staffa at the centre of London's cultural experience.

Turner conveyed a rich sense of Ossianic drama in his painting. Staffa's cliffs are greatly enlarged to dwarf the steamship on the sea below. A sinister swell of the sea is gathering. Heavy grey clouds have swung in from the west, the sea is cast in brown and near-black shadow. In the centre of the foreground is a thick band of black sea which cuts a dark horizontal across the picture. Staffa itself is barely visible through the clouds of mist and rain; as for the regularity of the basalt pillars of Fingal's Cave, so much admired for the previous half century, there is no sign of them in this murk. Turner could have been painting any coastal headland. His naming of the picture was perhaps part opportunism – it immediately brought a host of well-known associations – and in part, I would suggest, a brilliant provocation. The one distinct form is the silhouetted steamship and its long plume of smoke drifting across the centre of the painting, pointing to the obscured cave. The eye is drawn to the movement of the steamship, a motif of Britain's technological mastery of the world, even while it acknowledges the grandeur of the mass of Staffa. The island glows in the shafts of light breaking through the clouds – the land of a blessed nation. Turner's painting genuflected at the mythic status of Fingal's Cave while at the same time consigning it to the margins. What interested Turner more than the cave and the particularity of its geology or the myth of Fingal was the experience of wind, rain and sea. The wild scumbling of paint, scratching and striations, and the scraping and rubbing, reveal submerged layers of colour, immanent in the wildness. The speechlessness of the sublime was leading to increasing abstraction in Turner's work.

Peer deeply at the original (or a good reproduction) and on the steamship, deep in the dark, is a tiny pinprick of red: a light in a cabin. On the water near the ship, there are glints of red where the light is reflected. In this vast panorama of cloud and sea, the steamship appears small and alone, plying its way. This is underlined by the comparable fragility of the lone white gull flying over the sea in the immediate foreground. It is a painting full of foreboding and insecurity and echoes the point Pythagoras had made centuries before of the 'destitution and loneliness' of the Atlantic ocean. Keats had expressed a similar sentiment in a letter on his journey to Scotland: 'I am not certain how I should endure loneliness and bad weather together.'

Turner was fascinated by the vanity of human endeavours and wrote a rambling long poem on the subject entitled 'The Fallacies of Hope'. Several of his biggest pieces, such as *Snow Storm: Hannibal and His Army Crossing the Alps*, convey the folly of empire. The lone steamship expressed both the indomitable pluck of British imperial expansion and its shadow: the legacy of exile and emigration for the millions whom empire dislocated and transported.

Turner was ambitious, not just for his art and for recognition, but to create a new visual language for Britain. The sea was its setting. He was a patriot, his great hero was Lord Nelson, near to whom he was eventually buried in the crypt of St Paul's. He left a considerable number of his paintings to the nation, ensuring his legacy would last. Many of his paintings worked the theme of island nation. Epic painting of historical scenes was the most prestigious genre of his time, and his *Staffa*, with its heavy weight of association, was a form of epic painting. It was a representation of national destiny, acknowledging a glorious past as a spur to ever greater feats, and its impact reached beyond Britain.

Staffa was bought, unseen, by an American, James Lenox, through an intermediary in 1845. Lenox was baffled by it and 'greatly disappointed', and complained of its 'indistinctness'. Turner replied, unapologetic: 'You should tell Mr Lenox that indistinctness is my forte.' (Lenox overcame his disappointment and went on to buy another of Turner's paintings a few years later.) Meanwhile Turner's *Staffa* played an important role in American cultural life. Herman Melville was fascinated by Turner's work and its portrayal of what Melville called the 'full awfulness of the sea'. A few years after *Staffa* arrived in the US, *Moby Dick* was published, in 1851; the novel included a description of a painting surely based on *Staffa*: 'A boggy soggy squitchy picture truly, enough to drive a nervous man distracted. Yet was there a sort of indefinite, half attained, unimaginable sublimity about it that fairly froze you to it, till you involuntarily took an oath with yourself to find out what that marvelous painting meant.'

It inspired other American artists, including Winslow Homer. The meaning of Turner's *Staffa* was transposed onto a new maritime nation, which, in time, developed its own imperial ambition.

Staffa was perfectly suited for the role it played over this pivotal half century, not just because of its basalt columns, but because it was empty. Banks may have come across one family living there on his visit in 1772, but by 1800 even they had given up. The story went that the lack of shelter from the ferocious winter gales, and the meagre crops they would have been able to grow on the island's open plateau were enough to drive them off in search of an easier way of life. From 1800 on, the stream of visitors could contemplate the sublime and its Ossianic associations with the long-lost age of the noble savage without being troubled by the desperate poverty of Ossian's descendants. In other parts of Scotland these travellers recorded with horror the 'servitude' of the Gaels, even likening their plight to that of the slaves on Jamaica's plantations. In 1810, on neighbouring Iona, Sir Walter Scott admitted he was horrified when 'we were surrounded on the beach by boys and girls, almost naked, all begging for charity and some offering pebbles for sale'. But such disturbing social and economic realities did not intrude on the visitor's contemplation on Staffa; the island offered a blank canvas for the projected fantasies of the age.

Staffa's iconic representation as sublime linked the place with solitude and loneliness despite the swelling numbers of travellers. Staffa's visitors set the pattern: they experienced what they had already imagined from the plethora of accounts, poems and engravings in which Scotland's Highlands and Islands were empty and wild. This was an imaginative construction of the late-eighteenth-century elite. In reality the Highlands and Islands were neither. Literary critic Jonathan Bate points out that 'those who truly dwell in the place are never lonely, because they are attuned to collective memory, to old association – an almost exhaustive biographical and historical acquaintance with every object animate and inanimate within the observer's horizon'. The Romantic tourist's gaze represented a cultural disruption; it ignored or averted its eyes from the impoverished inhabitants to celebrate the beauty of the natural forms. When the tourist did engage with those inhabitants, it was with a view to furthering that cultural disruption. One traveller to the Highlands, John Dalrymple, commented in the 1750s that there was 'too much appearance of dead life', and he went on to expand on the possible 'improvements' which could be made, such as 'white cottages, trees and the sights and sounds of life'.

'Solitude', 'improvement' and 'trees' were three words which frequently cropped up in the writings of these travellers to Scotland in the late eighteenth and early nineteenth centuries, and they nodded to the ideals which framed urban Britain's view of the peripheral region of the Highlands and Hebrides. These travellers were not interested in finding company; they were looking for solitude and wildness. Alongside this Romantic ideal was the impulse to 'improve' the land, to make it economically productive within the new industrial economy. Both the Romantic and the improver were placing new demands on the land. Beyond that, they had little in common, one intent on a set of personal experiences to be gained from the landscape, the other measuring, mapping and reordering the land to achieve greater productivity. But both were essentially extractive and privileged personal interests, either for sensation or for income. Neither had much interest in the Gaelic culture they were pushing aside because, in their different ways, they both rejected tradition. Romanticism made this explicit and glamorous and claimed superiority for its enlightened views; unwittingly it helped to legitimize the ruthlessness of the improvers. Both expressed a belief in progress which brought a new form of hubris. 'Wild' and 'improvement' have been bitterly political words in these parts of Scotland ever since.

Neither Romanticism nor improvement would have taken such a grip on perceptions of the Highlands and Islands in this era if they were not rooted in a centuries-old belief, held by both Lowlanders and the English, of the Gael as a barbarian. King James VI had used the term in the sixteenth century to belittle and marginalize the Gaels' rival claim to political authority and saw the north-west of Scotland as a frontier country where civilization ended. After the defeat of the Jacobites at Culloden in 1746 and the brutal suppression of Gaelic culture, the Gaels were no longer considered a military threat. The Gàidhealtachd was cast in the role of a doomed culture, a lost cause. The xenophobic contempt of earlier ages was translated into indifference towards the economic circumstances of the people, and varying degrees of hostility to their language; this informed in different ways the enthusiasm of both the Romantic and the improver. The fact that some of Gaelic's most eminent poets were writing in the eighteenth century was entirely overlooked by Johnson, Banks and their many followers.

As the idea of the noble savage, uncorrupted by civilization, gained popularity in the eighteenth century, the attributes which had once been used as evidence of the barbarism of the Gael were now inverted. What had been described as the Gael's tendency to wild aggression now became bravery and valour; what had been dismissed contemptuously as impetuous and childlike became impassioned and expressive of deep feeling. The impact of this romanticization was to shroud Gaelic Scotland in an impotent nostalgia. 'The Scottish Gael fulfilled this role of the primitive ... albeit one quickly and savagely tamed, at a time when every thinking man was turning towards such subjects ... The Highlands were distant enough to be exotic (in customs and language) but close enough to be noticed ... Near enough to be visited but had not been drawn so far into the calm waters of civilization as to lose all its interest,' comments historian Malcolm Chapman.

Britain exported this idealization of the noble savage to North America, and it influenced some aspects of the relationship between early settlers and Native Americans. In eighteenth-century North America, the Gaels were renowned for their ability to negotiate and collaborate with Native Americans, and on occasion this was attributed by their English commanders to their common savagery. After the defeat at Culloden in 1746, Gaels were recruited in large numbers into Britain's armies. In the Seven Years War in North America (1756–63), the Scottish casualty rate was four times higher than that of England or America. The infamous comment of the British general James Wolfe was that it was 'no great mischief if they fell'. 'Savages' were recruited to fight 'savages' and both were expendable. In the British Empire such categorization became a frequently used tool by a country reluctant to shoulder the expense of a large standing army.

In the eighteenth century the Hebrides served the new British nation twice over. Its men joined its armed forces in disproportionate numbers, often recruited by clan chiefs anxious to secure their status in Britain, while its topography served Britain's process of national self-definition. It offered images of the enduring power of the natural world, unchanged by human history, at a dramatic moment of social and economic trans-formation, when Scotland's industrialization and urbanization was unparalleled in Europe in speed, intensity and scale.

The importance of Macpherson's Ossianic tales was that in the midst of the rationality advocated by the Scottish Enlightenment, led by the philosopher David Hume and the economist Adam Smith, they provided a counterbalance, a realm for intuition, insight and emotion. In an essay published in 1763 and afterwards appended to every edition of Macpherson's Ossianic works, Hugh Blair, Professor of Rhetoric at Edinburgh University, wrote: 'as the world advances, the understanding gains ground upon the imagination; the understanding is more exercised; the imagination less'. An image of the Gàidhealtachd had been created to assuage the anxieties of an age increas-ingly dominated by rational instrumentalism, but it had scant regard for the the Gàidhealtachd itself. The historian Malcom Chapman describes it as 'symbolic appropriation'.

The Hebrides had won a central place in European culture, but one tightly circumscribed by the defining characteristic of loss. The vitality of its Gaelic culture was subject to ignorance, indifference and prejudice. Its understanding of the relationship with land and place, and its culture of community, represented a profoundly different world view, and was pushed aside – or was actively suppressed – in a painful process of loss and conflict. Just as Banks, Scott, Turner and Mendelssohn were making Fingal's Cave a site of pilgrimage, the Gàidhealtachd found itself the subject of a dangerous process of improvement. This was a history which would dominate the rest of my journey north.

Meanwhile, the Hebrides has never lost its Romantic

reputation. The search for sensation, for the sublime and for solitude has proved a staple of its tourism industry. On the London underground Scotland sells itself with billboards of dreamy scapes of beaches and mountains with no sign of human inhabitation, designed to tantalize the weary commuter. Postcards and holiday snaps are framed by Romantic notions of the sublime. Few cultural movements have proved so durable. This Romanticism shaped my appreciation of Scottish glens as a child, and its fantasy of escape has been part of what has driven me on those many journeys north all my life, a set of associations as vital to transporting me to some remote headland as the petrol in the car's tank. I recognize Romanticism's erasure of the Gaelic past, but find myself caught still within its tradition. I appreciate how it has inspired me to begin the search for place, but increasingly acknowledge that it is a deceptive guide.

Romanticism's global appeal has written the most startling recent chapter of Staffa's history. The island was sold in 1986 to an American advertising executive. A long-time lover of Scotland, Jock Elliott Jnr was an account manager for one of the world's most successful advertising companies, Ogilvy & Mather, based in New York. He bought Staffa to give to his wife for her sixtieth birthday, and she then gave it immediately to the National Trust for Scotland. There is a small plaque on the island to commemorate the gift.

We headed back to Iona at the end of the day, the sun still bright but fast losing its warmth. The skipper had assured the passengers that we would see puffins; they had arrived in recent weeks, he told us, back from their long migration. Sure enough, as if on cue, we passed a small flock of puffins just offshore. Their puffed chests and erect heads gave them a look of comic self-importance. A small boy glanced up momentarily from his digital camera to declare with delight to his father that he had taken more than four hundred photos on the trip. Wordsworth would have wondered how much he was feeling of the wind and the sun on the water.

As I watched the puffins bobbing on the small waves, I was thinking about what it would be like to *own* such an iconic piece of land, and, having owned it for only a few days, what it would be like to give it away? The wealth of an advertising executive, built from selling things made by iconic brands such as American Express, IBM and Shell, had enabled this strange transaction: an American buying a symbol of nation, giving it to his wife, who then handed it over to the Scottish nation to become an international tourist attraction. This empty island has accumulated symbolic projections of vastly different histories.

PART II

Whose history?

We think place is about space but in fact, it is really about time.

REBECCA SOLNIT, *THE FARAWAY NEARBY*

5

Rum

*Never in all my 12 years in Gomorrah
[London] on Thames did I find any
Englishman who knew anything save those who
had come back from the edges of Empire where
the effect of the Central decay was showing,
where the strain of the big lies and rascalities
was beginning to tell.*

EZRA POUND, *GUIDE TO KULCHUR*

I

We sat on coils of damp rope on the harbour wall to eat our fish
and chips. It was chilly and a grey sky hung over us, promising
rain. The hot greasy chips warmed us inside out. My son Matt
and I were in company. Plump sleek gulls stalked along the
dock, and then stood within a few feet, subjecting us to a steady,
eager stare. They were as big as small dogs.

Mallaig is a distinctive combination of fuel fumes, rust, salt spray and bleak functionality. The clank, hum and banging of the west-coast port mixes with the intermittent shriek of gulls; boats are repaired, ferries loaded, and refrigeration units are filled and emptied of stock onto waiting lorries. Activity starts early and on occasion, when the boats came in late, continues into the night under the glare of fierce lights. Later the warden on Rum would tell us how the fledglings of the Manx shearwater are attracted by Mallaig's lights, mistaking them for moonlight, and on their maiden flight will stumble into the ganglands of Mallaig's gulls, where they are peeled and eaten as swiftly as a banana.

It was summer and we were back on the west coast, heading towards the Small Isles, as the Inner Hebridean group of Rum, Canna, Muck and Eigg are known. From Fort William, we'd taken the train to Mallaig for the ferry. The rail journey is now world famous thanks to its appearance in the *Harry Potter* films. At the head of Loch Shiel, the giant viaduct curves magnificently across the glen past the Glenfinnan monument, the imposing pillar to the memory of the Stuart adventurer Bonnie Prince Charlie. Then the train follows the shore of Loch Morar, Europe's deepest freshwater loch. A new mythology around the Scottish landscape has gone global, reinforcing the stereotypes of elusive and mysterious romanticism. Mallaig is where the romanticism runs out – a town of immaculate bed and breakfasts where the smell of fried bacon mixes with the rust and fish until mid-morning. Coming and going to the Small Isles always involves a stopover between trains and ferries in Mallaig, and that entailed the company of those uncomfortable dining companions.

Our first stop in the Small Isles was Eigg, where we camped at the northern bay of Cleadale, just over the water from Rum's looming cuillins. One of the first community buyouts in 1997, Eigg was a landmark in the struggle for land reform in Scotland; by 2013, its population had grown by 40 per cent. The community centre by the pier is the focal point of island life; the café was busily selling breakfasts, cakes and coffees. When the ferry came in, there was an influx of visitors and islanders exchanging news. Outside, there were bikes for rent and signs advertising kayak day trips. The community-centre noticeboard was covered with invitations to ceilidhs, coffee mornings and community meetings. The village shop was doing a brisk trade. It was easy to slip into first names with the people running these businesses, as they popped up every-where, one moment building fences on the shore in driving rain, the next scrubbed up to serve you a meal. There was an energy of making do, making a living, and making a commu-nity. We cycled the few miles past the lone ridge of An Sgùrr to the quieter township of Cleadale. Here, we dropped off to sleep to the beat of drums, carried by the wind in snatches over the sound of the surf. The party was still going as we ate breakfast, and when we got down to the beach, we found it petering out around a fire. Old armchairs had been dragged onto the beach for the festivities. Rum was to prove a sharp contrast with Eigg's vibrant air of conviviality.

For years I had examined Rum's dramatic outline through binoculars. On family holidays when my children were young, we sat on the end of the Ardnamurchan peninsula looking over to Rum. In the summer warmth of our visit to Eigg, Matt and I swam off the beach at Cleadale, and Rum's cuillins were mir-rored in the glassy surface of the beach as the tide retreated. 'There is a great deal of stormy magnificence about the lofty cliffs as there is generally all around the shores of Rum: and they are, in most places, as abrupt as they are inaccessible from the sea. The interior is one heap of rude mountains, scarcely possessing an acre of level land. It is the wildest and most repulsive of all the islands,' wrote the Scottish geologist John MacCulloch in 1824. Rum's peaks, surrounded by clear sea, made it a navigation point for boats on the searoads north/south, and west out to the Minch and back to the mainland. Its prominence explains the evocative names of Rum's mountains, which roll off the tongue like verses of a Norse saga: Hallival, Trollval, Ainshval and Ruinsival. The names of many significant land features in the Hebrides, especially those visible from the sea, originated with those great seafarers the Vikings, who navigated by the horizon's landmarks, while the names of places associated with the working of the land and fishing came from the Gaelic. Traces of these intertwined cultures are evident throughout the archipelago.

No other island has exerted quite the same degree of both fascination and revulsion as Rum. Its austere grandeur has been powerfully seductive, not least because it has been enjoyed largely uninterrupted by other people. Apart from Kinloch Castle and the handful of homes around Loch Scresort on the east coast, it has been uninhabited for nearly two centuries. Swathes of moor, mountain and rugged coastline are without a single dwelling and, usually, there is not a soul in sight. The small groups of day trippers have only a few hours before their return, which limits their explorations. On the long walks over to the island's west coast or up the mountains, we did not see a single person, a rare experience in the British Isles.

Rum's emptiness has made it a synecdoche in Scotland for the tortured history of the Highlands and Islands. Researchers, journalists, television camera crews and writers have kept coming back, as if to pick at the scab, questioning Rum's burden of history. Here on the edge of the Minch, the sea which lies between the Inner and the Outer Hebrides, the seemly accounting of a nation's history ran out. On Rum the 'rascalities', in Ezra Pound's phrase, could not be tidied up as heritage tourism or moved into a glossy history book. On Rum, I was moving beyond self-aggrandizing narratives of Britain and its cherished geographies of islands, edges and caves; I was heading into much more turbulent country, where the stories of loss and struggle are still alive. History here, for those who care to pay attention, is raw and contested: whose history counts and whose history is lost? Who gets to tell or write the story, and can past wrongs be righted? Rum's story is an abrupt, dramatic version of a process of enclosure and dispossession which took several centuries in England, and it feeds directly into the bloodstream of contemporary Scottish politics. As the Scottish historian James Hunter reflected when we met, 'In both Ireland and Scotland, there is a fascination with history; unlike in England, it has not been depoliticized.'

Rum tells a stark story of how land was once used, how it became a commodity demonstrating status, and finally how its emptiness was romanticized as wilderness. Nowhere in Scotland encapsulates more succinctly these transitions and the impact of the English innovation of individual landownership, which had repercussions around the world under the British Empire.

II

Not far from the pier where we landed on Rum, we followed a trail through woodland and heath under a leaden sky. After a short while we plunged into deeper woodland, where the moss lay over the rough ground like a luxurious velvet; our feet sank several inches into its softness. Lichen furred the tree trunks and dripped from branches. The sound of the sea was muffled in this copse. Beneath these trees and under this layer of moss were the remains of homes. The boulders which had once formed walls had tumbled into the undergrowth, but in a few places they were high enough to indicate a window ledge. Clouds of midges swarmed around our faces.

Later I learned that there are around twenty-four million midge larvae per hectare on Rum, an island infamous for them; that means perhaps half a million in an area of land two metres square. Carnivorous plants such as sundew and butterwort depend on Rum's midge feast to supplement the meagre nutrients of the moorland soils. Their leaves curl round the insects to enclose and secrete digestive enzymes. In one summer, a sundew plant can eat two thousand midges, but it is a tiny dent in a population of dizzying numbers. Midges – unlike their human hosts – have proved a resilient presence on the island.

Despite the midges, we stumbled around the ruins in the wood. It was one of the few places on Rum where I caught a glimpse of a time when the island had had a community, and could imagine its rhythms and smells of farming, fishing and family life: the cry of a child, the smoke of a turf fire, the grinding of oatmeal on a quern and the sound of a song. I was haunted by this sense of absence, of what was missing, of what had been lost.

The following day, after a night in the dilapidated Kinloch Castle, which serves as a hostel, we walked seven miles across the island to the wide bay of Harris, which faces west across the Minch to the Outer Hebrides, the islands south of Barra such as Vatersay and the cliffs of the abandoned island of Mingulay. Matt and I walked and talked in blazing hot sunshine for two hours on a track across the open moor. Fierce Highland cattle with wide horns blocked the track at one point; Matt likened them to street-savvy hoodies, their shaggy fringes shading their glowering eyes. We nervously pushed through and then encountered rather more gentle inhabitants: a group of flirtatious wild ponies. A welcome cooling breeze from the Minch greeted us on our arrival at Harris, where the grandeur of one of Rum's peaks, Ruinsival, sloped dramatically down to the rocky shore at one end of the bay. At the other end, the pebbled shore rose gently to a raised beach where the wild ponies, sheep and Highland cattle were grazing. The emptiness was all the more striking because the sharp sunlight picked out the ruins of around a hundred buildings and the lines of some of the most extensive runrig fields in the Highlands and Islands. These narrow strips of cultivable land which striped the slopes were shared out every year amongst the community and were used to grow the few crops which could survive the exposure to the sea spray and the wind. 'Lazy beds' was the misleading term for the gentle ridges built up by laborious labour with seaweed and sand gathered from the beaches to fertilize the soil and provide drainage; here was a gradual shaping of the land over generations, a hard-won intervention to nudge fertility out of the recalcitrant acid earth.

In most areas on the Hebrides, landlords replaced runrig with individual plots in the late eighteenth and early nineteenth centuries. The closely set homes were scattered and contemporary accounts reported the inhabitants' tears and lamentations at the disruption. But these radical agricultural developments did not reach Harris on Rum before the emergence of an even bigger threat, the Clearances, when the inhabitants were evicted from the island altogether. Harris' runrig was a relic of an ancient system of agriculture in which the small amount of arable land was carefully shared, a system which had lasted centuries, possibly millennia. Much of the island is only suitable for grazing, and in the summer women and children would move up to the shielings on the upper ground with the cattle to make cheese.

The ruins of four hundred shielings on Rum are a reminder of how this island once supported a population which reached a peak of 443 souls in 1796.

That period was a time of relative prosperity. The Napoleonic Wars had cut off sources of Spanish barilla, used in explosives, and the only substitute was kelp. Huge quantities of the slippery seaweed were gathered and carried by creel to be burnt to produce the ash. It was back-breaking work, requiring twenty tons of seaweed to produce just one ton of kelp. The bulk of the income generated by the sale of the kelp was taken by the landlord, and contemporaries were shocked by the hard labour the harvesting entailed as islanders worked in cold sea water to cut the seaweed from the rocks. The landlords ratcheted up rents to capture more of the small portion which went to the labourers. The traditional clan chiefs were eager to make money to maintain their status and prestige in the new economic system of the eighteenth century, and they saw kelp as a rare opportunity to make their Hebridean possessions pay. Samuel Johnson was horrified by what he saw on his travels in 1773, little knowing that worse was to come in the decades which followed. At the time, he commented that the Highland chiefs 'had already lost much of their influence, and as they gradually degenerate from patriarchal rulers to rapacious landlords, they will divest themselves of the little that remains'.

Rum had never offered prosperity or ease; the Welsh writer Thomas Pennant commented, after his visit in 1772, that the inhabitants 'carry famine in their aspect' because there was 'often a whole summer without a grain in the island, which they regret for the sake of their babes'. The land was unproductive, and the climate too harsh for better agricultural yields. On fifty days of the year there are gale-force winds, and Rum registers an annual average of four metres of rain. Yet despite the poverty, to the surprise of some travellers, Rum was rich in culture; in 1824 John MacCulloch described the 'smoky shelves' of the islanders' blackhouses, which contained not only 'the books of the ancients but of the moderns, well thumbed and well talked of'.

Rum is the site of the oldest human inhabitation in Scotland. Traces of Mesolithic settlements have been found in Kinloch on the east coast dating from nine thousand years ago. The sheltered bay with its area of level ground – on which Rum's castle was later built – offered space for a camp for these hunter gatherers. An archaeological dig in the 1980s uncovered an astonishing quantity of material: as many as 140,000 fragments of stone were found which were either broken stone tools or waste from working the stone. The extent of prehistoric activity can be attributed to Rum's distinctive bloodstone, an ornamental stone which ranges in colour from cream to green and even purple. The most striking pieces are deep green with red flecks of oxidized jasper, which can be worked like flint. Tools made of this material were traded throughout the region. It has been estimated that the camp was used for a thousand years before it was abandoned. By 3000 BCE there were farmers on Rum, the beginning of a tradition of agriculture which lasted the best part of 4,800 years, right up to the point when the runrig fields of Harris yielded their last harvest of oats.

All of this was explained to me in evenings at Kinloch Castle's hostel by a team of archaeologists from Edinburgh who were surveying Rum. We smoked cigarettes to keep the dreaded midges at bay as we sat on benches outside what was once the servant quarters. The archaeologists spent their days poring over plans and maps; they loaded up their Land Rovers with measuring tools for days out on the moors, and were piecing together the story of the intense human working and reworking of the land over thousands of years. Their task required patience and meticulous attention. Once they had surveyed Rum, they would move on to the next island. We discussed their work across the archipelago, the slow unfolding story – still with large gaps and questions – of how human beings had found a living, perched on this edge of the ocean.

The long history of human habitation on Rum came to a dramatic conclusion in the early nineteenth century. Rum's clan chief in 1815 was the respected Alexander Maclean, but he made a disastrous investment in kelp by buying the small island of Muck at precisely the moment the kelp boom collapsed when cheaper imports of Spanish barilla were resumed at the end of the Napoleonic Wars. Bankrupted, he was forced to let the island of Rum to a tenant, Dr Lachlan Maclean, who planned to make Rum profitable by farming sheep. The islanders were not needed; in the infamous contemporary phrase they were a 'redundant population'. In 1825 every islander was given a year's notice to leave. In 1826, three hundred men, women and children were herded onto two ships. An Edinburgh lawyer, Alexander Hunter, supervised the operation, and he admitted to a government committee in 1827 that some islanders 'were not very willing to leave the land of their ancestors'. A Rum shepherd, John McMaister, provided a rather more vivid picture: 'The wild outcries of the men and the heart-breaking wails of the women and their children filled all the air between the mountainous shores of the bay.'

For the thirty-seven-day passage to Canada, Dr Maclean provided thirty-five pints of water, eleven pounds of oatmeal and three and a half pounds of bread. Two years later, the remaining fifty islanders were removed. The Clearances were so thorough on Rum that Dr Maclean had to bring in people cleared from other places to work as shepherds on the new sheep farm. Eight thousand sheep were brought to graze on grass sustained by the fertility carefully accumulated in the soil over the preceding centuries. Dr Maclean's work was later praised by the New Statistical Account of Scotland; it was described as 'improvements' which exhibited both 'taste and judgement'.

This painful conclusion to the long history of farming communities on the island was the distant repercussion of the economic and social convulsions then gripping the Scottish Lowlands and England. The Hebrides were being relegated to a periphery – useful for the extraction of raw materials and as a supply of cheap labour – of an economic system centralized round the rapidly growing industrial and commercial heartlands of urban Britain. A profound change had transformed the role of the clan chief from warlord and protector to landlord. Rum's tragic history illustrates this brutal process of change. It was small comfort to the islanders that in due course Maclean fared no better in the volatile economic climate, was bankrupted himself and emigrated. In 1845 Rum was sold. A century before, selling land was inconceivable, when land, clan and chief were tied by bonds of mutual responsibility and loyalty, embedded in a culture of place and identity. All of that had been swept away. A largely empty Rum, no longer viable even for sheep farming because the pasture had been so badly degraded by overgrazing, was bought by an English aristocrat, the Marquis of Salisbury (father of the later prime minister), as a shooting estate.

Rum's story was echoed in the surrounding islands and across the Highlands. Mull to the south, Skye to the north and Barra to the west were subjected to comparably harsh expulsions of their inhabitants. Barra and South Uist were bought in the 1830s by the infamous John Gordon of Cluny, one of Victorian Scotland's richest men, and experienced some of the most brutal evictions. Islanders were chased down with dogs, bound and loaded onto the ships. Once on their journey, islanders from across the Hebrides encountered more hardship; according to contemporary accounts, on occasion they had to sleep in the open as they waited in Glasgow to embark for ships crossing the Atlantic. The ships were woefully inadequate, and the islanders arrived in Quebec malnourished and sometimes wearing nothing but a few rags. One medical officer in Quebec in 1848 wrote of his shock on seeing the condition of these emigrants arriving from Britain. Gordon declared himself 'neither legally or morally bound to support a population reduced to poverty by the will of providence'.

But providence had not produced the poverty. As the former clan chiefs became zealous landlords, they had imposed the new system of individual crofts, but ensured they would be too small to support the tenant, forcing them to take additional employment collecting kelp. A system of land use was established on the islands and the west coast to support the kelp boom, and after it collapsed the system simply produced abject poverty. The small plots led to a desperate overdependence on the one crop that appeared able to meet the burden of hunger – the potato – with disastrous consequences in the famine of the 1840s. Across the region, it was yet another catastrophe in the century since the defeat of Culloden, as the clan chiefs attempted to navigate their way from paramilitary power to economic wealth. The kelp rush and switch to sheep farming – part betrayal, part spectacularly ill-judged gamble – led to the emergence of an impoverished, precarious, landed peasantry, while the former chieftains fell into mounting debt or were bankrupted. Islands which had been held by a clan for centuries went on the market, advertised for sale in Edinburgh and London. Their new owners, enriched by their fortunes in the expanding industrial and imperial economy, were rationalists, men of the Enlightenment, and impatient with tradition. Ardent believers in what they described as 'improvement' and progress, they were largely unsympathetic to the casualties it might inflict. On Rum, the Marquis of Salisbury believed the population, then amounting to 161, was still excessive and demanded that a list of sixty names be drawn up for 'assisted voluntary emigration'; when there were delays in compiling the list, he insisted, 'I will allow no variation.' He duly had his way and fifty-nine islanders left for Nova Scotia.

In his book *The Making of the Crofting Community*, published in 1976, historian James Hunter describes the Clearances as 'a crime against humanity'. That conclusion was a direct challenge to the academic consensus of much of the previous 150 years, during which economic historians maintained that the Clearances may have been unfortunate but were largely unavoidable. Their contention was that the land could not support the weight of population, as was evident from the chronic poverty and rising incidence of hunger. In other agriculturally marginal areas of Britain (such as the Scottish Lowlands, South Wales or the north-west of England), the proximity of natural resources like coal provided employment for the displaced rural poor. In the Hebrides and north-west Scotland, there was no such alternative. Scotland's Central Belt was as foreign as North America. Reluctant to leave, the native population had had to be forced off the land, ran the argument.

Hunter's powerful book, with its vivid account of the callous brutality and extent of the Clearances, has been continuously in print since it was first published and, along with *The Highland Clearances*, a bestselling book by an English journalist, John Prebble, shifted the accepted narrative in Scotland. Tourist bookshops in the Highlands and Islands prominently stock both works, providing an account for any visitor wanting to understand more about the empty glens and ruined crofts. Since

Hunter there has been a shift as historians began to acknowledge the scale of the tragedy, though some have continued to
insist that the Highland landlords were in an impossible position, trapped in an 'economic vice', and even that they were
themselves victims of economic forces.

Hunter and Prebble were amongst a group of writers who
succeeded in moving the history of the Clearances from the
margins – it had always been vividly remembered and lamented
in Gaelic song and poetry – into a central position in Scottish
history and politics. There it has remained, liable to trigger
intense controversy and fuelling the long-running debate over
reform of Scotland's exceptionally centralized landownership
(half of the land is owned by less than five hundred people).
There have been intermittent calls for apologies to be made
for the Clearances. But who should carry the blame? Some
argue that the British government should apologize. As we
were shown round Kinloch Castle on Rum, the guide asserted
that the English were responsible for the Clearances, and when
I questioned her, suggesting that other forces may also have
been at play, a Canadian in the group regarded me with obvious
scepticism. Some argue that it is the Lowland Scots who should
apologize, and that their racism towards the Gaels legitimized
the process, while yet others hold the clan chiefs responsible.

James Hunter, reflecting on his forty years of writing and
studying Britain's troubled relationship with the Gaels, concluded, 'the difference between Ireland and Scotland was that
in the latter the British state was able to win over the elite and
they became agents of change'. He added, 'There was a sense of
betrayal by our own people.' It has profoundly marked Scotland.
He illustrated his point by remembering that as a boy growing
up in Argyll, he thought the local gentry – or 'toffs' as they were
known – who appeared every summer, were English. 'Their

accents were certainly English, upper-class English. They had been educated in England and lived there. I was amazed when I discovered that they thought they were Scottish, astonished to realize they were descendants of a family who had fought at Culloden.'

Racism, betrayal and imperial exploitation: three toxic elements have been incorporated into different readings of the Clearances. Nations have their foundational myths, the iconic chapters of their history which inspire and shape identity, and the Highland Clearances have assumed that role in Scotland. Few episodes in British history have continued to reverberate with quite the same intensity in contemporary debate. This is a history which will not go quietly into the past.

III

After our picnic on Harris bay, I lay back on the warm machair amongst the daisies, tormentil and celandines in the sun while Matt scrambled over the rocks on the beach below. Large damselflies and dragonflies were tipsy in the sunshine, veering erratically past my face, a flash of brilliant iridescent body. My head rested on our backpack and through half-open eyes I watched the sun glittering on the calm sea. It was one of those lavishly peaceful moments and I basked in the warmth, the smell of the sheep-cropped grass and the sound of surf breaking on the beach. Suddenly in the quiet, I heard the sound of a powerful engine. A small speck of a motor boat was coming towards the bay. The volume was explained by the insanely powerful motor, which seemed to chew up the sea, ploughing a great trough through the waves to carry its small number of passengers with great speed. It roared up to within twenty metres of the shore and paused. We could hear the sound of the guide's voice over the water. After twenty minutes or so, the boat's engines started up again and it took off, churning the surf behind it. Even after the sound had faded, we no longer felt alone. The intrusion had been jarring; it was a sharp contrast – of time, speed, and purpose – with the past millennia of human presence on Rum.

The Clearances have resonated so powerfully because they are a history repeated in many places around the world, where pre-industrial communal cultures have come into contact with capitalism, and resulted in bitter conflicts. They can be traced back to two radical innovations in land rights. The first was that land could be a commodity owned by one individual. Prior to the emergence of this idea in sixteenth-century England, there had been an 'essential belief that people everywhere had always held about owning rights to the earth, that they were subject to duties and obligations to gods and monarchs, and to families, clans and communities', explains Andro Linklater in *Owning the Earth*. Land had been the basis for the structure of community in peasant cultures across the British Isles and Europe. In the clan society of the Highlands and Islands, this took the forms of barter and military service, within strongly held patterns of relationship and loyalty anchored in the land and in a sense of place. That a piece of land could be owned in the same way as a horse or pot was not just inconceivable; it was a denial of the ties of relationship which bound people together. The anonymity and instrumentalism of a market economy in which land and people could be routinely used and exploited within a cash system proved to be deeply traumatic: it resulted not just in a loss of access to the land, but also in a loss of self-understanding.

The second innovation emerged as the Puritans founded settlements in North America in the seventeenth and eighteenth centuries, advancing a right to land which they deemed to be 'vacant'. Any land use which was not one of intensive human industry met the definition of vacant. In support of their claim, they quoted Biblical verses requiring that the land be fruitful. This was to have huge implications in the dispossession of Native Americans during the colonizing of North America, in which Scots played a prominent role, and these ideas flowed back to Scotland. Land had to be productive, and that meant it had to generate a monetary surplus; this was ordained by God.

These ideas also transformed rural England from the late sixteenth century to the mid-nineteenth century as successive waves of enclosure legislation deprived people of access to the common land on which they depended for grazing and gathering fuel. The commercialization of landownership prompted deep anxiety from contemporaries; one of the most eloquent English critics was William Cobbett, who commented in *Rural Rides*, published in the 1820s, that the new type of landowner 'looked to the soil only for its rents, viewing it as a mere object of speculation unacquainted with its cultivators, despising them and their pursuits, and relying for influence, not upon the goodwill of the vicinage, but upon the dread of their power'. Much of the anxiety flowed into a preoccupation with personal morality and respectability rather than into any effective political challenge. Similarly, in the Highlands and Islands, the Clearances were followed by a wave of fervent evangelical movements before a land-reform movement developed.

As in England, many writers, clergy and reformers in Scotland expressed anxiety at the country's huge social upheavals in the eighteenth and nineteenth centuries. No other country in Europe witnessed such brutal Clearances nor such rapid urbanization as Scotland. But these concerns were assuaged by arguments advanced by the Scottish Enlightenment thinkers, in particular Adam Smith, who famously wrote in *The Wealth of Nations* in 1766 that 'it is not from the benevolence of the butcher, the brewer and the baker that we expect our dinner, but from their regard to their own interest'. The seemingly self-interested pursuit of wealth could ultimately serve the greater good. Improving landlords were praised by contemporaries, and criticism was inhibited by a belief that this was progress. Part of what makes Johnson and Boswell's journals such a telling commentary is that they were confused over this issue. On the one hand Johnson wrote of the need for 'improvements' to make a barren land productive, and on the other he lambasted the greed of landlords and was horrified by the poverty he witnessed.

The contrast with the rest of Europe was striking; some of the same economic pressures on landlords were present but in most countries the fear of social disorder prevented the dismantling of time-honoured law and custom around land rights. T. M. Devine, the leading historian of the Scottish nation, draws a comparison with Denmark, 'where there was also a sustained attack on communal agriculture and inefficient patterns of landholding but it was managed very differently ... a degree of social benevolence ensured social stability with funds to help the transition'. In Scotland, there was no state constraint on the freedom of landowners, who used their political power in London to push through legislation which left the vast majority of the population with no legal rights to land.

Clearances happened throughout Britain but it is in Scotland that they have been so vividly remembered, and where they have taken on such direct political significance. The process of change in the Highlands and Islands was more abrupt and violent, achieved in half the time it took in England. The physical evidence has also proved more lasting; the emptiness of the Highlands and Islands speaks for itself, while in England the trauma of enclosures has largely been forgotten. The hedgerows and stone walls used to enclose the fields have even become the object of great affection in rural tradition. The gentry re-habilitated themselves as custodians of the land rather than cruel landlords; this was the depoliticization of English history to which James Hunter referred.

When Hunter explained to me how and why he came to write *The Making of the Crofting Community*, he identified two influences: first, E. P. Thompson's masterpiece *The Making of the English Working Classes*, and second, the impact of studying African history at Aberdeen university at a time when it was being radically revised, breaking away from the narrative of empire, explorers and missionaries, to tell the story of African people through their oral traditions. Hunter found resonances between the history of the Clearances and that of Africans sub-jected to British imperial power. He was fired by the histories of class struggle and anti-colonialism, and wrote his account accordingly.

The Clearances have become inextricably framed within both those debates and, as such, have been a powerful narrative engine for Scottish nationalism. It is a history which expresses a profound unease with capitalism and a belief that the human costs of its turbulent change can be intolerably high. Hunter's book was published on the eve of Thatcherism and it prefigured the Clydeside experience of deindustrialization in the 1980s, when the heart was ripped from a swath of tightly knit commu-nities – justified in much the same way as the Clearances had been, as part of an inevitable process of economic change.

Over time many of the landed estates of the Highlands and Islands were bought by Englishmen or were owned by Anglicized Scottish families. That allowed some to maintain that the Clearances were part of a process of colonization, and obscured the fact that they were the outcome of conflicts primarily within Scotland, although the improvers relied heavily on their alliance with the British state and its legislative commitment to private property rights. Rum was cleared by Dr Lachlan Maclean, but within a couple of decades it had been sold to the Marquis of Salisbury and remained in English hands until 1957. 'Arguments were made that the Highlands were the victim of English imperialism – this was historically nonsensical,' argues Hunter. Alex Salmond, the former leader of the Scottish National Party, has on occasion framed the historical relationship between England and Scotland as colonial. It is a characterization which masks a deep historical divide within Scotland itself.

The Clearances were the defining chapter in a two-hundred-year-long process of cultural loss and dispossession. Scottish military defeats had happened before the famous battle of Culloden, but it was the changes in land use which really triggered the collapse of the Gàidhealtachd. As Linklater points out, 'how land is owned shapes the way society is organized. Communal ownership requires an intensity of organization.' If land was the basis for community, once access to the land was lost, the relationships also were broken. Even the transition from runrig to individually owned crofts was traumatic, with homes being scattered into separate plots. Being forced off the land altogether was a catastrophic loss of an identity bound up with place. 'The earth comes to inhabit its inhabitants through story, art and music,' explained Linklater of the Australian Aborigines, and it was equally true of the Gaels. After they lost the land, and thousands emigrated, the Gaelic language went into steep decline. This catalogue of cultural loss has been a powerful strand in Scotland's self-image, and the losses have fed a deep resentment of England's studied indifference. Romantic travellers continued to paint their watercolours and muse on Scott's works; on a visit to the Highlands in the late 1840s, after a generation of Clearances and a potato famine had devastated the region, Queen Victoria wrote that they were 'most delightful, most romantic' and that 'all seemed to breathe freedom and peace and to make one forget the world and its sad turmoils'.

On the beach at Harris in Rum I tried to imagine what had been lost over those decades of the nineteenth century. For hundreds, probably thousands of years, countless lives had been lived entirely within the circumference of this bay and the Minch's wide horizon. Everything that was needed – food, shelter, clothing and transport – had to be found and fashioned from this landscape. Imports would have been few and far between, and it would have been a life of ceaseless labour. Anyone visiting the Hebrides and the north-west coast of Scotland is haunted by the disturbing pathos of this history. As Neil Gunn wrote in *Off in a Boat* in 1938, 'wherever we went in the West we encountered it, until at last we hated the burden of thinking about it'. The Scottish Atlantic coastline is an often inhospitable place and yet a people had found a way to survive on the rocky slopes and thin soils, and had developed a rich tradition of poetry, song and music, from which they drew dignity and independence of spirit. The history of the Gaels has always been a source of unease in Britain, challenging its cherished, self-serving ideals of progress, civilization and a just order.

IV

As if this history was not enough for Rum to bear, there has been more. The reason for the motorboat's noisy arrival in the bay of Harris was in part the stunning beauty of the coastline, but it was also because of an extraordinary monument. Prominent on the machair just above the shoreline stands a mock Grecian temple. Eighteen heavy Doric pillars, closely placed, support the roof and its imposing granite gable ends. It is all for effect, as the number and proportions of the pillars vastly exceed what is required to support a roof made of timber and slate. A low iron chain is slung between fourteen short stone posts to mark the surrounding lawn, another grandiose flourish. Inside the temple, open to the Atlantic gales, lies the stone tomb of John Bullough, an industrialist from Accrington in Lancashire.

He bought Rum as a shooting estate from the Marquis of Salisbury in 1888. He shipped in enough deer to make its description plausible and spent a few weeks on the island during shooting seasons. Rum again symbolizes the fate of a wide swathe of the Highlands and Islands; sheep farming quickly exhausted the land's meagre fertility, and profits declined. The emptied, overgrazed tracts of land were bought with the new wealth of Britain's industrial elite. Status was still intimately bound up with ownership of land and the only place where it was possible to buy the desired quantity was Scotland (much of England's land was entailed in family trusts). Land in Scotland's north-west was no longer expected to provide food or an income, it had instead become an opportunity for personal fantasy. In addition to Rum, John Bullough bought another, grander estate in Perthshire, where he specified that he should be buried. But his son George landed on the quixotic scheme of digging up his father's body from its first resting place and moving it to a mausoleum on the uninhabited west coast of Rum, an island he had only occasionally visited.

Further up the slope behind the mausoleum, we stumbled on an even stranger sight. Amongst the turf, sheep droppings and boulders were the ruins of an arch and a half-buried wall covered in brightly coloured Italian tiles and mosaic. The tiles, in gaudy reds, greens and yellow, bore the initials JB. This was the first Harris mausoleum for John Bullough, a vault dug into the hill with an interior covered in tiles. When a visiting correspondent from *The Times* likened it to a public lavatory, George had his father's sarcophagus removed and the vault blown up. All that was left behind was the debris. George abandoned Italian tiles and turned to the most solemn and imposing of material and form: granite and Greek. When the sun set behind Barra across the Minch, the mausoleum cast a long shadow over the turf of the empty bay.

George Bullough has been delicately referred to as 'volatile', even by the standards of other Hebridean incomers. Whim and the wealth to indulge it have played a central role on these islands in much of the last century and a half. Even in this crowded tradition, he stands out as the stuff of fables. The lonely mausoleums are the least of it.

George Bullough spared no expense in the building of his castle at Kinloch on Rum's eastern shore, completed in 1900. The entire edifice and its surroundings were imported and arrived on Rum as if from another world: the red sandstone was quarried, dressed and brought from Arran; a quarter of a million tons of topsoil were brought from Ayrshire for the landscaped gardens, golf course and bowling green. A large domed conservatory was built on the south side of the castle, and to the north a short distance away was a complex of walled gardens and hot houses in which to grow muscatel grapes, figs, peaches and nectarines. Six domed palm houses with freshwater tanks were home to turtles, a pair of alligators and humming birds. He imported the deer, game birds and trout he intended to hunt and fish, but also frogs and wild goats. He experimented with 120 species of tree. For three years, three hundred workmen were employed constructing this fantasy castle, and they were even paid a small supplement to wear kilts. Fascinated by innovation and comfort, Bullough's castle was one of the first in Scotland to have electricity, central heating, an internal telephone system and opulent plumbing. The shower offered a variety of options by which water could pummel, douse or gently spray the body from several directions. Bullough brought in a range of cars to ferry him the short distance from the pier, where his luxury yacht docked, to the house. More astonishing than all these inventions was the Orchestrion he installed in the castle at immense cost. It mimicked an orchestra by working off a punch-card system to play a range of forty musical instruments. Imported from Germany, it had one revealing drawback: no volume control. In the end, apart from summoning guests to dinner, it was rarely used.

A century later, the castle's pink sandstone is crumbling, too soft for the fierce Hebridean gales; the conservatory and its exotic flowers and fruit have long since disappeared. The alligators' sojourn proved particularly short-lived after a breakout terrified a guest. Only the humming birds are still at the castle, stuffed and encased in glass after a breakdown in the heating system killed them.

We stayed in the servant quarters of the castle, which now serve as a hostel; the windows of our bedroom were placed high up in the wall so George Bullough's guests could come and go without being seen by curious servants. We sheltered from the midges in a sitting room dominated by an enormous wooden mantelpiece with a heavily carved Adam and Eve; the former sported a magnificent Edwardian handlebar moustache. Matt took up residence in a deep armchair placed in a turret; appropriately enough, he was reading *Harry Potter*. I wondered how a child experienced the merging of fiction, fantasy and reality in such a place.

Kinloch Castle was one of the strangest places in which I have ever stayed, owing in part to its opulence and in part to its sense of absence. The last Bullough left in 1957, but little has changed since the 1900s. The curtains and upholstery were slowly fading and the fabrics finally fraying; the huge rugs of dead animals shot on foreign travels were wearing thin; the lashing of winter rain was seeping into the structure of the house; but in every other way it was still the house where Bullough entertained his raucous shooting parties. The smell of cigars and whisky seemed to hover in the billiard room, despite its state-of-the-art ventilation system; the sitting room of Bullough's wife, with its chintz flounces and French affectations, echoed to the sound of chilly gossip and flirtation. I wandered through the unkempt garden and stumbled on a statue, bridge and folly amidst the undergrowth; in the flower beds, lupins, poppies and daisies battled with ferns and weeds. The place was redolent of a very particular historical moment at the end of the century: the last days of an ageing monarch's reign, one widely regarded to have been glorious, which had taken Britain to unprecedented wealth and power. But the self-confidence had given way to a nagging sense of insecurity as Germany's industrial strength grew apace. This brash but insecure hubris made the place disturbing.

Kinloch Castle can be seen as a memorial to the tensions and brutality which were woven into the running of the British Empire. The dead humming birds summed it up, captured in their life-like brilliant colour perching on a branch in the dusty glass case. The place was full of stuffed animals. Stags' heads peered from every wall – this castle was designed for their comfortable killing. Stuffed fish, harpooned in tropical waters, hung in their glass cases. Teeth gleamed in the flattened heads of the tiger skins on the floor of the Great Hall, where the oversized trophies of Bullough's travels were displayed. Tall bronze incense burners and vases two metres high had been presents from the Emperor of Japan after Bullough lent him his yacht, and the room's centrepiece was an almost life-size bronze monkey-eating eagle. In the library, there was a model of two Japanese wrestlers, clenched in combat. At every turn lay evidence of fascination with the violence of this imperial culture, and the model of masculinity required to maintain it. The photograph albums of Bullough's world tour in the 1890s included chilling images of crucifixions in Burma – a practice introduced by the British – and public executions in China. Killing animals and people had become a routine experience for the nineteenth-century British elite;

the rituals of shooting parties and imperial wars bound the two nations of Scotland and England most tightly together. The elite moved seamlessly from metropolitan power to their play-grounds – the hunting and shooting – on the periphery thanks to sleeper trains. 'We may go to bed in Euston and wake on a western sea loch; we may sit at the play one evening and be on a Scots moor after breakfast,' wrote the Scottish novelist John Buchan.

The castle was not built as a permanent home. It was designed for parties. Sixteen guests could be accommodated, with over a hundred servants brought in to attend to their com-fort. Given the high windows and the curious arrangements by which no servant could ever witness the activities of the ball-room – food and drink were served through a hatch – rumours have flourished ever since. Music-hall girls brought by private charter from Glasgow were likely; homosexual orgies were rumoured. The castle was only used as the party house it was intended to be for less than two decades. By the time of the First World War, most of its male staff were fighting in France, while Bullough himself had moved on to other interests, such as race horses, and the construction of other opulent homes in southern England.

After the desperate poverty of the previous century, a form of wealth had arrived in the Highlands and Islands, a spillover from the immense earnings of Britain's industrial and imperial economy. The Bulloughs' wealth was the proceeds of the labour of Lancashire's working class. It barely touched the lives of those living in these places; on the Hebrides, only a small number were employed as servants and ghillies. The gates to the castle on Rum were kept shut; the few islanders had little contact with the Bulloughs or their personal servants. The son of Bullough's ghillie, Archie Cameron, wrote in his memoirs of how, as a child, he dreamt of raiding the conservatories for their luscious fruit, but never dared. He remembered how he and his six siblings would receive an orange to share on special occasions.

The builder of Kinloch Castle, George Bullough, had little interest in the industrial empire that his brilliantly inventive grandfather and shrewd father had built up. Howard and Bullough's Globe Works was the biggest employer in Accrington in the late nineteenth century, exporting textile machinery all over the world, but while George Bullough was shooting deer on Rum and buying racehorses, the firm was increasingly threatened by competition. Bullough's interest in innovation was reserved for his own domestic comfort. In the 1930s, the Globe Works was amalgamated with other Lancashire textile companies, and in 1993 it finally closed down. The wealth of Accrington proved short-lived, lasting less than a century, and a large portion of it was diverted to rot and crumble in the damp of a Hebridean island.

Here was a spectacular failure of the British elite. The self-made industrialist, intent on social acceptance, had sent his son, George, to Harrow to become a gentleman, giving him a taste for a life of conspicuous consumption and leisure. Accrington's working classes had funded Kinloch Castle, but the money would have better served the town's own future; by the twenty-first century it was one of the most deprived in England.

V

A year after my trip to Rum, I returned to Eigg, just across the water, and its beautiful Cleadale Bay. The crofts cluster beneath steep cliffs amongst a patchwork of fields. Many of the small plots have been abandoned and the brilliant egg-yellow of ragwort blazed in late August. Beyond the fields, the deep blue of the mountains of Rum sat on the horizon. On a walk early one Sunday morning, I found a sign on a croft gate, announcing that it was a museum and was open. I pushed past the glossy green shrub looming over the small wooden door. The door was unlocked and I found myself in a tiny croft. A bedroom was to one side, a kitchen to the other and in front of a small backroom a steep wooden ladder led to an attic. It was 'Morag's Croft'. A notice explained that Morag had returned to live here for the last ten years of her life, and after she left for a care home on the mainland, her family decided to leave the house untouched as a museum. It was never locked, the notice added. There was a calendar on the wall for 1993.

The floor was concrete, there was no running water and the only source of heat was the iron range in the fireplace. A folder gave details of Morag's long life, most of which she had spent in service to the owners of Eigg, the Runcimans, who lived in London. Only in the last chapter of her life did she return to the place where she had been born, moving into the old family home next door to her brother, who had built a new house and still worked the land.

Her life had partly overlapped with that of the Bulloughs, in time and in geography. She had also moved between metropolitan England and the Hebrides. She acquired sophisticated urban tastes. A long strand of plastic pearls was draped over her dressing-table, a silk 1950s dress hung on a rack alongside a pale lemon blouse trimmed with lace; on the kitchen dresser, there were fine bone-china cups and saucers. Tables were covered with home-made embroidered tablecloths. But the chairs were made from timber salvaged from the shore; paper cut-outs had been plastered to the wall to imitate wallpaper. The attic was full of the tools of crofting: a butter churn, scythes for hay making, pails, and a pair of tough wooden boots with soles made of metal nails.

Morag's life had bridged the gap between the periphery and the centre, between the rural crofting culture of the Hebrides and the Runcimans' world at the heart of London's political life (Lord Runciman, of the family shipping dynasty, had a long, distinguished political career and his wife was one of the first women MPs). The latter is the stuff of history books, the former we can only glimpse from fragments – such as this wonderful croft – by chance. I sat in Morag's rough wooden chair by the hearth, looking out of the window above her mangle to the cuillins of Rum, beyond which lay the opulence of Bullough's castle. The two homes echoed with the presence of their owners on either side of the Sound of Rum, but they represented a vast gulf in life experience. In both there was a sense of intimacy with the past; it seemed possible that Morag might step into the room at any moment to offer tea.

Her father had rented the croft in the early 1900s, but on the condition that he would have to leave at any time when called upon to do so; he was specifically exempted in the terms of his lease agreement from the legislation giving crofters some security of tenure. Morag was one of four children and the stories of her siblings were those of Britain's twentieth century. Her brother Duncan served on the Atlantic convoys in the Second World War; he was honoured for volunteering to go down into the bowels of a ship to dispose of an unexploded shell, thankfully surviving. Her sister Mary was comparably brave and awarded the Burma Star for her service in Burma, India, Sudan and Italy for the Queen Alexandra's Royal Army Nursing Corps. The small backroom, where some of these siblings might have slept, had a few children's books. One of them was on geography, and it described how the world was divided into races; it specified a complex stratification according to which there were middle and upper barbarians, and upper and lower savages. Throughout, it emphasized the duty of empire.

The two homes, Kinloch Castle and Morag's Croft, illustrate how empire found its way into the furthest corners of Britain, leaving the imprint of its ideology both on those who profited from it and on those required to defend it. Underpinning both were the quiet, unremembered lives of the servants dedicated to the daily tasks of sustaining life, the cooking of meals, washing of laundry and making of fires. 'If we had a keen vision and feeling of all ordinary human life, it would be like hearing the grass grow and the squirrel's heart beat, and we should die of that roar on the other side of silence,' wrote George Eliot in *Middlemarch*.

VI

In 1957 George Bullough's widow was persuaded to sell Rum to the Nature Conservancy Council. Headed by Max Nicholson, the council dreamt up a radical plan to return Rum to nature. No visitors or development would be allowed and only selected scientific research teams would be able to visit. Rum became known as the 'Forbidden Isle'; the Bulloughs had never encouraged visitors and now the official conservation bodies did the same. Rum would be a laboratory and nature would be left to take its course, observed by scientists. 'Rum is an island which has been put to work, to effect not only its own salvation but also that of other islands and the vast tracts of the mainland which are also suffering from degraded bioproductivity,' ran the Nature Conservancy Council's proposal for Rum in 1957. Long-running research projects were undertaken into its deer population. Looking back in 1994, Nicholson, slightly defensive, reflected on the key role Rum played in the development of nature conservation: 'Our practical comprehensive knowledge of how ecology works – of population equilibrium, response to environmental change and interactions of competing species or of predator and prey – was practically nil. We were making it all up. The message was plain. If we were serious we must have a larger tract of totally separate land on which visiting and living would be strictly controlled so as to minimize human impact. And we must, by a blend of toughness and persuasion, show all concerned that this was how it must be.'

It was another form of fantasy drawing on a cultural tradition which privileged the wild, empty and remote. It was as astonishing in its way as Bullough's fantasy island. Rum had assumed a salvific role in the approaching environmental crisis. These early environmental scientists denied the ten millennia of human presence on Rum and how it had shaped the island's ecology. For several decades the 'Forbidden Isle' was subject to one of the longest-running studies of deer populations in the world. In time a new understanding of human ecology emerged, which recognized how nature and human activities interconnect. After the formation of Scottish National Heritage in 1992, the management of Rum shifted and a community land trust was set up to develop a viable future for the small population which has settled on the island in the last few decades, and to support a school and shop. Meanwhile, the castle has become the subject of confusion and uncertainty; urgent repairs requiring millions are needed but no one so far has been willing to find the money to prop up Bullough's folly.

On our last day on Rum, Matt and I climbed Hallival, following the stream up through the forest, swatting the midges which gathered around our faces and which were breeding above the pools of black water. The bloodstone pebbles in the waterbed glowed red in the rapids where the peaty water ran yellow. Only when we were finally above the tree line did the assault from the midges abate. Kinloch Castle had disappeared behind the curve of the hill, and all around us lay stretches of wind-bleached grass, studded with the brilliant blue of lochans reflecting the sky. Small streams glinted white in the distance as they ran over bare rock. We searched the blue sky for Rum's famous eagles. Under our feet, the sphagnum mosses gave way to rocks and scattered grasses as we climbed. Tons of this soft wet moss, which has healing properties, were gathered from hills across Scotland in the First World War and loaded onto trains to be transported to hospitals where it was used to dress soldiers' terrible wounds.

Once high enough to be surrounded by the peaks of Rum's cuillins, we paused for lunch. The scree-covered slopes glittered in the midday sun, the calm remains of the huge volcanic chain which, sixty million years ago, created the dramatic contours of this coastline and its islands, from Rockall hundreds of miles to the west and St Kilda, to Skye, Ardnamurchan, Mull, Arran and down to Ulster. These are remains of the three million years of volcanic activity when the earth's crust stretched and the North Atlantic began to emerge, separating Greenland and Europe. Liquid rock rose from as deep as sixty-two miles along cracks and vents. As the magma welled up, the land surface bulged into a dome over two miles high before collapsing, with explosions of hot ash and gas, and creating the massive blocks of rock found on the northern rim of Rum's cuillins. A shallow volcano, sixty-two miles wide, was formed. The complex igneous rocks of Rum bequeathed by this tumultuous volcanic history fascinate volcanologists; one went so far as to say that Rum was 'the most stupendous succession of volcanic phenomena in the whole geological history of Europe'. The comment has been dismissed as an absurd superlative, but to my mind it is testimony to how, on Rum, even the most circumspect scientist can be carried away.

Away to the east, Skye was laid out in its full length; we were on a level with the small cumulus clouds which brushed the peaks of its cuillins as they drifted past. To the west we could see the Western Isles stretching from Lewis in the north down to Mingulay in the south. Somewhere in that long strand of land on the horizon was my next island, Eriskay.

Even up here, amongst these magnificent peaks, the place was defined by absence. The silent stillness of this upland is deceptive; at night, it teems with life as its inhabitants return, under cover of darkness. Between a quarter and a third of the world's population of Manx shearwater raise their young on Rum. They live at sea but return to burrow into the soft scree and earth of the cuillins to lay their one egg. Their droppings enrich the growth of green which cloaks the slopes in summer. At night they return to feed the chick with fish and squid, their squabbling a breathless bubbling of sound, almost that of a baby's gurgle. This unearthly sound on the mountain in the night became the stuff of myth for the Vikings and Gaels.

The shearwater still intrigues and astonishes scientists. It winters at sea off Brazil and Uruguay, a journey of over six thousand miles from Rum; it has been estimated that some birds have flown five million miles over the course of their lifetimes. A shearwater may do nearly two hundred miles in a few days to gather food for its chick. These enormous distances are only possible because of the remarkable economy of its flight as it glides on stiff wings, low over the slope of a wave as it 'shears' the water using the energy of the wind off the water's surface. Its narrow, elegant wings are perfectly adapted for this glide, but make it difficult for the birds to take off from level ground. They have to use the steep slopes of Rum's cuillins to launch themselves. The fledgling grows to a weight one and half times that of the parent, so fat that when squeezed, oil drips from its beak – islanders used to waterproof their shoes with it. The fat supports the fledgling as it makes its maiden flight thousands of miles south. Thereafter, most of its life is spent shearing the waves of the Atlantic ocean from South America to the Hebrides, with annual forays onto land only to breed, spending a few weeks on Rum on its summer visits.

That evening we headed back to Mallaig on the ferry as the sun broke intermittently through grand, ragged grey clouds in the west, and Skye's Cuillins rose above us to the north. We were accompanied by shearwater gliding over the steely grey swell and dip of the sea, and at the stern of the ferryboat frills of foam left behind a white trail of our route. After days of walking

Rum, I had begun to dream of the island. The textures of the place marked my sleep: the hairy lichens; the surfaces of different rocks under my hand; the soft land under my feet, springy with sphagnum suddenly giving way to dark peaty water; the sun-warmed breath of the cropped turf scattered with daisies, and the crunch of the glittering scree on the cuillins. This experience of touch and feel had crept into my mind. It passed after I had returned to the urgency of the city, its pavements and worn parks, but the memory hung on, a way of thinking versed in the land. The roar beyond silence.

6

Eriskay

*The essence of the nation is that the people have
many things in common, but also have forgotten
much together.*

ERNEST RENAN, *WHAT IS A NATION?*

I

From the top of Ruinsival on Rum there is a view which takes
in the full extent of the Western Isles, the 120-mile stretch of
fragments of land and crumbling rocks, also known as the Long
Island or the Outer Hebrides, which stalls thousands of miles of
Atlantic swell. In the far south lies Mingulay, abandoned over a
century ago, then north to Vatersay and Barra, linked by a causeway. Next the Sound of Barra as one heads north to Eriskay, and
the long thin string of South Uist, Benbecula, North Uist and
Berneray, also all now linked by causeways. After Berneray lies
the Sound of Harris, a treacherous strait scattered with dozens of
small islands and skerries, before the largest islands, Harris and

Lewis, shoulder into the North Atlantic, ending finally in the far northern tip at the Butt of Lewis. These islands are strung along the ocean edge like the lights of a seaside promenade.

'Outer' was the word geographers used to describe this edge of the European continent. It is an adjective that came to be applied in time to Mongolia, space and London. It keeps eclectic company, reflecting different definitions of the centre and periphery. The shifts in usage track how understandings of space – national, global cosmic and urban – have changed.

From various vantage points on islands in the Inner Hebrides, I had studied the shape of this Long Island horizon. Sometimes it was caught as a sharp silhouette against the setting sun before a thick bar of cloud descended and blotted out all evidence of it. There were days at a time on the Small Isles when none of it was to be seen and visibility extended no further than a few metres of foam breaking on the shore in the wet whiteness as the rain fell out of the sodden air. It seemed implausible that beyond it lay land.

For the final sections of my journey, I travelled alone. As I drove the car down the jetty at the harbour in Oban into the bowels of the ferry for Barra, I felt a moment of elation that a long-held dream was taking shape. A routine event for some around me, although I fancied that it may have been as momentous for the elderly lady I later sat next to, for different and unknowable reasons. She barely moved during the four-hour journey except to turn the pages of the Bible in her hands, headscarf tied under her chin.

Ferry journeys were a hiatus: I had left but not yet arrived, and I loved the sense of suspension. We moved sedately across the calm Minch, a blue sea below the blue sky in a cold wind. While the good lady read her psalms, I read about the world's oceans, and how they are filling up with vast floating fields of plastic, and how our mild British climate is balanced delicately on the enormous global movements of water which wash around our shores. I broke off to watch the hills of Morvern on one side and those of Mull on the other slip by as the ferry headed up the Sound of Mull, then pushed out between north Mull and the tip of Ardnamurchan, before setting a course north-west to Castlebay, the main harbour on Barra. Through binoculars I could see the beaches on the Ardnamurchan peninsula where we had flown kites with the children, gathered mussels and swam during family holidays several years before. Tucked into a cleft in the hills was the one-roomed blackhouse where we had stayed, and had sat in the evenings to watch the sun set, if we were lucky, behind Barra.

Approaching the small harbour of Castlebay, and Barra's bare hills, it felt as if I had travelled a long way. I should have been in another country. Yet as I disembarked, I was greeted with a big YES sign for the Scottish referendum. It was still Scotland, part of the UK, as the saltire and YES flags flown from signposts, outside tents and in windows repeatedly reminded me. Part of the same fractious multinational conversation, although from Barra, Edinburgh seemed as distant as London. But despite the familiarity, there was something subtly different.

On the edge of an ocean and the edge of a continent: I felt an unsettling sense that I was both at home and abroad – in its meaning of 'widely scattered', of being 'beyond the confines of home'. The etymology of 'edge' is closely related to 'point', 'sword' and 'corner'; these meanings capture the subtle sensation, uncomfortable and also exhilarating, of these bare islands offering so little shelter from the presence of the Atlantic ocean.

This edge is precarious. Every winter brings periods when ferries and flights are cancelled or delayed, as storms break over the islands and bring down power lines. A few days of no electricity during a power cut are a familiar seasonal irritant. There are days when the mainland, and its safely predictable comforts and convenience, disappears from view beyond the Minch. Then the islands are thrown back on the resources of their own communities, their kindness and self-reliance. This is a place where people look out for each other. On my second day, an islander noticed at the petrol pump that my car tyre was a bit flat, and insisted I follow him back to his croft several miles away where he had a pump.

On this edge, various possibilities obscured elsewhere are apparent. Here, in the Outer Hebrides, the great projects of British state power have never been completed. The basic building blocks of nation of the last half millennium – faith and language – were never established. Either they were quietly subverted, or the reach of effective state instruments fell short. The impact of this was compounded by the indifference of successive governments to building the transport links (cheap ferries and flights) which might have knit the islands more closely to the mainland. The result is a distinctive island culture. Barra and the neighbouring islands of Eriskay and South Uist never experienced the full force of the Reformation; some Catholic practices seemed to have continued, so that when Irish missionaries arrived in the early seventeenth century, they found a warm reception. The islands have remained Catholic ever since. Protected by their Catholic clan chief, the MacNeils, the islands were exempt from three hundred years of passionate Protestantism which defined Scottish and British national identities. 'Catholics were referred to as outlandish, meaning they were not just strange but were out of bounds, did not belong and were therefore suspect,' comments the historian Linda Colley in *Britons*, her history of the eighteenth century. Outlandish: this was the history which endeared Barra to my father, a staunch Catholic and enthusiastic yachtsman. The island held a particular place in his imagination, and as he lay dying in an east-London hospice, he talked of his voyages to Barra and the Outer Hebrides.

By the nineteenth century, the Protestant Society for the Propagation of Christian Knowledge was sending missionaries to the Hebrides. Only a few islands in the Western Isles held out and remained Catholic, served by Scottish-born priests mostly trained on the Continent, in particular at the Scots College in Valladolid in Spain, where the seminarians spoke Gaelic and English alongside studying Latin. The Hebridean parishes were large and the priests were too impoverished for any means of transport; their work involved walking as much as giving the sacraments. But by the nineteenth century, they had scraped resources together to build churches, placed prominently so that no one could be in any doubt about the islands' Catholic identity. Above the harbour at Castlebay stands the church and above that, up on Heaval, the highest hill, is a Virgin and Child, who look out over the islands south to Mingulay. The day I visited, I bumped into several making the steep climb along the worn path; at the foot of the statue someone had left a box of ashes. The Virgin is a site of local pilgrimage.

On Eriskay and South Uist, there are roadside shrines, with their plaster Madonnas, at many corners and junctions. The Catholic identity is proudly asserted, literally at every turn. The most imposing of these markers is Our Lady of the Isles on South Uist. A pillar of granite over nine metres high, she stands on a hill above the road heading north. What makes this Madonna so significant is her position beside a military base, part of the radar tracking for the South Uist missile-testing range on the coast below. Behind the Madonna, on the summit of Ruabhal, is a large compound with a prickle of masts and satellite dishes. The tall fences are topped with barbed wire, and notices threaten trespassers with the Official Secrets Act.

The statue was commissioned at the height of the Cold War in 1957, when the Ministry of Defence first proposed a missile-testing range and a new military town on the island. It was paid for out of islanders' donations and was the initiative of a local priest who feared the Catholic Gaelic culture would be destroyed. The tall Madonna holds her young son standing in her arms, his hand raised to bless the Atlantic. Down below by the shore lies the range, housed in a quietly sinister conglomeration of warehouses and now run by a private security firm, Qinetiq, which rents it out to other countries for missile training. To the north, across the causeway, is the military base on Benbecula, with its small airport, barracks and town of terraced streets for personnel and families. These bases are linked to that at St Kilda, forty-five miles out to sea in the Atlantic.

In the first few days in Castlebay on Barra, I felt that my ferry had gone adrift and that I was in Ireland. One evening I was drawn into a ceilidh when the restaurant was cleared for dancing. It was a monthly social and most of those attending were women. I found myself dancing in my walking boots alongside these soft-voiced, motherly women in their pretty dresses. On the Saturday of my visit, the whole island came alive for a wedding; a marquee was erected on the machair and a long cortège of cars wound round the island and made its way up to the flower-filled church. The celebrations could be heard all the following day as the music reverberated around the harbour.

The Western Isles have the highest rate of religious observance in Britain. While the southern islands are staunchly Catholic, North Uist, Harris and Lewis are devout Free Church Presbyterians. The two denominations represent two poles of British Christianity, yet there is no history of tension or conflict. These are places unlike any other in the British Isles. Aspects of culture and a rural subsistence economy survived the powerfully centralizing history of the British imperial state until well into the twentieth century. The local and national bump up against each other in a gently messy way, but unlike in most other places, it is the local which has repeatedly had the edge. Long Island has maintained a distinctive parochialism – a word so often used derogatively (an indication in itself of the success of the centralizing project) yet its original meaning is a devotion to local place and an acceptance of the responsibilities that entails. It is a quietly rebellious, proudly self-referential place.

This is the north-west and I had arrived, and I understood why Louis MacNeice chose such a prosaic title for his book *I Crossed the Minch*. The crossing did seem to explain something very significant. I intended to meander along this edge – I was not in a hurry, given how many years it had taken me to get there – heading north, listening to its stories and people. I spent a day kayaking around Barra, alongside rocky outcrops, looking through the crystal-clear water at waving fronds of seaweed the colour of deep rust, orange and chocolate brown. I walked Vatersay's machair, scattered with mauve orchids, white daisies and pale yellow buttercups, in drifting misty rain. I sat on rocks and watched the oystercatchers, and in the evenings I joined convivial fellow travellers as we discussed how they were going to vote in the referendum on Scottish independence. They may have been divided in their political opinions but they shared an energetic passion for their country's beauty as they described the multiple ways they had explored it, climbing Munros (the peaks over 1,000 metres), walking long-distance paths and here – in the more low-lying topography of the Western Isles – walking every hill over a certain height.

II

Few Britons could point to Eriskay on a map, tucked into the
Sound of Barra with its many small islands and skerries. Eriskay
is only 2.5 miles long and 1.5 miles wide. Low rocky hills, a few
lochs, dunes and a long sandy beach – in other words, a small
Hebridean island like dozens of others up and down the archipelago. Unlike many of them, it has not been abandoned, and
is now linked to South Uist by a causeway. Since the ferry from
Barra docks there, it could even be described as busy, with a
scattering of houses, a pub and a shop.

Eriskay may have a modest demeanour, but it has a striking
way of inadvertently finding itself the site of national – and
international – dramas. Three histories over two and half
centuries have transfixed their respective audiences. The
island's Catholicism is traceable through all three, fostering a
culture in which forms of subversion, rebellion and challenge
could find purchase. The first is famous: Eriskay is where
Bonnie Prince Charlie landed when he arrived from France in
1745. The Jacobite chapter in the history of the Gàidhealtachd
had finally caught up with me – and I was to discover that
my lack of interest until now was itself a crucial part of that
history.

The celebrated story of the Stuart pretender might have been
enough history for one small island, but Eriskay cropped up in
another national story, this time in a dusty corner of Victorian
intellectual history, more than a century later, when a young
Englishwoman arrived in search of evidence of the paranormal. This is one of those obscure tales which rarely makes it
into history books, but vividly exposes the feel of an age, its
anxieties, hopes and strange fantasies. It brought Eriskay to the
attention of some of the most pre-eminent thinkers of the day.

Thirdly, Eriskay was the setting for a famous tale which became much loved in the immediate aftermath of the Second World War, prompting a novel and a classic black-and-white film still shown on television every Christmas. *Whisky Galore!* established a deeply affectionate portrait of the Hebrides in the national imagination.

These myths are all powerful but so disparate that I found their convergence on this one patch of land intriguing. What kind of cultural fault lines made possible these three histories: the beginning of an invasion in one century, earnest delibera-tions in another, and delighted laughter in the last? What can Eriskay's stories tell us about the making of myths, and how they flourish on the edge?

It was an eerily still Monday morning when I arrived on Eriskay, and the low cloud seemed to muffle every sound. I parked the car and walked up a gentle slope behind the dunes and across the hill to Loch Cracabhaig. The white cotton grass bobbed on delicate stalks, the brightest points in the greys of sky, sea, loch and rock. Looking east, the hill loch seemed brim-ful from this point, its steely water only separated from the grey of the Minch beyond by a thin strip of land. Not a soul was about as I headed back towards the island's township. Here, amongst the houses dotted over the hillside, washing hung optimistically on the line and someone was mowing his garden, carefully manoeuvring the mower around the rocky outcrops. The even-ness of this lawn was very foreign to these rock-strewn islands, but the grass grew thick and vivid green, like the artificial turf flung over market stalls in London street markets. An air of busy, neat domesticity hung over the place.

Below spread a magnificent stretch of dunes and silver-white sand, Coilleag a' Phrionnsa, the Prince's Strand, visible from the ferry as it plies the short distance from Barra. Prince Charles

Stuart landed here on 23 July in 1745 after his long voyage from France, carried piggyback from the French navy ship through the surf in driving rain. These dunes and hills were his first experience of Britain, the kingdom he had been plotting for while growing up in Europe. The prince had brought seeds of the seashore convolvulus flower, so the story goes, and he scattered them on the strand, where they have flowered ever since. His first night on British soil was spent in a turf-roofed cottage, along with the 'seven men of Moidart' who were accompanying him, a band who represented between them the four nations – English, Scottish, Irish and French – which would fight for Jacobitism. There was also an Italian valet, but he is never counted and his story never told. He had a strange ringside seat on history. What did he make of the soggy enterprise and its bold, implausible ambition, while he endeavoured to dry his master's clothes and find a warm meal?

There was to be precious little of either comfort in the eleven months which Prince Charles spent in Britain, his only experience of the country, he claimed (bar an extraordinary incognito trip to London in 1750, four years after his attempted invasion). Eriskay had been chosen as the landing point for the Stuart prince in the hope of winning the support of Alexander MacDonald of Boisdale, head of one of the most powerful Catholic clans. The chief arrived on Eriskay the following day to meet the prince, but refused support without full French backing for an uprising. After a brief sojourn, the prince left Eriskay for Arisaig on the mainland. He did not find much enthusiasm there either, but just as it seemed that the prince's plans would come to nothing, his fortunes took a dramatic turn. When he raised his standard a month later at Glenfinnan, at Loch Shiel in Moidart, he had an army, and by the middle of September he had taken Edinburgh. He had rallied the

Gàidhealtachd, inspired that at last they had a chance to recapture power in the Scotland they believed rightfully belonged to them, and to reinstitute Gaelic at its heart. Within five months of landing on Eriskay's strand, the Jacobites had taken Manchester, and shortly after, Derby. They were 127 miles from London.

It was an audacious challenge to the new nation of Britain, and probably the closest that the British monarchy has ever come to violent upheaval. London was in a state of panic in late 1745. But the decline in the Jacobite fortunes was almost as swift as the rise had been. In a fateful discussion with his leading supporters in Derby, the prince was persuaded not to march to London, but to return to Scotland. By April 1746, he was facing the well-equipped and disciplined armies of another young man, the Hanoverian Duke of Cumberland, on a windswept moor above Inverness. A series of disastrous decisions, including a misjudged night march in a bid to ambush Cumberland, led to a catastrophic defeat at Culloden. Poignantly, it has been estimated that a quarter of the Jacobite forces slept through the battle of Culloden, exhausted after their night of tramping through mud and heavy rain. They awoke to be slaughtered. The bodies of Jacobite soldiers were heaped into piles and targeted with cannon fire in the bloody aftermath. A campaign of indiscriminate killing and terror followed throughout the Highlands and Islands in a final bid to destroy the Gàidhealtachd. One historian has described it as 'verging on ethnic cleansing'. The prince fled.

For the young British nation, it was a formative experience: it exercised brutal state suppression to dismantle the social structure in the Highlands and Islands through terror and to erase the cultural identity through a range of new laws, which included a ban on the wearing of tartan and the carrying of arms. These measures were combined with new ways of gathering detailed information through surveys as a way to establish control, ultimately leading to the establishment of the Ordnance Survey. The aftermath of 1745 proved to be a template for imperial suppression and some of those involved went on to use similar methods in their careers in the empire.

On the beach at Eriskay, the only sounds were the hum of the ferry's engines as it intermittently plied back and forth to Barra, and small waves rippling to the shore on the grey day. Through the dunes, there was a faint path studded with daisies made by the passage of feet, while on either side in the longer grass stood yellow buttercups and sweet-scented clover. The path wandered over the uneven ground to arrive at a modest commemoration cairn, built by the children of Eriskay primary school in 1995, 250 years after the handsome Parisian aristocrat landed.

Many places across the Hebrides and the west coast boast of their link to the Stuart prince. George MacLeod, the founder of the Iona Community, recounted how, as a boy of nine, his father had told him on a trip to Iona, 'I want you to talk to Mrs McCormack. She's eighty-five years old and I want you to shake hands with her.' His father explained, 'When she was nine years old, she shook hands with a Mrs Campbell, who was then eighty-five years of age, and Mrs Campbell when she was nine stood at exactly this point on the jetty and watched the boat going down the Sound of Iona taking the prince back to France.' MacLeod concluded, 'Now that was a wonderful education. Two handshakes away from Bonnie Prince Charlie.'

Despite the catastrophe which his defeat unleashed on the Gàidhealtachd, Charles Stuart has been revered by many in the centuries which followed. Later on my journey I came across a recently erected handsome stone memorial on the boundary between Lewis and Harris. Shaped like a teardrop, it stands, over two metres high, on a hill beside the road. It marks a place where the prince landed as he fled his pursuers after Culloden, and overlooks the upper reaches of the magnificent Loch Seaforth. The steep hills plunge to sea level, and between them a section of open sea is visible, with Skye in the distance on the horizon. Engraved on a plaque are the words: 'It is to the eternal honour of all the Hebrideans that regardless of their loyalties, he was not betrayed to the authorities.'

He was a prince whose power came from European rivalries and the myths he could spin about his dynasty. French promises of military support failed to materialize, but the Stuart cause has shown remarkable longevity, lingering on in the imaginations of at least two nations, Scotland and Britain, inspiring devotion as well as suspicion. As I stood by the cairn on Eriskay, amongst the clover and daisies, the story of '45 seemed characterized by sheer improbability. How could a cosmopolitan young courtier have persuaded the Gaels to place their faith in him, and how could he have led an army with no prior military experience to within striking distance of London, the new global maritime and commercial powerhouse? Even one of the historians of the period has admitted that this chapter of history is 'stranger than fiction'. It certainly has many of the elements of a novel: colourful characters, unexpected victories as well as a great defeat, an extraordinary escape which involved near-capture several times and feats of endurance across rough country and stormy seas pursued by the full force of the British state. To cap it all, the prince's survival owed much to the bravery and ingenuity of a young woman from South Uist, Flora Macdonald, who took in the fugitive prince and negotiated safe passage to Skye, taking him as part of her party disguised as an Irish maid.

Despite, or indeed because of, such rich detail, it has been a difficult history for historians to write. The adventure began in the world of eighteenth-century espionage, full of courtly intrigues, misunderstandings, rumours, absurd claims and counterclaims, and it thrived on more of the same once the prince arrived in Scotland. The assembling of reliable facts has proved elusive. No sooner had Cumberland's troops finished at Culloden than the fight began over how the history was to be written and by whom. As in a fairground mirror, nothing appeared as it seemed. Was Prince Charlie a remarkably determined, fearless young man, or a risk-taking chancer who abandoned his men and escaped to a miserable alcoholic decline?

There are books passionately arguing the case both ways. Even some historians, those would-be paragons of objectivity, have admitted that on Jacobitism there can be no neutrality; everyone has had to take sides, because this eighteenth-century chapter is so deeply embedded in the narratives of four nations: Britain, England, Scotland and Ireland.

I had never been interested in the Jacobite history; it was the Clearances which provoked me into reading Scottish history. I was baffled by the tourist-packaged romanticism I had intermittently stumbled upon in places such as Skye. But this is another chapter which refuses to slip quietly into history books. In recent decades, a generation has rewritten the history and, in so doing, contributed to a new national backstory for Scotland. Even the descriptions of Jacobitism's improbability and strangeness – indeed my own lack of interest – were the outcome, it was argued, of a deliberate strategy to belittle and dismiss the nature of the challenge. The Hanoverian British state and its advocates had not only to crush the Stuart armies but also to win the hearts and minds of Jacobite sympathisers throughout the Atlantic archipelago. To do so, the prince was cast as an effete aristocrat whose wild armies fought musket shot with broadswords and never had a serious chance of victory. According to this telling, the whole episode was a freak of history with no lasting significance. But historians such as Murray Pittock have argued that, on the contrary, the Jacobite armies were well organized and armed, and they could have taken London. In his view, their astonishing success was because Prince Charles drew on deep antipathy to the 1707 union of Scotland and England, and because his support came not just from the Gaels but from throughout Scotland. His rallying cry as he took Edinburgh was prosperity for Scotland and an end to the union. The Stuarts had a vision of a multi-kingdom monarchy, 'a federative Union rather than an incorporating one'. A large part of their appeal was that they drew on an ancient historiography of Scotland as a distinct kingdom with its own identity through a thousand years of conflict with its bigger neighbour, England. In this version of history, Scotland played the part of the heroic David against Goliath.

For the British state in the eighteenth century, these were dangerously subversive ideas, and Britain has never wanted them in the history books. The words of the great English historian G. M. Trevelyan are symptomatic: he described the Highlanders in 1745 as 'barbarians' in pursuit of a 'fantasia of misrule', and the Highlands as 'an Afghanistan ... [which came] within fifty [*sic*] miles of the modern Athens'. Britain wanted a benign national narrative of its development and, revealingly, the title of the relevant volume of the New Oxford History of England, published in 1989, was *A Polite and Commercial People 1727–1783*. What the British did not want represented was an aggressive Anglo-British supremacy which ruthlessly centralized power and suppressed challenge in its religiously plural and multinational kingdom.

British historians have claimed that in the eighteenth century a coherent national unity emerged; in her book *Britons* Linda Colley defines this British identity as Protestant, imperial and anti-French; in so doing, she downplays the internal fault lines within a Britain that included subjects who were Irish Catholics and Jacobite Scots. She became the British establishment's historian of choice; she was invited to give seminars at Downing Street when Gordon Brown, a Scot with a passionate interest in the union, was Chancellor of the Exchequer under the Labour government. The BBC commissioned her to deliver a series of essays to open the momentous referendum year of 2014. The eighteenth century had become the most politically relevant chapter of British history for both Scottish nationalists and British unionists alike. It was a political battle fought in history books as old traditions were reinterpreted to address new preoccupations, before it found an echo in the streets, community centres and church halls of Scotland in the referendum campaign.

Once the Jacobite rebellion had been violently crushed and its history relegated to a colourful concoction of Highland barbarism and Stuart dynastic claims, British commentators conceded its romanticism. A tale of hopeless bravery of a doomed people, '45 was used to reinforce the inevitability of the supremacy of British nationalism. Once the escapade had been deemed improbable, Britain could appear magnanimous in tolerating quaint Jacobite rituals, symbols and ceremonies. Within a few decades, the British state was even laying claim to them, thanks to the efforts of Sir Walter Scott and his devotee, Queen Victoria – the joint inventors of the modern British monarchy. They grasped that charisma, symbols and mythology would sustain the monarchy against the revolutionary challenge facing Europe in the early nineteenth century. They used Jacobitism, still powerful nearly a century after its ostensible defeat, for their own ends. Their trump card over the Hanoverians was the authenticity of a clear lineage stretching back centuries. In contrast, the Hanoverians had been hoisted onto the British throne after no less than fifty-eight others in the line of succession had been rejected for holding the wrong religious faith. Prosaic, dull and German, the Hanoverians were the bargain basement of European royalty, and struggled to win the affection of the British people.

Scott carefully grafted his version of Jacobite romanticism onto the British monarchy in 1822, in the famous pageant he orchestrated for George IV in Edinburgh, the first visit by a reigning monarch to Scotland since 1650. Bagpipes and kilts, the symbols of the crushed Gaels, were rehabilitated as props for a modern monarchy. The Jacobites had pioneered the use of propaganda, ceremonies, relics and souvenirs; drinking glasses and lady's fans, for example, were engraved with Jacobite symbols. Queen Victoria followed suit, and helped by her husband Albert, another scion of German royalty, she built her castle at Balmoral with its ersatz Scottish medieval architecture. The royal couple toured the sites – including Staffa – and painted the inevitable watercolours. This was no passing fad for the queen, who continued to take a close interest in the Scottish royal dynasty. In 1889, in the midst of another Jacobite revival (of magazines and drinking societies), she agreed to be patron of an exhibition of alleged Jacobite relics in London. It included no less than fifteen locks of hair and eleven pieces of tartan belonging to Prince Charles. Queen Victoria recognized that the Jacobites' quasi-religious practices brought the mystique and romance needed to reinvent the monarchy, using symbol, national pageant and propaganda. It was extremely successful, securing the monarchy as one of the most resilient foundations of the British state on both sides of the border.

The longevity and popularity of the British Royal Family owes much to its assiduously maintained Scottish identity, particularly during the First and Second World Wars, when it had to overcome its German origins (and habit of finding spouses in Germany). Lady Elizabeth Bowes-Lyon, a new infusion of Scottish blood, proved to be the most admired royal since Queen Victoria. Queen Elizabeth II has carefully cultivated her Scottish connections, going so far as to name her first born Charles. She chose a Scottish public school, Gordonstoun, for her sons' education; Scotland was her favourite holiday destination, either at Balmoral or on cruises through the Hebrides (one of the queen's favourite places is reputed to be a beach on Rum, and she took a young Prince Edward and Princess Anne to visit St Kilda). Every year she attends that gala of Scottish pageantry, the Braemar Highland Games. Today's Royal Family owes its origins in large part to Germany and Greece, but it is its Scottish heritage that it chooses to highlight, dressing in kilts and tweeds for photocalls and documentaries. Prince William chose to attend a Scottish university, St Andrews.

When Prince Charles wanted to live incognito as one of the people in 1987, he headed to that spectacularly atypical part of his future kingdom, the island of Berneray, off North Uist, and lodged with a shepherd for a week before the world's media arrived. It was a choice of destination rich with symbolism: Prince Charles in hiding in the Hebrides – again.

III

On the road above the Prince's Strand on Eriskay, which takes the campervans from the ferry north towards the Uists, is a shrine. A small enclosure sits within the white picket fence with a garden of geraniums and benches for visitors around a statue of the Virgin, in white with gold trim, and at her feet are offerings of fresh pink carnations. The dedication records that the Virgin Mary appeared to three children in 1917 in Fatima, Portugal and gave them a message, 'Pray and do penance for the sins of the world.' The shrine's bright paint is visible from almost every home in the township and to all the cars arriving from Barra.

The Catholicism of the Hebrides shocked successive generations of visitors in the eighteenth and nineteenth centuries, and they seized upon it as evidence of the backwardness of this edge culture. But they were also intrigued by its coexistence with elements they believed to be relics of pre-Christian folklore. One of the first to gather accounts of the song, poetry and stories was John Francis Campbell. He seemed almost embarrassed by his subject, and wrote in his introduction to the collection of Gaelic folklore he published in 1860–62 that they were 'light mental debris' and a 'museum of curious rubbish about to perish'. He maintained that the modernity of railways, newspapers and tourists would 'drive out romance'. By the end of the nineteenth century, Campbell's misgivings had given way to a passionate reappraisal, supported by the growing folklore movement which celebrated the survival of a distinctive, rich Gaelic folk culture in the southern Outer Hebrides. The songs, music, poetry and folk tales were a treasure trove, a vibrant cultural patrimony disappearing from the rest of the British Isles, the last vestiges of a pre-industrial rural culture, it was suggested. There was an urgent need to gather the fragments of this dying culture.

The most famous collection of Gaelic folklore is that of Alexander Carmichael, who spent half a century gathering material, conducting hundreds of interviews all over the Hebrides, particularly in South Uist, Eriskay and Barra. 'Perhaps no people had a fuller ritual of song and story, of secular rite and religious ceremony than the Highlands. Mirth and music, song and dance, tale and poem, pervaded their lives, as electricity pervades the air,' claimed Carmichael, himself born on the island of Lismore in Argyll. It represented, he continued 'an admirable union of elements in life for those who have lived it so truly and intensely as the Celtic races have done, and none more truly or more intensely than the ill-understood and so called illiterate highlanders of Scotland'.

The first two volumes of Carmichael's vast collection of Gaelic stories, poetry and songs, *Carmina Gadelica*, were published in 1900 (four more volumes followed in later years). There were prominent accounts of omens, signs, apparitions and the 'two sights' or 'second sight', an ability to foretell the future, in particular, a death. Such beliefs could be unsettling and some believed they required blessings, holy water and prayer to propitiate these unruly spiritual forces; it is not difficult to see how the Catholic priests had come to an accommodation with these folk practices. But busy and prosperous island fishing communities such as Barra, Eriskay and Uist were now cast as repositories of a 'uniquely mystical if also pessimistic way of life', concludes historian James Hunter. The Gael of the Hebrides had come to stand for everything that late-nineteenth-century urban industrial Britain was not: spiritual, poetic, musical, sensitive, intuitive, impulsive, imaginative and mystical. Hovering over this idealization was the legacy of the Ossianic controversy and the lingering doubts over authenticity.

'As the logic of commercial utilization permeated the land, it gave to the remaining enclave of commercial uselessness the radiance of a disappearing authenticity,' writes cultural historian Peter Womack. A social and spiritual renewal could be found in the roots of British rural cultures, proposed the Folklore Society, founded in 1878. Gaelic culture in the late nineteenth century and at the beginning of the twentieth century was used to inform a process of British self-definition and, at the same time, to illuminate perceived British moral and spiritual failings. These ideas were taken up by many artists and writers, most famously the Irish poet W. B. Yeats in the Irish literary revival, the Celtic Twilight.

This renewed fascination with Gaelic Hebridean culture was partly inspired by the writings of the Frenchman Ernest Renan, who drew on his childhood upbringing in Brittany to expound a theory of nations and identity, positing the Celtic Atlantic peoples as visionary dreamers. Carmichael, said Renan admiringly, was gathering 'the divine tones thus expiring before the growing tumult of uniform civilization'. The Ossian themes of the romance of a doomed civilization were being reworked for a new century. The projection onto the distant north-west assuaged an 'intellectual unease', comments cultural historian Malcolm Chapman, 'perhaps in part triggered by the misery and squalor of industrial areas, the loss of old habits and their replacement by a transient, cosmopolitan, shifting and impermanent society where wage labour moved whenever and wherever it must'. Salvation would come from this rural Atlantic west. Renan, Matthew Arnold (an Englishman) and Kuno Meyer (a German) all announced that in the Celt there was a spiritual imagination in danger of being crushed by the calculating utilitarianism of their times. It was another instance of cultural appropriation by the dominant culture for its own ends; yet again, the Hebrides was defined by its 'otherness'.

At the turn of the twentieth century the urgent task of col-lecting Gaelic folklore fell to amateurs – Carmichael was an exciseman on the islands. Another of those amateurs was a Catholic priest on Eriskay, Fr Allan MacDonald, a handsome, charismatic and intelligent man. Visitors were intrigued by his dedication to his parishes, first on South Uist and then on Eriskay, and he ended up as a character in at least one novel. Amongst his many duties, he listened to his parishioners' songs, poems and tales; some included accounts of strange lights, eerie sounds and the untoward behaviour of animals and weather. He took meticulous notes. Much of the material he accumulated over years of compiling his journals were from monoglot Gaelic speakers. It represented a remarkable collection.

'A bird with a terrible scream was observed to flit across the island from time to time at night,' ran the story of the Eriskay Alarm Bird in MacDonald's notebooks in 1887. No one had seen its like before and one man heard it 'push against his door and to make as much noise in moving about his door as a man would'. The following autumn an outbreak of measles killed many young people, including the man's only daughter, the notes continued. Another story told of how a man standing outside his house saw a group of the dead coming towards him: 'He felt hot as if oppressed by the warm breath of many people. He felt himself being sped away with rapidity as if he were riding a horse at a furious speed, and he could feel the hair of his head brushed aside by the rapidity of his movement through the air.' He found himself transported to the graveyard seventeen miles away, and then back home again. Some of the instances of second sight, MacDonald noted, foretold deaths, like the time the twelve-year-old Marion MacRury saw two adults whom she did not recognize pass by the schoolyard on Eriskay; a short while later, the schoolteacher died.

MacDonald established a reputation for careful documentation and was much respected by Carmichael. In 1894 a young woman, Ada Goodrich-Freer, asked Carmichael for help with an unusual project. The attention of the recently founded Society for Psychical Research in London had been drawn to the rumours of second sight in the Highlands and Islands. An enquiry into a phenomenon believed to be in danger of disappearing along with the rest of Gaelic folklore was urgently commissioned. The wealthy Catholic Marquess of Bute agreed to fund a researcher, and this enthusiastic young woman put herself forward as qualified for the job. Goodrich-Freer did not speak a word of Gaelic, had no knowledge of the Hebrides and little of Scotland, but as an assistant on an occult journal she had established some useful connections. She declared in her application an appetite for the outdoor life, an ability to walk up to sixteen miles a day, and a facility for talking to 'peasantry' derived from her Yorkshire background. She may have lacked qualifications, but she made up for it with an abundance of charm. A number of her letters have survived in the Marquess of Bute's archives, showing how she carefully sustained her patron's interest in the enquiry. She won over Carmichael, who wrote in one letter that an associate was as 'charmed as we all are with Miss Freer'. On another occasion, shortly before she made a visit to Eriskay, Carmichael wrote to Fr Allan regarding her imminent arrival, saying, 'I heartily envy you.' The local newspaper, the *Oban Times*, even reported that during her long visits 'she appears to be a favourite among Highland people'.

During her three visits to Eriskay Fr Allan gave her unrestricted access to his many notebooks; perhaps he was as fascinated by this beautiful young woman as she was by his parishioners' tales. Fair-haired, with finely arched eyebrows, she must have been an arresting figure on Eriskay. A photo has survived of her sitting on one of the island's beaches with the handsome Fr Allan and another of his guests, Walter Blaikie, the publisher of Carmichael's work. Goodrich-Freer looks evasively away from the camera. She recognized the value of the notebooks to furthering her own ambitions, and drew extensively from them in her writing over the next few years.

In 1895 Goodrich-Freer delivered an interim report on her research to 'a very crowded general meeting' in Westminster Town Hall; the great minds of Victorian intellectual life were enthralled by the tales she told, which she maintained had been 'sought out [in] the most remote spots accessible', gleaned from the 'fisherman in his herring boat, and the travelling "merchant" in his gig, in the blacksmith's forge and the manse kitchen'. There was no reference to Fr Allan. Neither was there much specific detail on second sight, as commissioned by the society, but she brushed such concerns aside, insisting this was only an interim report and the full detail was still to come. Chairing this meeting on Eriskay was no less a person than Henry Sidgwick, the society's first president, Cambridge Professor of Moral Philosophy and one of the most prominent thinkers of the century. Founder of Newnham College for women and advocate for a host of good causes, he was passionately interested in the potential of psychic phenomena. He was not alone. The society counted among its members several MPs, lawyers, a physics professor and clergymen such as the writer Lewis Carroll; honorary members included luminaries of late Victorian society such as William Gladstone, the critic John Ruskin, and the poet Alfred, Lord Tennyson.

The fascination with psychic phenomena was part of a cultural movement exploring a range of spiritualist and unorthodox religious experiences. In the late nineteenth century many were searching for new models of belief as their faith in Christianity came under increasing question. There were hundreds of societies all over the country and famous mediums were widely sought after for consultations and lectures. Séances, speaking with the dead, furniture moving, curtains twitching were part of this rich culture of bewildered Victorians. The Society for Psychical Research claimed it used rigorous scientific methods, but alongside its research there were also famous imposters, celebrated exposures of fakes and long-running legal disputes. The ambitious and inventive could find unexpected status in this field, particularly women, and they played a central role. Goodrich-Freer had both ambition and inventiveness, and history has proved a harsh judge of her for it. After her lectures, Goodrich-Freer went on to write a book, *The Outer Isles*, published in 1902, which drew on MacDonald's notes. But former allies became disillusioned and Carmichael wrote to Fr Allan that she was 'not altogether what she seems', and that 'we hear from various sources that Miss Freer is not genuine and some call her a clever imposter'. The final report never appeared; she failed to provide the definitive evidence the society insisted upon. Then she fell silent, and her name disappeared from the society's archives.

Many such intriguing characters flit through a few pages of obscure history books. But several decades later two researchers resolved to find out who exactly Ada Goodrich-Freer was. They picked apart her fabricated birth, age, family, name and upbringing. They discovered she had been an orphan without family background, little education and no financial resources. At the age of nearly thirty-eight, with astonishing chutzpah she passed herself off on Eriskay as a twenty-four-year-old, and by the time she died, she had reset her age again, misleading her husband by twenty-three years.

One of the researchers, the distinguished Gaelic folklorist John Lorne Campbell, could not forgive her for the extensive and unattributed use of Fr Allan's notebooks and her handling of a payment due to him from the Marquess of Bute whereby the priest ended up with a fraction of what had been proposed. In his book *Strange Things*, Campbell's contempt is relentless, but despite Goodrich-Freer's taste for self-dramatization and her habit of hinting at her own spiritual powers, she is owed some admiration for how adroitly she moved through this overheated world of spiritualists, intellectuals, aristocrats, priests and folklorists, impressing all of them. But her success, such as it was, proved brief. Mixed up in various controversies over haunted houses and the mysterious suicides of leading psychical researchers, Goodrich-Freer fell from favour. She wisely left London, and travelled to Jerusalem, where she married before ending up in America.

Meanwhile Eriskay continued to feature on visitors' itineraries. Marjorie Kennedy-Fraser, the Scottish singer and composer, arrived in 1905 with the Celtic Revivalist painter John Duncan, just in time to discuss Gaelic songs with Fr Allan before his early death from pneumonia. Inspired by the islanders, she recorded their singing, and went on to arrange and publish collections of music over the following two decades. Her *Songs of the Hebrides* were celebrated, the four volumes published at intervals before, during and after the First World War, and were used in schools and drawing rooms all over Britain (although later commentators regarded her interpretations as bearing little relation to the originals). Several of her arrangements became iconic, such as the 'Eriskay Love Lilt' and, in particular, 'The Road to the Isles', which she dedicated to the 'lads' fighting in France in the trenches. Played by a piper on the beaches of Normandy on D-Day during the Second World War on the orders of the Scottish commanding officer, Lord Lovat, it has found its way into several films and into the regular repertoire of military bands.

For some folklorists, the Gaelic cultural traditions represented a living past. Academics kept their distance and it was only in 1951 that the School of Scottish Studies was set up to study the traditions of Scottish rural life. That ushered in a growing respect for the sophistication of Gaelic culture and a body of serious research into the language and literature developed. There was recognition of a distinctive and unique perspective; John Lorne Campbell reflected on his lifelong fascination in 1967, writing that the 'Gaelic mind' existed in a 'vertical plane' of an 'amazingly long' historical continuity, which stretched back to Viking times and was infused with 'a sense of the reality and existence of the other world of spiritual and psychic experience'. In comparison, Campbell suggested, the modern European was 'horizontal, possessing breath and extent', but without a depth in time, so even the names of one's grandparents could be forgotten. Campbell had alighted on exactly the same detail used by Orwell in *Nineteen Eight-Four* to define a loss of identity.

IV

On the shore near the cemetery is Eriskay's pub, the SS Politician. It was named after Scotland's most famous shipwreck: on 5 February 1941 the 8,000-ton cargo ship the SS *Politician* blundered into the shallow sound of Eriskay and ran aground. It had been on its way to join an Atlantic convoy and sank with its cargo of cotton, bicycles and, most famously of all, 250,000 cases of premium whisky destined to pay for American loans to Britain to fight the war. At a time of strict rationing, the *gu leoir* – the Gaelic word for 'abundance', Anglicized as 'galore' – was so improbable that it seemed the stuff of fiction. As indeed it was to become.

The crew was rescued by islanders, and word spread quickly of the ship's cargo, the automatic property of HM Excise. The salvage firm took the cotton and bicycles, but oily water in the hold made it difficult to extract the whisky, and after a month the effort was abandoned. The islanders could not believe their luck. Small boats set out every night to collect the whisky. The islanders donned old clothes to protect themselves from the oil – even some of their womenfolk's old dresses, so the story went – to slither around in the hold for the precious cases. Neighbouring islands joined the spree and drunkenness was endemic for a few months. Rumours spread of informants and there were a handful of arrests. The wreck was finally blown up, but not until an estimated 24,000 cases of whisky had disappeared into crofts and byres all over Eriskay, Barra and Uist. This warranted a few paragraphs in the local papers, until one of the most exotic characters to have ever settled in the Hebrides,

Compton Mackenzie, turned the tale into a bestselling novel, *Whisky Galore.*

The pub has a large conservatory overlooking the machair and the sea. The day I visited, it was virtually empty; the bartender was in discussion with a customer about a memorable evening the night before. I got talking to a middle-aged Glaswegian eating lunch. He had been born on Eriskay and had lived there until he was ten; after several decades, he started coming back regularly, and he grew intent as he explained just how much he loved the place. The walls of the pub were covered in old photos of the SS *Politician*, and the amused young bartender showed me a still-unopened bottle salvaged from the wreck. The whisky glowed in the brown bottle against the light from the sea outside.

Mackenzie lived just across the water from Eriskay on Barra throughout the war. He was there for the whisky bonanza of 1941, but it was not until 1946 that he published the book for which he is best known. The film soon followed in 1949. Mackenzie was an unconventional character, a Catholic, a founder, in 1928, of one of the early nationalist parties, the National Party of Scotland, and Governor-General of the Royal Stuart Society. Born in County Durham, he was an Englishman who had redefined himself as a kilt-wearing Scot, a man whose love of islands (Capri, Herm, Jethou in the Channel Islands, the Shiants in the Hebrides) finally landed him in Barra. In *Whisky Galore*, Mackenzie portrayed a resourceful island community which defied the authorities to salvage and hide the whisky. It was a celebration of the anarchic, the rebellious and the particular against the petty, onerous and sometimes nonsensical regulations of the wartime state. The film helped define post-war notions of Britishness with its plucky humour and gentle satire of the class system and officious bureaucracy. The audience's sympathy is squarely with the Gaels, who outwit the authorities. It was Scotland's version of *Dad's Army*, but with pioneering cinematography of the Hebridean coastline.

In this crowd-pleasing plot, there is something more unexpected. Mackenzie placed a deeply sympathetic Catholic priest in a central role in the novel, and the lead character converts to Catholicism: challenging material for a largely Protestant British audience. He littered the book with Gaelic sayings and phases (for which he provided a glossary), at a time when Hebridean children could still be forbidden from speaking Gaelic at school. He depicted the sole middle-class Englishman as absurd, humourless and pompous. He even had a dig in one passage at the misty-eyed romantization of the Hebrides, with a spoof of the popular contemporary guidebooks by Alasdair Alpin MacGregor (a bitter feud ensued). Only in the last chapters of the book did he fall back on a trusted Scottish literary tradition, used by both Sir Walter Scott and Robert Louis Stevenson, in which the English and Scottish were reconciled in mutual affection and respect. The ageing mother of the groom, a Cockney, announces that, for all her love of her native city, she has 'fallen in love' with the Hebridean island. The islanders take her to their hearts in an emotional union which in the book (though not the film) is more prominent than the romantic denouement.

The Hebrideans were lodged in the imagination of the cinema-going British public as a gallery of lovable rogues, the 'local character' was bequeathed as a requisite feature of Scottish rural life. He (and it was almost always male) defiantly resisted modernity with an independence of spirit out of kilter with his times – a plot reworked in the later film *Local Hero*. This was the Gaels' history of subversion, updated for the twentieth century. *Whisky Galore* was Mackenzie's farewell gift to the Hebrides and to Scotland. His interest in Scottish Nationalism had waned. He sold up and left, returning to the social whirl of London parties, which he now described in letters to friends as 'civilization'.

Charles Stuart, Ada Goodrich-Freer and Compton Mackenzie: all three only fleetingly set foot on Eriskay's rocky hills. All brought it fame – of vastly varying kinds – creating myths which reverberate to this day. All three spun stories to serve their own ends and used the distance of this Atlantic edge to find licence for their myth-making. Beyond that, these three had little in common.

What strange re-ordering of historical narrative might we find if, instead of structuring it by *when* it happened, we structured history by *where* it happened. A history jumble sale, in which the odd, delightful and significant sit alongside each other. What other kinds of unlikely historical bedfellows, like these three, might it produce?

I shook myself from such odd musing. On Eriskay, the washing was still hanging on the line, limp in the damp air. It was time to head north again.

7

Lewis

*The islander is caught in a net of contradictions
imposed on him by his history, and ... to live
from the centre of what he is, is far harder
than for those who have been luckier with their
geography and their history.*

IAIN CRICHTON SMITH, *TOWARDS THE
HUMAN*

I

The journey from Eriskay north to Lewis was eighty-five miles
over four causeways and a ferry, and it took me over another
Hebridean anomaly, a land boundary between two islands,
Harris and Lewis. Entranced by the understated charm of the
Uists, Benbecula and Berneray, I explored their machairs rich
with flowers and miles of sandy beach. The midsummer days
dawned early and I woke to the sound of corncrakes a few feet
outside the window of the old blackhouse which served as a

hostel. On walks over the machair and beaches, the air vibrated with a cacophony of birds, an intensity of song and flight unlike any I had ever experienced, setting all my senses alert. On the long beach at Tobha Mòr in South Uist I came across an incongruous reminder of my London life: an office chair had been brought in by the ocean, and now it was propped up with an absurd air of self-importance on an outcrop of rock looking out to sea. One armrest had been carefully mended with tape. I wondered about its origins and long journey. A sampling of the tons of plastic which circulate the globe was scattered amongst the shells and seaweed: brightly coloured bottles, odd shoes, buoys, bits of old rope and fishing crates. Later I came across a tree trunk lodged in dunes, which had made its way from the Caribbean. Thousands of miles of ocean stretch west from this Uist shore to the Americas. The Atlantic connects the Long Island of the Outer Hebrides with Iceland, Greenland and the Arctic in the north, and to the south, the Caribbean, Brazil and Africa. With my back to Britain, facing out to this wide salty world, I felt an unparalleled sense of space. It was a precarious perch on the planet's surface, for the land on which I was standing was a narrow strip only six miles wide in places, riddled with inlets and pockmarked with lochans. The oceanographer Callum Roberts points out that since 71 per cent of the world's surface is water, 'earth' is a misnomer. Planet Water. On the Uists, this recognition has perhaps always been present. It has long been a source of anxiety.

'No man could conceive, no imagination could realize, the disorderly distribution of land and water that is to be seen in these Outer Islands, where mountains and moor, sand and peat, rock and morass, reef and shoal, freshwater lake and salt water loch, in wildest confusion, strive for mastery,' wrote Alexander Carmichael in the introduction to his collection of Gaelic folklore, *Carmina Gadelica*. He went on to quote the nineteenth-century Scottish man of letters John Blackie:

> *O God-forsaken, God-detested land!*
> *Of bogs and blasts, of moors and mists and rain;*
> *Where ducks with men contest the doubtful strand,*
> *And shirts when washed are straightway soiled again!*

North Uist is known as a 'drowned landscape' buried under layers of peat, bog and hundreds of small lochs. Most drowned landscapes, such as Doggerland in the North Sea, are under water, long since lost to sea level rises. This Uist landscape is not quite drowned; rather, it seems to be *drowning* – the lochans appear on the point of finally brimming over and reconnecting to one another, and to the ocean. The cream water lilies glow in the peaty black water. Yellow irises line streams and spill over marshy ground. Above, low hills emerge briefly before they disappear into low-lying cloud and thick mists roll in, wrapping you in a damp, claustrophobic embrace.

In Lochmaddy's arts centre, Taigh Chearsabhagh, in North Uist, I visited an exhibition of the New York-based Latvian artist Vija Celmins. Her work traces the complex patterning of the surface of water in intricate woodcuts which are so precise and detailed that they can take her a year to make: a practice of patient, attentive study of matter in constant motion. (She was flown into North Uist from New York to give a talk, and seemed disorientated; 'How far am I from Riga?' she asked her audience.) She described her images of the surface of the ocean or the night sky as 'impossible', reminding us of 'the complexity of the simplest things'. Her attention to the detail of water suggested a way of honouring the Gaelic belief that the sea is a blessed place, more so than the land. The belief reveals the appreciation of the fecundity of the sea and recognition of the recalcitrance of the thin soils and rock on these islands.

On a map the Uists' intricate pattern of land and water looks like lace, pale brown land crumbling into the blue water. The Uists helped me to understand why 'solid ground' is often a term of endearment. These islands are amongst the most vulnerable landscapes in the British Isles to rising sea levels from climate change. I was haunted by the fate of a family who, in 2005, left their coastal croft in a winter storm in South Uist to seek safety and were drowned just a few miles from their home.

Once on east Harris, there is plenty of solid ground. But it also has a strangeness of its own. It is more rock than earth, quite literally unearthly. The south Harris peak of Roineabhal is a rare anorthosite rock 1,500 million years old, the same rock which makes up much of the moon's mountains. Stanley Kubrick filmed his sequences of Jupiter here for his 1968 film *2001: A Space Odyssey*. When islanders were cleared off the fertile machair on the west coast of Harris in the Clearances, they moved east to this rocky coastline, known as the Bays, where they grew potatoes on the scraps of land between the boulders, some no larger than a metre or so square.

These disorientating alien landscapes took a new form when I reached Lewis. I was heading to the south-west of the island, to Uig, and as I drove over the moor, the mountains which marked the boundary between Lewis and Harris dominated the skyline to the south. The road peters out on this south-west coast, leaving a stretch of nearly thirty miles of rugged uninhabited coastline where the mountains meet the sea. Uig itself is a wide bay of huge beaches framed by twisting slabs of ancient rock. In the distance, beyond the headlands of the bay, the dull roar of the sea where it beat against the cliffs was like the hum of a motorway. On the sheltered beaches, the waves calmed to a gentle rhythm as they rolled over shining sands. The hills beyond the beach rose in great swags and folds of grey rock like the carcasses of exhausted elephants.

A layer of peat bog carpets the central plateau of Lewis, riddled with lochans, with only the occasional croft in this undulating watery land. Most of the townships are along the coast. The two roads which cross the moor from east to west run dead straight, accompanied by the swoop of telegraph wires strung between poles. Islanders drove at terrifying speeds as they overtook me. After my first visit in the summer of 2014, I returned several times to Lewis over the course of a year, and each time I crossed Barabhas Moor, its character was strikingly different. On the first occasion, in late June, the heavens opened, and the car drummed with the beating of heavy rain. For a few miles in the thick grey I could not see more than a few metres in front, but it was brief, and afterwards shafts of sunlight shot between cracks in the low cloud to light up patches of green-gold land, silhouetted as long thin strands between shining water. On a return visit later that year in early November, the moor was the colour of burnt umber; brown and orange grasses smouldered under grey clouds. When caught by sunlight, they flared into splashes of rich yellow against the sombre dark of the heather. The tips of the iris leaves were rust red in the thick clumps along the road. There had been heavy rain, and the streams were swollen, and the brimming lochs seemed ready to spill. Patches of blue sky were reflected on the road where the puddles unfurled like blue satin ribbon. The Lewis poet Iain Crichton Smith writes of an 'untaught sky', and after experiencing the mercurial, unruly nature of inland Lewis, I saw the aptness of his phrase.

Later that winter, towards the end of January, blizzards buffeted the car I was driving as they tore over the undulating plateau one night. In the gaps between storms of snow, moonlight broke through, splashing a weak grey light on the lochs. At one point the wild gusts flung a flock of what looked like small birds across the road like litter. Only a deer seemed impassive in the storm as my headlights picked out the glint of her eyes. She stood beside the road as I passed. These moors are not always dramatic; on some days, grey cloud and smirr drain all contrast from the land, leaving an unmerciful bleakness. The poet Louis MacNeice likened them to 'the colour of grizzly bears or burnt toast'. It is a volatile, shape-shifting land, which outsiders often perceive as either a place of hostile threat or tedious uniformity. This central moorland plateau has defined the island of Lewis; before good roads were built it was difficult to cross, and the sea was the main means of communication for the communities which clung to its coasts. Each of the four corners of Lewis has a distinctive character, where people have made a home and a living squeezed between sea and moorland, and the threats they both represent.

The size of this island has made it distinctive in the Hebrides; where smallness and intimacy had been characteristic of many islands on my journeys, Lewis is big. As one land mass, Lewis and Harris (the boundary relates back to the claims of rival clans) is the third largest island in the British Isles after Britain and Ireland. It dwarfs more famous islands such as the Isle of Wight, Skye or Guernsey, but has a fraction of the population. Yet, despite its size, it can still get lost and I began to notice how it is sometimes missed off maps of Britain used in adverts. A sloppy graphic artist can disappear this mass of land. It is a problem even more familiar to the Shetlands. Southron geography can be careless.

Being forgotten has been a part of Lewis' history. James VI of Scotland, who became James I of England and Ireland, wanted to 'plant policy and civilization in the hitherto most barren Isle of Lewis'. In the late sixteenth century, he backed colonies in both Northern Ireland and Lewis, but he gave up on the latter, while the plantations in Northern Ireland have marked Irish history ever since. The Gaelic chief on Lewis fought off the king's Fife Adventurers (still the cause of relief and pride by the Leòdhasaich, the Gaelic term for the islanders) and the island was left to run itself. Only in the nineteenth century did outsiders start imposing their versions of improvement.

Lewis's separateness has generated a fierce sense of identity, arguably more powerful than any other I experienced in the Hebrides. It has a sizeable population (nearly 19,000 of the Western Isles' total of just over 26,000), and a town, Stornoway, with proud civic self-respect. Yet a harsh history has left its legacy in these Western Isles; it has the highest rate of fuel poverty in all Western Europe and one of the lowest household incomes in the UK. The Leòdhasaich chafe at the way they have been portrayed in national media, which tends to focus on their religiosity and alcoholism, but the mainland fascination with the distinctiveness of Lewis persists. Lewis is the biggest stronghold of Gaelic in Scotland and over half the population speak the language. It has some of the highest rates of churchgoing anywhere in the UK, dominated by a number of strict Presbyterian denominations, including the Free Church of Scotland and the Free Presbyterian Church of Scotland. Religious belief here has offered powerful consolation in times of cultural and social crisis; in the nineteenth century, the fervour of the dramatic conversions at mass open-air services was such that at one it was reported the altar cloths were drenched in tears. To this day, differences over doctrine, beliefs about homosexuality or the style of services cause schisms; music – hymn singing and instrumental accompaniment such as organ playing – continues to be a particular source of contention. The large churches stand at road junctions, surrounded by a large skirt of functional car park, and often different Presbyterian denominations face each other; they are starkly intimidating as they loom up across the moors. In recent years, there have been inroads in the strict sabbatarianism, with Sunday ferry sailings for example, but some children's playgrounds still carry signs warning that they are shut on Sunday. Stornoway was deathly quiet on a Sunday, bar the morning and evening flurry of churchgoing, with the ladies in their hats, heels and smart dresses.

It is telling that Lewis gave its name to Britain's oldest rock, one of the oldest in the world: Lewisian gneiss is three billion years old, two thirds as old as the world itself. On a winter's day at the Butt, Lewis's most northerly point, where the sea smashes into the shattered cliffs, there was an indomitability in this exposed windy point of land before the North Atlantic. 'I love [Lewis] for its very bleakness, for its very absences. I think of it as a place beaten upon by winds, an orchestra of gales which bend the fences like the strings of a musical instrument. If it has noises, they are not supernatural ones, they are in fact the noises of our own obdurate world,' wrote Crichton Smith, who introduced me to this island long before I ever arrived, his poetry and prose informed by a deep sensitivity to the local, and yet characterized by his urge 'to connect the parish to the universe', as critic Matthew McGuire puts it.

In the winter sunlight Lewis was absurdly beautiful and cruelly cold. Uig seemed the kind of place where Narnia's Snow Queen might have had her castle. The fast-changing light and rugged contours ensured that no two moments were ever the same, and in the shifting kaleidoscope all manner of magic seemed credible. On the shore at Timsgearraidh the old graveyard is the site of a legend, according to which a Norwegian princess, after a visit back to her homeland, offered second sight to an islander in return for being allowed to return to her grave. He became known as the Brahan Seer and went on to use his magical gifts to become famous across Scotland in the seventeenth century for predicting the future.

On this visit, the light snow picked out the lines of the *feannagan*, the lazy beds, which scarified the slopes of the hills running down to the belt of dunes. A lodge, built by the nineteenth-century owner of Lewis, James Matheson, stood proud on a hillside looking out to sea. The large white building looked as if it had been dropped by helicopter, without a bush or tree to offer shelter. Arthur Ransome was a regular visitor there for a period after the Second World War, and used Uig's astonishing landscape for a novel, the last in the famous *Swallows and Amazons* series.

Thick marram grass cloaked the dunes, and in the snow it shone a brilliant, pale blond. Off a dead-end road here, in the farthest north-west of the British Isles, one of the most striking archaeological finds ever unearthed in Britain was discovered. Ninety-three artefacts were found in a dune in 1831: seventy-eight carved chess pieces of walrus ivory and whale teeth, fourteen tablemen (pieces for another board game, similar to backgammon) and one belt buckle. The carving of the chessmen is exquisite, the detail still crisp after nearly a thousand years. Historians have pieced together their history. They were probably made in Trondheim, Norway, between 1150 and 1200 CE and brought by a merchant heading for the Norse towns of Ireland whose journey was interrupted on Lewis. The chessmen are evidence of the wealth and power of a northern empire whose trade routes stretched to Greenland, with its stocks of precious raw materials such as walrus ivory, and down to the Norse lands of the Isle of Man and to Dublin.

Lewis was on the main shipping route of this international network of patronage and tribute spanning the North Sea, from Scandinavia across the North Atlantic. The Norse (also known as Vikings) settled Lewis for the best part of four hundred years, until the Hebrides were ceded to the Kingdom of Scotland by the king of Norway in the Treaty of Perth of 1266. In the Icelandic sagas there are many references to the Norse Hebrides, indicating their importance in the North Atlantic empire ruled by the Norwegian kings. On Lewis, many place names – such as Uig, Siabost, Laxay and Bostadh – indicate the lasting Norse influence. The Outer Hebrides was known as the Innse Gall, the land of the foreigner, by Gaels on the Scottish mainland. Some part of Lewis' distinctive character is derived from this meeting of two cultures, and the most powerful evidence of that is the Lewis chessmen – or, as they are known on Lewis, the Uig chessmen.

In a small office in the back rooms of the British Museum, amongst piles of papers and books, the curator Irving Finkel offered me gloves so that I could handle a few of the chessmen. According to close analysis, they have barely been used. Their compact forms were carefully designed to be stable on the chessboard, and were shaped with a shrewd eye to longevity; there were no delicate necks to snap, or outstretched limbs to break. They sat squatly in the palm of my hand, satisfyingly solid. The texture and colour of the material was beautifully rich: a browned cream which gleamed in the small room, and they were silky smooth to the touch.

The chessmen reflect the sophisticated hierarchies of the court and the complex relationships between temporal and spiritual power, and between king and queen. They express a society accommodating change as it absorbed new standards of courtly life from southern Europe. The elegant folds of drapery are characteristic of the Romanesque style of the twelfth century, with its Europe-wide flourishing of ideas and creativity. The graceful Celtic intertwining incorporates the Gaelic culture of the Atlantic seaboard. Yet the violence of a ferocious-frontier raiding people is evident in the warriors, who chew their shields – a habit of the mythical berserkers mentioned in the Icelandic sagas. The kings' swords rest on their laps; the sedentary, intellectual pursuit of chess was one of the arts expected of royalty, who were no longer defined simply by their martial skills. This was a society in which queens had a prominent role;

two hold horns, a container often used for money. All seven queens raise their hands to their cheek in an eloquent gesture believed to denote thoughtfulness and wisdom, a reference to their role of advisor to the king. Their worried faces seem to express the anxiety of their uncertain times.

The Lewis chessmen have fascinated both the erudite scholar and the most nonchalant of tourists; their bulging eyes and grimaces are cartoon-like in their emotional charge. They have become emblematic of a North European seafaring medieval culture: powerful, sophisticated, cosmopolitan and clever. They have found their way into *Harry Potter* films and children's cartoons. The tiny forms have become iconic, shorthand for an ancient North Atlantic sensibility.

That objects of such sophistication should turn up on a remote beach has given rise to many tales. Uig crofter Malcolm Macleod was said to have come across a stone kist containing the pieces while pursuing an errant cow; he believed he had stumbled on 'an assemblage of elves or gnomes upon whose mysteries he had unconsciously intruded', according to an account in 1851. It is thought that they passed through several hands, including a Stornoway merchant who earned himself a small fortune, selling them in Edinburgh in 1831. Eleven of the pieces were bought by the Scottish Society of Antiquaries, and the British Museum bought the rest. They have been regarded as some of the most remarkable medieval artefacts in the two museums' collections ever since. The pieces form part of four incomplete chess sets, leaving the tantalizing possibility that more figures are buried somewhere in the sands of Uig.

In the last decade a strange twist in the story of the Lewis chessmen has seen them emerge as a trophy of national identity claimed by several countries. There has been a sensitive discussion between Scottish and British curators on the role of

Lewis. Was it just a chance shipwreck which led to the pieces' arrival on Uig's beach, or was it a reflection of the status and wealth of an owner in Lewis? No Scottish curator has disputed that the chessmen are likely to be Norwegian in origin, so the Scottish claim to the pieces depends on the possibility that they were the property of a Leòdhasach rather than the chance survivors of a shipwreck or theft. The differences of opinion were relatively amicable, but in 2007 a Scottish National Party minister in the devolved government asked the British Museum to give the chessmen 'back'. The British Museum's then director, Neil MacGregor, maintained that it was Norway who was entitled to ask for them 'back', not Scotland. But the British Museum has picked its way carefully, and six of the figures were loaned long-term to Lewis' new museum in 2015. The British Museum gives exhaustive detail on the loans and travelling exhibitions which have taken the chessmen all over the world.

Matters became even more complicated in 2010 when a former Icelandic parliamentarian published an article arguing that the chessmen were made in Iceland, not Norway. It sparked an ill-tempered argument with Norwegian and British archaeologists. Icelandic craftsmen were trained and worked in Trondheim, and the two countries were intimately related at the time the chessmen were made, so the debate has been detailed, focusing on the shape of the knights' horses and the presence of bishops on the chessboard. National prestige was at stake. The Icelandic parliamentarian Guðmantur Thórarinsson argued, 'in addition to Iceland's literary tradition, the country boasted a highly developed culture of decoration and carving'. The chessmen were the 'true flowering of a uniquely Icelandic culture', wrote fellow author Einar S. Einarsson. Their claims appeared in reports in the *New York Times* and the *Daily*

Telegraph. Emboldened, Thórarinsson produced a booklet, and gave lectures in Iceland and in Edinburgh. The response from Norway was combative. Chess player Morten Lilleøren defended the pieces' Norwegian origin in exhaustive detail, with references to similar artefacts from across Scandinavia; he was concerned that Thórarinsson's theory was gaining ground, and argued that it was riddled with 'faults and oversights'. Meanwhile, the response from Scotland was scathing: Alex Woolf from the University of St Andrews described 'Iceland as a bit of a scrappy place full of farmers. The pieces are also exquisite works of art. You don't get the Metropolitan Museum of Art in Iowa.'

Thórarinsson was unrepentant as he expounded his theories to me at length, just before he headed off on his first visit to the Southern Isles, as the Hebrides are known in Iceland. He had an amateur's pleasure at provoking the establishment experts. At a recent conference the debate had got heated, he told me, and he was accused of 'politicizing the issue'. He explained how the chessmen were a central part of his bid to establish the reputation of a remarkable twelfth-century woman carver, known from contemporary texts as Margaret the Adroit. Her skill in carving walrus ivory was famous, and he wanted a statue erected in her home town. He declared himself delighted to be getting enquiries from the US, the UK and Iceland about his ideas and about the remarkable Margaret. In 2015 an American writer, Nancy Marie Brown, even developed his thesis into a book, *Ivory Vikings: The Mystery of the Most Famous Chessmen in the World and the Woman Who Made Them*.

Nineteenth-century nationalism was largely defined by its linguistic and musical patrimony: song, poetry, music and literature were the elements used to delineate and express identity. In the late twentieth century, it shifted to material objects, which became powerful symbols of national prestige, suggests the former British Museum director and cultural historian Neil MacGregor. When the objects concerned are the product of multinational empires, it inevitably leads to controversy. The small ivory figures are caught between competing political narratives: Iceland's quest to restore self-confidence and national pride in the aftermath of its catastrophic financial crisis of 2008; Scotland's move to position itself alongside Greece (in its struggle over the Elgin Marbles) and as the victim of English greed. Meanwhile the British Museum maintained the calm complacency of ownership, insisting their acquisition was fair and their stewardship magnanimous. All recognized that the Lewis chessmen have a political importance precisely because they speak of an older distribution of power, another political geography of centre and periphery that has contemporary resonance for nations such as Scotland and Iceland.

It is a remarkable story which Malcolm Macleod could never have imagined would be the outcome of his day herding his cow. In a poignant footnote to his brief involvement in the saga, he and his family were cleared from the land shortly after. There is not much at Uig to represent the fame these figures have brought the place apart from a large wooden carving of a chess piece, a king, in the dunes beside the road, where the occasional tourist poses for photographs.

II

A short walk in a stiff Atlantic winter wind along Uig beach brought me to the croft of Malcolm Maclean, who recounts another complex tale of history and identity which has fitted awkwardly into nation-building. Malkie grew up in Govan, the urban heartland of Glasgow, but both his parents were

from Lewis, and he was sent back every holiday to stay with
relatives. He developed a passionate attachment to Gaelic, and
has lived most of his adult life on Lewis. By way of explaining
how he looked at Gaelic history, he showed me an unfamiliar
map. It was a satellite image which faced west to the Atlantic
and placed the Hebrides in a swathe across the centre of the
page, with Ireland dominant on the left, and mainland Scotland
tailing away off the bottom of the page. It was a disorientating
reminder of how mapping relies on cultural conventions so
that the north sits at the top of every page and the south at the
bottom. It is easy enough to turn the compass points round –
or even upside down; Malkie pointed out that we say we go
down south, but in Gaelic south has always been up. Malkie's
map showed Ireland as the dominant land mass, and mainland
Scotland as peripheral, with the Hebridean archipelago as an
arc of islands stretching north-east towards the Faroe Islands
and beyond to Scandinavia. These were the lands of the Gaels
for more than 1,500 years. Sharing a language and culture, they
were known as the Scoti. They moved back and forth across
the islands, absorbing on occasion incomers such as Norsemen
from Norway. Over the last five hundred years, the Gaels were
progressively beaten back, divided and marginalized in a process which Malkie described as 'indubitably colonization'. The
Gaelic-speaking communities bordering the Atlantic from the
Butt of Lewis down to the tip of south-west Ireland are the last
fragments driven to the edge.

The Gàidhealtachd was a testing ground for the English,
Scottish and later British states; over several centuries these
states weakened complex social systems, destroyed power
structures and generated the notions of cultural superiority
which legitimized their supremacy, explained Malkie as the
light drained from Uig's mountains beyond the window of

his croft. To his mind, this was a conflict within Scotland, between Gaels under the Lord of the Isles and the mainland Scots, long before the English were involved. The Gaels had founded Scotland, but they lost their kingdom as the Scottish court abandoned Gaelic; the last Scottish king to speak Gaelic was James IV (1473–1513). The Edinburgh-based monarchs became increasingly hostile, so by the late sixteenth century, James VI referred to Gaels as 'wolves and boars'. Jacobitism was the Gaels' last attempt to win back their country, and it foundered when their Scottish opponents found an ally in the Hanoverian state, intent on finally crushing them. In this reading of Scotland's record, Malkie and others have claimed that historically the Gaels preferred the indifference of England to the contempt of Edinburgh. It seems an insidious distinction. Malkie knows his history is contested by some and flatly rejected by others. That is part of why he is so emphatic; Scotland's history has been shot through with a particular complexity, he argues. The country has been both colonized and colonizer, and out of that bitter experience both the colonized and the colonizers were recruited, in disproportionate numbers, into two centuries of conflict and expansion in the British Empire.

The Gàidhealtachd challenged the British state centralized in London; one of the weapons of the establishment was either systematic indifference or wilful ignorance. Johnson infamously dismissed Gaelic as 'the rude speech of a barbarous people'. By the time Louis MacNeice published *I Crossed the Minch* in 1938, after nearly two centuries of travelogues about the Gàidhealtachd, he was not embarrassed to admit he didn't even know the islanders spoke another language (he had been educated at Marlborough, Wiltshire, and Oxford) and said as much in his opening pages. The condescension was part of the way in

which the Gaelic periphery was disempowered and fragmented
(a history which had tragic results in Ireland). Crichton Smith
describes growing up as a Gael as a 'snake pit of contradictions
because of an accident of geography and a hostile history' in
his collection of essays, *Towards the Human*, written as the use
of Gaelic reached its nadir in the 1980s. 'We are born inside a
language and see everything from within its parameters; it is not
we who make language, it is the language that makes us . . . The
imperialism of language is the most destructive of all,' he writes.
'For the islander to lose his language . . . would be to lose to a
great extent the meaning of his life, and to become a member
of a sordid colony on the edge of an imperialist world.'

Like many other islanders, Malkie sees himself first and
foremost as a Gael; his Scottish identity is secondary. He knows
that this position does not fit neatly into the politics of Scottish
nationalism. He believes one of the values of his perspective is
its undermining of entrenched political positions. He has spent
time in Northern Ireland, where he has been able to move
between its communities, sharing Gaelic with the nationalists
and a Protestant heritage with the Ulster Unionists.

'In the European Union forty million people regularly speak a
minority language, and the map of the sixty minority languages
bears no relation to national boundaries,' said Malkie, pointing
out that nation states have never fully encompassed the overlap-
ping multiple identities which have criss-crossed the European
continent.

Since the 1980s and his first groundbreaking cultural projects
promoting Gaelic – a touring exhibition on landownership,
an arts centre in Stornoway – he has witnessed a dramatic
reversal in attitudes towards the language. The steep decline
from 250,000 speakers to 60,000 over the course of the twentieth century has slowed. There has been a Gaelic literary

revival, led by the towering figure of the poet Sorley MacLean, from Raasay off Skye. A raft of other poets, including the Leòdhasaich Derick Thomson and Iain Crichton Smith, have won international recognition. The Gaelic College of Skye, Sabhal Mòr Ostaig, was set up as a centre of study and learning of the language. Thousands of children now attend summer Fèisean camps all over Scotland, introducing them to Gaelic music, dance and culture. Political pressure led to Gaelic broadcasting, the use of Gaelic as an official language, and bilingual signposts across Scotland. Yet, despite the support, Gaelic speakers on the islands themselves are still in decline, and opinions in Lewis on the future of the language were divided when I raised the issue. Some argued that the support had come too late, some that the jury is still out, while others were more confident of Gaelic's resilience, pointing to their children texting in the language to argue for its vitality. Gaelic's decline on the islands is compensated for by a new interest in Edinburgh and Glasgow, where there are Gaelic schools. Inevitably there have been critics who argue that millions have been spent on a language that only 1.1 per cent of the Scottish population actually speak, and that Gaelic signposts in areas of southern Scotland where it has allegedly never been spoken is absurd tokenism. But Malkie sees it as the 'healing' of a great historic injustice. It is a long-overdue acknowledgement, he insists, of how much the Gàidhealtachd has contributed to Scotland, militarily, economically and culturally.

Back in London, I was explaining this history to a friend, and he rolled his eyes with boredom. It was so long ago, he maintained. But who decides when a history is old enough to become irrelevant and why? Histories are always being unearthed, repurposed to fit new preoccupations. (In 2015, Richard III's reinterment after six hundred years prompted national ceremony and interest.) A great champion of the islands, the former Labour Cabinet minister Brian Wilson, who lives on Lewis, commented to me that 'there's a fine line between indifference and suppression'. These two strategies of domination are a disconcerting combination, and Lewis has been the subject of both.

Every nation has its lost histories of what was destroyed or ignored to shape its narrative of unity so that it has the appearance of inevitability. The British Isles with their complex island geography have known various configurations of political power. Gaelic is a reminder of some of them: the multinational empires of Scandinavia, the expansion of Ireland, and the medieval Gaelic kingdom, the Lordship of the Isles, which lost mainland Scotland, and ultimately was suppressed by Edinburgh. The British state imposed centralization, and insisted on English-language education. Only the complex geography of islands and mountains ensured that pockets of Gaelic have survived into the twenty-first century.

What would be lost if Gaelic disappeared in the next century, I asked, when I visited hospitable islanders who pressed me with cups of tea and cake. There is a Gaelic word, *cianalas*, and it means a deep sense of homesickness and melancholy, I was told. The language of Gaelic offers insight into a pre-industrial world view, suggested Malkie, a window onto another culture lost in the rest of Britain. As with any language, it represents another way of seeing the world, which makes it precious. Gaelic's survival is a matter of cultural diversity, just as important as ecological diversity, he insisted. It is the accumulation of thousands of years of human ingenuity and resilience living in these island landscapes. It is a heritage of human intelligence shaped by place, a language of the land and sea, with a richness and precision to describe the tasks of agriculture and fishing. It is a language of community, offering concepts and expressions to capture the tightly knit interdependence required in this subsistence economy. Gaelic scholar Michael Newton points out how particular words describe the power of these relationships intertwined with place and community. For example, *dùthchas* is sometimes translated as 'heritage' or 'birthright', but it conveys a much richer idea of a collective claim on a land, continually reinforced and lived out through the shared management of that land. *Dùthchas* grounds land rights in communal daily habits and uses of the land. It is at variance with British concepts of individual private property and these land rights received no legal recognition and were relegated to cultural attitudes (as in many colonial contexts). Elements of *dùthchas* persist in crofting communities, where the grazing committees of the townships still manage rights to common land and the cutting of peat banks on the moor. Crofting has always been dependent on plentiful labour and requires co-operation with neighbours for many of the routine tasks, like peasant cultures across Europe, born out of the day-to-day survival in a difficult environment.

The strong connection to land and community means that 'people belong to places rather than places belong to people', sums up Newton. It is an understanding of belonging which emphasizes relationship, of responsibilities as well as rights, and in return offers the security of a clear place in the world. A Leòdhasach and Gaelic speaker, Agnes Rennie pointed out to me that the Gaelic greeting is 'Where are you from?' and 'Who do you come from?' in contrast to the English, 'How are you?' The identity of place and family matter more than personal wellbeing and health. This understanding of family stretches back generations, so identity is situated in the context of a continuum of the dead as well as the living. The dead remain as central reference points, and graveyards are prominently sited on these Hebridean islands so that many live within sight of their ancestors' graves.

Tellingly, in English, 'belonging' is defined in the *Oxford Dictionary* as a matter of property, as in *belongings*. There is a further definition closely related to status: 'having the right personal and social qualities to be a member of a particular group'. Yet dig deeper and the word originated from the Old English *gelang*, which indicated something much closer to the Gaelic sense; it meant 'at hand, together with'. Buried in the etymology of the word is an understanding of the power of closeness, of touch and how that generates solidarity. The sentiment cropped up in the conversation with Agnes – who still crofts her land in north Lewis alongside many other activities – when she insisted, 'I couldn't conceive of living on this land without getting my hands dirty. It keeps me connected with the place.'

Gaelic's attentiveness to place is reflected in its topographical precision. It has a plentiful vocabulary to describe different forms of hill, peak or slope (*beinn, stob, dùn, cnoc, sròn*), for example, and particular words to describe each of the stages of a river's course from its earliest rising down to its widest point as it enters the sea. Much of the landscape is understood in anthropomorphic terms, so names of topographical features are often the same as those for parts of the body. It draws a visceral sense of connection between sinew, muscle and bone and the land. Gaelic poetry often attributes character and agency to landforms, so mountains might speak or be praised as if they were a chieftain; the Psalms (held in particular reverence in Gaelic culture) talk of landscape in a similar way, with phrases such as the 'hills run like deer'. In both, the land is recognized as alive.

Gaelic has a different sense of time, purpose and achievement. The ideal is to maintain an equilibrium, as a saying from South Uist expresses it:

Eat bread and weave grass
And then this year shall be as thou wast last year.

It is close to Hannah Arendt's definition of wisdom as a loving concern for the continuity of the world.

Gaelic's colours are pastel rather than primary, with a large number of words to describe variations of blue, green, grey and white. There are three words for different shades of blue-green alone. A large vocabulary is dedicated to hydronymy, where water and land meet in skerries, outcrops, cliffs, and headlands. The place names of the shoreline often refer to the distinctive sounds of water; it suggests an ear acutely attuned to the sound of waves breaking on landforms so that a coast can be navigated at night. The Ordnance Survey maps offer only a tiny glimpse of this relationship with land and sea, which translated into a practice of dense naming; every rock, outcrop or patch of land is named, 'even to places the size of a spade', writes Newton.

'Every place has a memory, so you hear people say that this is where so and so lived, or where someone fell off the rock,' said local historian Bill Lawson. 'Memory is woven into the land in a way that people moving in from the south can never understand. Memory is maintained by the community, so there was no need for headstones in a graveyard. Everyone knew where everyone was buried.'

Communal history is embedded in the landscape. 'Places became co-extensive in the mind not only with personal and ancestral memories but with the whole living community culture,' suggests Newton. Place is a 'touchstone of identity'. Lawson agreed, illustrating the point with an anecdote of two soldiers meeting in Canada in the eighteenth century. They established each other's identity by a detailed recitation of the features of the glen from which, it turned out, they both came.

Listing places is a characteristic of Gaelic poetry, and often the list is prefixed with 'I can see'. This is not interpreted literally – the places might be far apart – rather, as Newton put it, 'the internal vision of the poet and performer reconstructed his ancestral territory with the mental map created by the performance itself, reaffirming his identification with people and place'. The Scottish writer Neil Gunn describes this memory and knowledge as the 'hidden landscape' lying beneath the physical, which is largely unrecognized by visitors who come in search of 'remote wilderness'. Several times I was shown around a part of Lewis by islanders, and as they talked about its past and its myths, my understanding of its hidden history slowly began to emerge and I saw it with new eyes.

This hidden history is as much about human relationships, the structures of community which ensured survival, as it is about the observation of physical phenomena. Gaelic has a set of terms with no exact equivalent in English; for example, Crichton Smith points to the word *cliù*, which roughly translates as 'reputation', but has the meaning of usefulness to the community and brings prestige. Such understandings are fading, but are still present on Lewis. *Cliù* ensures negligible crime: 'that would forfeit *cliù*, one's status in the community and that would last, because of communal memory, to the end of time ... There was no need for a policeman because the community itself passed judgement, and a judgement more rigorous than any the police could impose,' wrote Crichton Smith. On the other hand, the community generated a powerful hold; it was as 'delicate as a spider's web. If you pulled one part, the rest would tremble,' wrote Crichton Smith in the 1980s. One is known, and one's parents and grandparents are known. But within that web there was also tolerance of individuality, even eccentricity, pointed out Malkie. In a small community, differences have to be negotiated, often on a daily basis, often with wicked humour.

Crichton Smith recognized that the strong community was double-edged (he left the island to study and only returned as an adult, for visits) but described this belonging as a sustaining force, in which one is 'held up in its buoyancy as a swimmer in water'. You are known so well that there is no requirement on you to prove or sell yourself; acceptance is not provisional and, within that, there is a sense of security which can endure emigration and long absences. Knowing one's place, both the physical environment of land and sea and within the relationships which sustained daily life, was at the heart of the Gaelic language.

III

Uig's population has roughly halved in the last forty years. From Malkie's croft, in the early dark of winter, I could see the light of a croft in the distance and one other closer by. In that huge bowl of hills and bay, the two lights seemed fragile company; occasionally, headlights appeared on the hillside several miles away. (Perhaps it helped explain a curious enthusiasm across Lewis for street lighting, which blazed against the darkness even in places with only a few homes.) On the road south from Uig, the townships of Mangursta and Mealasta had similar stories of population decline. The lights were going out one by one along this rugged coast and it filled those left behind with despondence. They remembered the busy crofting communities of their childhoods. Population loss has dominated the island's history in the last century, and has played its role in the decline of Gaelic in its rural Hebridean heartlands.

Lewis has always had a tradition of migration; throughout

the nineteenth century islanders emigrated or left for seasonal work in the herring industry or agriculture. But the loss was countered by population growth, which reached its peak in the 1890s. The twentieth century saw the number of islanders steadily fall. The tragedy which triggered that decline was the First World War.

I returned to Lewis, once more, the following summer. In the middle of quiet residential streets in Stornoway rises the hill of Cnoc nan Uan. On its summit stands a ninety-metre granite tower which dominates these suburbs – and the view of the island from the ferry as it pulls out of Stornoway's harbour to head to Ullapool. This elegant tower is a sobering welcome to new arrivals and a last comment to departing visitors; it was the grand culmination of all the war memorials I had noticed every few miles along my journey north through the Hebrides. The lettering on these memorials was always small and the names close together, such was the quantity of casualties, even on tiny islands such as Vatersay, south of Barra, where the population has only ever been a handful of households.

Lewis had the highest proportion of its population serving in the First World War of anywhere in the British Isles. This reflected a tradition of military recruitment in Scotland, particularly amongst the Gaels, beginning in the aftermath of Culloden. A staggering 90 per cent of sons of the manse in Scotland had volunteered by 1915. Lewis also had the highest proportion of casualties: 17 per cent of those serving died in the conflict; the ratio of deaths to the general population on the island was twice the national average. The crowded plaques and depopulation were closely connected: the loss of so many young men was a catastrophe for islands whose rural and fishing economy relied on them. The First World War brought a final tragedy to Lewis on New Year's Day 1919. A ship heavily packed with excited demobilized servicemen was caught in heavy seas on its return to Stornoway. HMS *Iolaire* went down on rocks known as the Beasts of Holm, just outside the harbour, with the loss of 174 lives.

I made my way out to the Beasts of Holm, beyond Stornoway's suburbs and new windmills, to the memorial on the shore. The Minch glittered bright blue. The mountains of Skye and Rum lay to the south, and over to the east, on the mainland, I could see the peaks of the Assynt. Yachts and the occasional fishing boat slipped past on their way into Stornoway. Sheep were nibbling the grass round the small granite pillar dedicated to the *Iolaire* disaster. The calm of this early July day made it all the more shocking: the boat was only six metres from the shore as it went down. The men were within sight of this low grassy headland, but the ferocity of the waves made it hard for them to get ashore. Islanders tried to help, separated from brothers, neighbours, friends and sons by a narrow stretch of water. In the following days, the waves brought in bodies along with the presents they had been carrying for their children, wives, mothers and younger siblings. Trinkets and toys such as rag dolls were washed up in the rock pools by the tides.

It reminded me of my great uncle Norman, whose letters home from Gallipoli and France in the First World War often included discussion of the presents he would bring home for his little sisters – my grandmother and great-aunt – from his leave in Cairo and then Paris. Gift shopping had been a consolation for these travelling soldiers. MacNeice made several references to the gloomy nature of the Leòdhasaich on his visit, twenty years later; I thought of my great-grandparents' grief at the loss of their two sons and how it passed down the generations. The devastation of my grandmother, when she was told, as a twelve-year-old, to go away and read a book as her parents and family servants were shaken with grief at the loss of a second son. At every war memorial on my journey, I found those who shared a surname: the frequent listing of brothers, cousins and relatives.

After visiting the Beasts of Holm, I drove up the east coast of the island, and walked along the cliffs above Tolsta Head. The day was extraordinarily clear, yet the weather forecast was predicting imminent heavy storms. My feet sank through the crust of dried sphagnum as I scrambled across bogs. At the cliff edge I watched the swell of the waves over the pink and tawny gold of the seaweed-covered rocks sixty metres below. Through the binoculars I could see swarms of jellyfish, pink and purple, moving through the turquoise sea. In the distance the mountains on the mainland were palest blue and white, with clouds of pale gold. The colouring was like some exquisite Austrian baroque, and the Minch lay as smooth as shot silk.

IV

The townships of Lewis were traumatized by the war, and its losses triggered a wave of emigration during the 1920s and 1930s. The tight communal structures were fast unravelling. In the early 1920s, three ocean liners bound for Canada swung north from Glasgow and picked up hundreds of young Leòdhasaich. For the crofting communities of the islands, it represented another devastating loss of the labour on which they depended; eighteen men came from the village of Siabost alone. Of the three hundred who boarded the *Metagama* in Stornoway, all but twenty were men, and the average age was twenty-two. Most were heading to work on farms in Ontario. Just before the ship slipped anchor, the *Stornoway Gazette* reported that the pipe bands were stilled, and the Leòdhasaich gathered on the deck for prayers in Gaelic. 'It was an affecting scene and there were tears in many eyes, for not a few of the lads who had come away from the pier light-heartedly became very quiet and thoughtful as if they only then realised that they were going to put thousands of miles of land and sea between them and Lewis Isle.'

The sailing caught the imagination of newspapers on both sides of the Atlantic. It represented the failed hopes of a generation; not even the war's victory had brought the longed-for land reform. Without land, and with a sharp decline in the herring industry, many felt they had no choice. The *Stornoway Gazette* pressed for government initiatives to stem the flow, understanding only too well how the loss exacerbated the decline of remote rural communities. 'The islander has never had the chance of staying where he is: history has condemned him to departure,' Crichton Smith commented half a century later.

These emigrants' descendants now return to visit. Canadians and Americans were frequent companions on my travels; forty million people around the world claim Scottish descent. Often well into late middle age, their spirit of enquiry and adventure was inspiring. On the top of a mountain pass in Harris, I met an American couple as we admired the view over to Skye and the mainland. With the swift directness of many Americans, we were quickly exchanging family histories and life stories. They were cycling through the Hebrides, and, with delight, they confessed they were nearing their eightieth birthdays. This journey was a form of pilgrimage, the woman told me, following the paths of her ancestors. She launched into a detailed description of a family tree which mapped continents, islands and oceans. Her exhilaration was infectious.

Many of these modern-day pilgrims find their way to the genial Bill Lawson. He grew up in Ayrshire and trained as a surveyor, but ever since he was a teenager he was drawn to the Hebrides. He learnt Gaelic and became fascinated by the stories the elderly told him. He saw that their memories were dying with them, and began to take notes. Friends asked if he could help them trace their genealogies; in due course, the hobby outgrew his day job and he was dealing with requests from all over the world at his family history centre, Seallam! There, on the wall, were the two Gaelic questions of identity which Agnes Rennie had mentioned: 'Who do you belong to? Where do you belong?' Belonging is in short supply in the twenty-first century and Bill has made it his life's business, literally, to help people find answers to both.

His work has the methodical approach of his training as a surveyor. Over the last few decades he has studied census returns and the registers of births, deaths and marriages, and then added oral-history accounts to piece together family-tree sheets for 9,000 households – a total of 40,000 people. He showed me the painstaking pages of notes. Bill has traced the generations who lived on a particular croft and compiled neat files of names and dates and places. It's a mapping of people and places which crosses the Atlantic to Cape Breton and Nova Scotia on the eastern coast of Canada to the Gaelic communities there, and round the world to Australia and New Zealand.

Emigration was already part of Hebridean life when Samuel Johnson visited in the eighteenth century, as islanders faced rising rents from their landlords. He sensed the pressures which were forcing people to take the drastic decision to emigrate: 'No man willingly left his native country,' he wrote, lamenting the 'dispeopling' of Skye. 'Some methods to stop this epidemic desire of wandering which spreads its contagion from valley to valley, deserves to be sought with great diligence ... For nobody born in any other parts of the world will choose this country for their residence; and an island once depopulated will remain a desert.'

There was a big surge in emigration in the 1850s after the Clearances and the potato famine; 10 per cent of Harris' population left in just three years between 1852 and 1855. Particularly evident across the Highlands and Islands, emigration was a feature across Scotland through the nineteenth and twentieth century, despite the country's growing industrial wealth; for much of that time, it was only just behind Ireland and Norway in the proportion of emigrants to population in the European emigration league. Many took the most obvious route of departure – the sea – and made their way west to Canada and America; only later in the century, with better railway connections, did they head south to the cities of Scotland's central belt.

'There's a fashion to say, "Poor islanders, having to emigrate", but a lot of them couldn't get away quick enough given the opportunity,' said Bill. 'I'm asked who was to blame for so many leaving, and I jokingly reply, "The doctors." They had eradicated smallpox. If you had ten children and four acres of rock, you couldn't feed them all. But there was also a lot of forced emigration. It had to happen, but it didn't have to happen so brutally.'

The first generations of emigrants were usually illiterate and letters were few. Emigration was like a death. In time, easier communication and more frequent transport links enabled families to keep in contact across continents. Bill's collection includes a letter from a woman in Cape Breton writing to her sister in Lewis in 1868 after fifty years. Dictated to her son, she poignantly detailed relatives' births, marriages and deaths, both in Canada and at home in the Hebrides, a web of family relationships across continents.

'A couple from Canada came in recently trying to trace their family, who had moved from Lewis to Quebec. We narrowed it down, and it turned out I knew his aunt. He and his wife were in tears. I could show them the land where their people might have lived. Ancestors are part of you, whether you know it or not,' said Bill.

He has helped hundreds of people from all over the world find their ancestors and identify the townships where they lived. He has built a museum out of the stories. The sepia photographs in the museum offer a moving record of this global scattering. A map of the world has pins clustered in corners of the globe such as Patagonia, the Falklands, New Zealand and the fringes of north-east Canada. Hebrideans were believed to be able to cope with isolation, poor weather and sheep, so they were specifically recruited to colonize such far-flung parts of the empire.

Emigration has declined but young people still routinely leave for jobs and more opportunities on the mainland, leaving a population skewed towards the elderly. The Hebrides is one of the few areas of Scotland where the population is in decline, though the rate has been slowed. For a long time parents have been left to grow old alone, as MacNeice describes in his poem 'The Hebrides':

> *Over the fancy vases*
> *The photos with the wrinkles taken out,*
> *The enlarged portraits of the successful sons*
> *Who married wealth in Toronto or New York,*
> *Console the lonely evenings of the old*
> *Who live embanked by memories of labour*
> *And child-bearing and scriptural commentaries.*

There was a mobility here not found in rural communities further south in England. A common employment route for young men in the past was the merchant marine, which took them all over the world. When the herring industry was at its height, young Leòdhasaich women followed the season from port to port, round the north of Scotland to Peterhead, Aberdeen and south to Great Yarmouth, gutting and packing the fish. A perception of the Hebrides is that it was cut off and isolated, but the reverse was true. Being on the edge brought a network of connections to places such as Toronto, Quebec and Auckland, rather than London or Edinburgh.

This global diaspora had often maintained a powerful Gaelic identity through successive generations. Several Leòdhasaich enthused to me about a novelist who closely captured the spirit of the Gàidhealtachd: Alistair Macleod was a fourth-generation Scottish Canadian. Was there a particular tenacity to Gaelic heritage? I could trace a line back through my grandfather, a Farquharson, whose own grandfather had moved south to London. A true Gaelic name: at the Culloden battlefield I discovered it was one of the clans engraved on a plaque – five hundred Farquharsons are believed to have fought for the Jacobite cause.

IV

Hundreds of islanders emigrated to provide labour for the expanding empire after the First World War because there were so few opportunities in Lewis. What so many of these young people wanted was land, but the two men who bought the island in succession, and were to dominate its history for nearly a century, would not consider it. Their plans for the island did not include easing the pressure in the overcrowded crofting communities. Both were men who made immense fortunes through the extraordinary opportunities of empire.

From the neatly cropped lawns of Stornoway's War Memorial, I could see a startling sight over the roofs: trees. Thousands of tall, graceful mature oak, beech and ash cloaked the hillside and, between them, patches of grassy parkland. After only the occasional beleaguered copse and battered pine plantation on my journeys in the Hebrides, here were 600 acres of woodland. No less extraordinary were the grassy meadows with no sign of heather, reeds or outcrops of rock. Someone had cut out a patch of English countryside and floated it up the Minch. The trees had come from all over the world: Japanese black pine, sugar maple, Chilean pine, Monterey cypress, western red cedar, and hinoki cypress. They were an intriguing monument to empire, a collection which reflected one of the empire's most powerful families, whose interests stretched from the Far East to Canada. Along the winding paths and bridleways amongst Himalayan honeysuckle, gunnera, bamboo and wild cherries, the Matheson family could survey their exotic collections of plants. Or they could retire to their castle and its conservatories to enjoy the tropical flowers. What the family built and planted on Lewis has no rival in the Hebrides.

On a prominent terrace overlooking the loading docks for the ferries in Stornoway harbour, there is an imposing memorial to James Matheson and his wife, Mary Jane, who together built Lews Castle and planted this wood after James bought the island in 1844. A scantily clad marble nymph stands on a pedestal with lengthy dedications to the pair; true to classical cliché, the nymph's arms are stumps, her eyes stare madly from under a stone canopy. 'In life a consistent Christian, possessed of those social Virtues conducive to the happiness of others, and truly has it been said of him that he was a child of God living evidently under the influence of His Holy Spirit,' runs the dedication, and beneath, 'Well done thou good and faithful servant ... enter thou into the joy of the Lord (Matthew XXV.21)'.

It is a remarkable epitaph for a man who made his fortune selling opium to China. In 1832 Matheson and his fellow Scot, William Jardine, founded what is today one of Asia's biggest multinationals, Jardine Matheson. Scots played a key role in the empire in the eighteenth and nineteenth centuries (more than a third of all British colonial governors were Scottish between 1850 and 1939), and nowhere more so than in Hong Kong. Jardine Matheson was the central player, building its fortune on China's demand for opium, an illegal but lucrative trade. By 1838 the British were selling a massive 1,400 tons of opium a year (equivalent to a sixth of the world's production in 2006), despite Chinese attempts to ban the trade. The Opium Wars followed when the British government, persuaded by Jardine and Matheson among others, sent gunboats in support of the drug dealers. A young politician of Scottish descent, William Gladstone, denounced the war as 'unjust and iniquitous' and the opium trade as 'an infamous contraband traffic', but the protests were swept aside. After the British victory and a humiliating treaty for the Chinese, Jardine Matheson was able to take full advantage of its position to open up the Chinese economy to British imports and the flourishing opium trade. The Qing dynasty had been fatally undermined and in the ensuing Taiping rebellion of 1850–64 an estimated twenty million Chinese died. By the early 1900s 25 per cent of the Chinese male population was using opium, a rate of addiction which has never been equalled.

Matheson had made so much money by his mid-forties that he retired from business and dedicated himself to a parliamentary career and life as owner of Lewis. He built his baronial castle in Stornoway and planted his trees, while his public works, undertaken to mitigate the potato famine in Lewis, earned him the respectability of a baronetcy. As in other parts of rural Britain, these imperial fortunes acquired by dubious means – slavery, piracy, selling arms and drugs – were invested in an ideal of landed squirearchy.

Jardine Matheson has interests ranging from supermarket chains to property and luxury cars. It recently marked its 175th anniversary with a brochure which made one brief reference to the opium the company traded, before dwelling on its biggest export, tea. It recounted how the company has survived political collapse, revolution and war as it adroitly adapted to every new regime over a century of tumultuous Chinese history. It attributes its success to the two Scottish founders, Jardine and Matheson, who instilled a 'strong work ethic, an independent spirit, financial prudence, business foresight and a determination to succeed'. That is not how most drug barons have been described.

V

In 1917 the Matheson family sold Lewis to a man who also founded a major multinational, Unilever, and whose career of empire-building was even more spectacular. Of all the eccentrics attracted to this edge, Lord William Leverhulme was the most brilliant, autocratic and flamboyant. He first visited the Hebrides on a yachting holiday with his wife. Many years later, having amassed his fortune manufacturing soap on Merseyside, he saw Lewis as the perfect challenge for his formidable energies in his retirement. At Port Sunlight, Cheshire, he had built a model village and huge factory on Merseyside marshland, and now he dreamt up a magnificent scheme to provide secure employment, comfortable homes and decent lives for the islanders of Lewis: a state-of-the-art fishing fleet and canning factories whose products would be exported all over the UK to dedicated retail outlets. Initially, he met with some enthusiasm from the islanders: he was an industrialist with an unmatched reputation for well-funded paternalism and he was proposing to solve the wretchedness of Hebridean poverty.

Leverhulme saw the Hebrides as, above all, a problem to solve. In his view, cleanliness was one of the great benefits of civilization, and the housing he had built in Port Sunlight, his model village for his workers, was designed to be clean, spacious and filled with light. On Lewis he was horrified by the traditional blackhouses, where humans and livestock shared the same living space, separated by a low partition, and a fire burnt in the centre of the room, the smoke escaping through the thatch. The smoke blackened the interiors of the houses and damaged people's lungs. 'They leave the people in houses *not fit for kaffirs*,' wrote a shocked Leverhulme. For a man who believed in the empire as the bearer of progress, prosperity and harmony, the Hebrides was a terrible failure in Britain's own backyard.

To persuade the islanders of his vision, Leverhulme took a party of Leòdhasaich to Merseyside. I followed them. Even now, over a century later, Port Sunlight is astonishing: avenues of trees border the broad roads, edged by lawns and stone-flagged paths. Shrubs cluster round the cottages, roses bloom in the flower beds, children play on the green lawns by the fountains. It expresses an ideal of English domestic architecture. In the middle of the factory-workers' cottages stands the resplendent Lady Leverhulme Art Gallery, with its prestigious collection of paintings, furniture and sculpture. Leverhulme believed art could elevate and inspire even the humblest factory worker, an idea which amazed many of his contemporaries. He wanted to design a whole new society, and to do that he built schools, a gym, hospital, auditorium and church. The working hours of his factories were shorter than many others – he even campaigned for a six-hour day – to enable his workers to enjoy hobbies such as gardening, reading, drama, sport and choirs. The result would be a hard-working, clean, law-abiding, sober workforce for his factories, in sharp contrast to the overcrowded, disease-ridden slums of the Lancastrian industrial towns. In some ways his dream succeeded; the rate of infant mortality was halved in Port Sunlight.

But there was a catch. Leverhulme wanted to be in control of every detail in his town and he enforced detailed regulations against such things as keeping hens or hanging out the washing. He picked his tenants by hand and had them evicted if they did not conform. In Port Sunlight his company officials could inspect homes at any time to ensure that standards of cleanliness and respectability were maintained. In the son's biography of Lord Leverhulme he made a masterful understatement: 'Lever's strength of will and originality made him unsuited to any sphere of activity other than one in which his could be the sole deciding voice.'

Lord Leverhulme's plans for Lewis went adrift over a fundamental clash of world views between the industrialist and the islanders. The basis of all progress, Lord Leverhulme once wrote, was the 'universal law of self interest of the individual', the 'persistent, consistent and uninterrupted effort of every right-thinking man to better his condition … a principle as unvarying as the law of gravitation'. To his frustration, Leverhulme found that there were many on Lewis who did not share this understanding, or had a profoundly different interpretation of 'bettering' one's condition. What the islanders doggedly insisted upon was land for crofts, and that was the one thing that Leverhulme refused to consider; he did not want an island of contented crofters, he wanted a workforce for the fish-canning factories he planned in Stornoway.

The islanders believed that only land provided them with the security they craved after a century of loss. Exasperated by his intransigence, they resumed the protests and land raids – organized acts of trespass or squatting of Leverhulme's land used for hunting – which had been a feature of Lewis for forty years. They did not share Leverhulme's optimistic calculations about the potential of fishing in the Hebridean seas. Nor did they trust the volatility of the world economy, with its potentially crushing impact on fragile peripheral economies like theirs. In the end, they were proved right on both counts, and Leverhulme's extravagant plans foundered when the price of herring collapsed in the aftermath of the First World War.

While his plans in Lewis were unravelling, Leverhulme was also attempting to build a new society in the Belgian Congo in Africa, based on wage labour for the collection of palm oil. In both places he wanted a biddable workforce, and he offered hospitals, schools, railways and roads in return. In the Congo his company struggled to find willing workers, and resorted to a catalogue of coercion and abuse. Tellingly, in Port Sunlight's museum on the life and work of Leverhulme, I could not see a reference to the great failures of either the Congo or Lewis.

Infuriated by the islanders' independence of spirit, he lost patience with the Hebrideans and decided to give up. In a remarkable gesture in 1923, he offered to give the islanders his land. The town of Stornoway took up his offer and the woods of Lews Castle became a park. Two years later he died, his company saddled by debts from the debacles in both Lewis and Africa. It has been estimated that he lost nearly £1.5 million in his Hebridean adventure, a huge sum at the time. Few traces remain of his involvement on Lewis; the War Memorial, for which he made a hefty donation, has proved his most lasting legacy.

In Port Sunlight Leverhulme was buried in a stone tomb in the gothic grandeur of the church he had built. His effigy lies next to his wife's under a vault, his baronet's robes of velvet and fur, carved in stone, wrapped around him.

VI

Matheson and Leverhulme had the money and power to ensure their histories were recorded and elaborate memorials erected to their memory. Books have been written about their deeds, and corporate marketing departments still pay tribute to their foresight and business skill. In contrast, much of the history of the islanders themselves came close to being lost in the twentieth century as the communities were eroded by death and emigration. Their history did not get taught in the schools or churches. Scottish schoolchildren routinely learnt English history – 1066 and the Tudors – while in church they learnt the biblical history of the Jews. They did not learn about the struggles of the Clearances, how communities were uprooted and villages disappeared, nor of the protests and land raids of the late nineteenth century, triggered by desperate land poverty. In the 1970s, a few pioneering individuals (such as Bill Lawson) began to take notes and record interviews with the elderly to capture their memories. Local history societies sprang up all over the Long Island; in Lewis alone, there are around twenty which gather information, develop archives and local museums. They trace the abandoned villages, and how families moved from place to place in search of habitable land. One of the areas where this has been particularly pronounced was the rocky south-eastern area of the island known as Lochs. Large swathes of this mountainous area are virtually uninhabited and on the recently published wild land map of Scotland it ranks in the highest category. But before the land was cleared for deer, it supported thirty villages. In the community shop at Ravenspoint, alongside the milk and bread, there are dozens of booklets recounting the histories of the local townships. These are not for the tourists but for local people; this is history designed to be useful.

Four major stone memorials have been erected in different parts of Lewis to mark key confrontations in the late nineteenth century during the Crofters' War, as the protests across the Hebrides were known. Frustrated and overcrowded, people demanded land reform (encouraged by the growing protests in Ireland). Alarmed by the unrest in both Ireland and Scotland, Gladstone (of Scottish parents) and his Home Secretary, William Harcourt (who had some affection for the Hebrides after yachting holidays), were sympathetic. In 1883 the Napier Commission was set up to travel across the Highlands and Islands to gather evidence on the land question. It led to the Crofters' Holdings Act of 1886, in which Gladstone's government conceded an important point of principle: the rights of private property were not absolute, and in the designated crofting areas the rights of those who lived on and used the land were to be recognized. For the first time crofters gained some measure of security of tenure and rent control and a Crofters' Commission was set up as a form of tribunal. But progress on the release of land to create new crofts, a measure of land distribution, was to remain painfully slow well into the twentieth century, as was evident during Lord Leverhulme's ownership of Lewis.

At Baile Ailein, on the main road from Tarbert in Harris to Stornoway, stands the handsome Memorial to the Heroes of Lochs, a dry-stone structure echoing the beehive huts of the

Celtic monks. It marks a key moment in 1887, when hundreds gathered from the villages on the rocky coasts of Lochs to demand land from Lady Matheson. These overcrowded villages had absorbed those cleared from the other parts of the peninsula. In a carefully organized protest, later known as the Pàirc deer forest land raid, hundreds set up camp and built bonfires on which to roast the deer they had poached. Journalists were invited and their vivid newspaper reports of the spectacle reached parliament, prompting the government to send police reinforcements to quell the unrest. Six men were arrested and taken to Edinburgh to be tried, but the sympathetic jury took only half an hour to find the men not guilty. Their names are engraved on the memorial. It was seen as a great victory, but it did not lead to significant land redistribution and the land raids continued. Unrest spread to all corners of Lewis and large open-air meetings attracted thousands, who walked for miles to join the protests in places such as Uig, and Griais in the north-east, all now commemorated in the prominent stone memorials.

This energetic remembering of local history has turned around a historic narrative of loss and decline and instilled a new pride in the island's communities, believes Malkie. The period of the land raids, from the 1880s through to confrontations with Lord Leverhulme in the 1920s, provides a history of protest, resistance and self-assertion. Erecting the monuments was a political act to present a narrative of agency from which islanders could draw inspiration.

The process of remembering and commemoration has had a dramatic impact in the last ten years, agrees Agnes Rennie. She points to the fact that half of the land in the Hebrides is now in community ownership, following the passage of land reform in 2003 by the devolved government, which introduced a community 'right to buy'. Two thirds of Hebrideans are now living on land they own for the first time in three hundred years. There are still delays in some areas and, on occasion, owners have held out, but it is a dramatic achievement, bringing at last some resolution of a painful history.

Agnes herself is chair of the 56,000-acre community land trust in the north-west of Lewis (Urras Oighreachd Ghabhsainn). They celebrated their launch in 2007 by staging a play about the land raids on the estate once owned by James Matheson and Lord Leverhulme, when a detachment of the Royal Marines suppressed the protests.

'It was a history which people had forgotten because they had been so busy coping. There is a great capacity for coping here. We have used culture as a great resource,' said Agnes, laughing.

'People will say, "Someone sang a sad song at a ceilidh to cheer us up".'

For Agnes, language and history are interlinked. One leads to the other. 'If you don't understand Gaelic, you don't understand the land. There is a sense of place in that landscape – names associated with people, events tied up in particular places. There is a sense of connectedness to the past, to people who fought or who emigrated to Canada. This is what gives such emotional impact to land reform.'

To make the point, Agnes' husband Frank pulled a well-thumbed book down from the shelves. It was an account of Lord Leverhulme's brief and ill-fated ownership of the island. He turned to the description of an open-air public meeting in 1919 at Griais, just north of Stornoway, at the height of the unrest over land. Leverhulme exerted all his formidable powers of oratory to impress his audience with plans for factories, clean homes, electricity and railways. He seemed on the point of winning over his audience until one crofter spoke up: 'We attend to our crofts in seed-time and harvest, and we follow the fishing in its season – and when neither requires our attention we are free to *rest and contemplate* ... Lord Leverhulme! You have bought this island. But you have not bought us, and we refuse to be the bond-slaves of any man. We want to live our lives in our own way, poor in material things it may be, but at least it will be clear of the fear of the factory bell; it will be free and independent.'

The Griais confrontation was an iconic moment in the islanders' struggle with modernity, believes Frank, and it continues to inspire islanders, himself included, in their work on sustainable rural development. Many islanders recognize that the Gaelic heritage – the language and the way it has shaped their perceptions and culture – has been the crucial resource with which to imagine and defend a very different way of life and set of values to that of the mainstream. In the community land trusts, it has found expression.

'Local decision-making has given people a sense of self-worth. It's not utopia but there is a sense of empowerment and that brings a new self confidence,' said Agnes.

This new optimism has been strengthened by Lewis' potential for renewable energy. The island has some of the strongest, most continuous winds anywhere in the British Isles. Its frequent gales and its plateau of low-lying land makes it one of the best sites in Europe for wind power, and the potential for marine wave power and offshore wind turbines is likely to be even bigger. On the coast where Agnes and Frank live, strong winds can fling the waves a hundred metres or more into the air, and in winter the sleet drives horizontal across the undulating fields. Their sturdy house creaks like a boat in its buffeting force.

Communities which have struggled with poverty for generations are poised on the brink of a gold rush. Who benefits from this resource has already been the subject of one bitter struggle, reminiscent of that with Lord Leverhulme a century earlier. A wind farm was proposed in 2005 across much of the Barabhas moorland of north and central Lewis. It would have been the largest wind farm in Europe, with 234 turbines, their wings the size of a jumbo jet's. Each needed large concrete bases, six metres deep, and the connecting roads and cables would have required removing thousands of tons of peat in this rare moorland. It was suggested that the project would bring jobs and a modest income for the communities affected. The project divided the island and prompted a passionate campaign by some islanders to protect the moorland which has been part of their families' history. In a dramatic example of Neil Gunn's 'hidden landscape', islanders articulated the meanings of a landscape which to outsiders seemed bleak and empty.

The proposal was finally rejected in 2008 by the Edinburgh government on the grounds of environmental damage to a moor which is the subject of several national and international designations. It was the huge scale of the wind farm which provoked opposition from many islanders. The scale was a function of the requirement that the project bear the cost of building the electricity cables to carry the energy generated back to the mainland. It added a huge burden; an infrastructure built to distribute to the periphery now needed to gather electricity from the periphery. Since the failure of that project, community land trusts in Lewis have been investing in wind power on a much smaller scale, working with inhabitants to reduce the impact on the moors, and generating significant income from the proceeds.

The response to the Lewis wind-farm project bore many similarities to the successful resistance to a superquarry in south Harris in the 1990s. The proposed Lingerbay quarry would have effectively removed a mountain and created a hole a mile deep below sea level, over a mile long and half a mile wide. The rock was to be used for road construction in the south of England. The Leicestershire-based company had come to Harris for the stone because planning guidance had specifically ruled out quarries of this scale in England and Wales, for fear of public opinion. In support of its planning application, the quarry company argued that the area was remote, and even drew on Sir Walter Scott's journal as evidence of its meagre cultural value; 'high sterile hills ... I have never seen anything more unpropitious,' Scott wrote from a boat at sea – he never landed on the island.

The maps the quarry company used abandoned the Gaelic names for the numerous lochans and replaced them with numbers. The land was stripped of its cultural identity and emptied of its history in a bid to take control – a process akin to that applied to borders of African countries, drawn arbitrarily with a ruler. Words such as 'wild', 'remote' and 'empty' were used in a deeply political way by the developers, and resented as such. Edward Said, in his critique of imperialism, wrote of a 'geography which struggled', and he proposed that it was the 'residual integrity of the local which provided hope of resistance' in a process of 'reclaiming, renaming and reinhabiting' the land. That was what unfolded in Harris and Lewis.

In their campaign to rally resistance the islanders of Harris relied heavily on two Gaelic concepts to explain their understanding of place: *dùthchas* expresses the collective right to the land of those who use it; and *còraichean* expresses the idea of people belonging to the land. They argued for a future for Harris in tourism, crofting and fishing rather than a form of economic development which would be environmentally damaging and bring little direct benefit to the island. One resident eloquently summed it up: 'Another reality prevails in Harris: language, religion, culture – the whole of everyday life – are embedded in tradition, not in consumption. Tradition should not be confused with the past; it could better be described as the meaning of the past, distilled into the present and cared for, with a view to handing it on to future generations.'

The sense of local place on these islands is powerful and deeply attractive to some incomers, who can bring new skills and energy. But the survival of the island's distinctive world view is precarious, dependent on the strength of numbers and their continued commitment. More battles lie ahead, claims geographer Joseph Murphy, who walked nearly 1,200 miles along the west coast of Ireland and Scotland, exploring how Gaelic-speaking communities have resisted the imposition of big commercial developments. The UK's commitment to increase wind power from 6 per cent to 31 per cent by 2020 will put increasing pressure on the Western Isles as a 'resource periphery', he predicts, explaining that these places will always be deeply contested, as the dynamics of capitalism – such as the short-term pressure of share prices – come up against profoundly different local cultures and precious natural environments. Being on the edge is likely to continue to offer a history of struggle.

That conflict is perfectly illustrated by the analysis tool used to plan wind farms. A Geographical Information System (GIS) combines vast information databases with mapping and modelling to identify suitable sites across the country. It recognizes certain types of knowledge, such as wind speeds, the distribution of buildings, and existing electricity distribution infrastructure. It calculates detectable noise levels and the costs of connection to the grid. But this wealth of information does not factor in community memory of where people have lived and the stories of their lives and of their ancestors, or the power of place as symbol and identity. It stands at the opposite pole to the Gaelic way of talking about place; it subtracts all human relationship.

This is the placelessness which capitalism requires to ensure that the flows of capital, people and resources can be ordered to achieve economic efficiency. Local belonging, which impedes or slows down those flows, has to be undermined and eventually eliminated. The dystopian endpoint is that everywhere becomes a kind of anywhere, all distinctive characteristics erased. Metropolitan elites who determine cultural status subject the local and the parochial to dismissive contempt; as the radical sociologist Manuel Castells succinctly summed it up, 'elites are cosmopolitan and people are local'.

'Knowing one's place' has become a derogatory comment

about class hierarchy, but the local is where people live their history and geography and both are infused with emotional attachment and personal identity. History, as Orwell points out in *Nineteen Eighty-Four*, was the basis of identity, and thus freedom. 'The historic role of capitalism itself was to destroy history, to sever any link with the past and to orientate all effort and imagination to what is about to occur,' writes critic John Berger. If, as we are repeatedly told, the future is cast as a place of nightmares, the present is then fraught with instability and anxiety.

Just as capitalism threatens to turn place into abstract space, it threatens to make human relationships a calculation of self-interest. On both these counts, Gaelic has proved to be a resisting force. It provides a language in which to experience how the living and the dead are connected and held by relationship, thus relieving the burden of individualization, with its often neurotic quest for affirmation and recognition in which all forms of relationship and solidarity – whether of family, neighbourhood or nation – become brittle and provisional. No one saw more clearly than Crichton Smith the freedom to be gained in breaking free of such tight communities, as well as the loss in doing so. Here was the sensibility which so powerfully resonated with me years before I reached Lewis. 'I see in Britain, a plea for a home, for a name, for attention,' wrote Crichton Smith.

VII

I needed to make one last visit before leaving Lewis, to a weaver of the famous tweed. Every conversation I had had on the island included a reference to its most famous industry. It may be known as Harris Tweed, but most of it is woven in Lewis.

Agnes' father was a weaver, and she grew up with the clickety-clack sound of the loom. The sons of another woman I talked to worked in the mill at Siabost where they spin the thread. Almost everyone in Lewis has some connection to the industry in one way or another.

The modern-day Harris brand, one of the oldest in the world, owes much to the enterprising initiative of Lady Catherine Herbert, owner of Harris, who sent two sisters to Paisley, the great centre of Scotland's textile industry, to learn new weaving techniques in a bid to revive the islands' economy devastated by famine in the 1840s.

Like many Harris Tweed weavers, Norman McKenzie works in a shed in the garden. He returned to Lewis after a career as a dentist in Glasgow, and took up weaving with his uncle's old loom. Bits of wool scattered the floor beneath the Hattersley single-width loom, a machine which bore witness to the durability of early twentieth-century British engineering. The only power came from his pedalling; it was like cycling up a gentle slope, he explained. On a single-width loom, there are 696 threads in the warp and the warp is sixty metres long. His wool comes from the Siabost mill, up the road, where I had watched the laborious process of mixing the dyed wool and spinning it into yarn. Different coloured yarns were measured out in ratios according to a recipe and were split into smaller and smaller pieces in enclosed rooms by big spinners. The carding then reduced them to single fragile filaments and straightened them into long gossamer-light strands which whirred past on the huge machines. It was this mixing of colours which gave Harris Tweed its distinctive depth of colour. Norman showed me his favourite cloth and I bought a length. As I write, it sits beside me in the London autumn sunshine. I can see yellow, red and pale blue, and then my eyes begin to dance and perhaps there is green and white also. The closer I look, the more the colours reverberate in a myriad of different shades.

Five shuttles of different-coloured wool pulled the weft through the warp, barrelling from side to side as the loom frames rose and fell. In an hour Norman makes three or four metres of cloth, but it was an old machine and it often broke down. Even on the latest looms, the wage is not much above the national minimum, but in the Western Isles, where jobs are not plentiful, it is crucial for the economy. After an hour and a half, Norman has to take a short break as the concentration required is so intense. Weaving is highly skilled work. 'There is so much to watch,' he said. As he wove and his feet pedalled, one hand checked the shuttle while the other smoothed and felt the cloth for imperfections. I was fascinated by the hypnotic sound and sight of an activity which has left such an imprint on our imaginations and which frequently crops up as metaphor. The anthropologist Tim Ingold uses it to describe all of life: 'this tangle is the texture of the world ... beings do not simply occupy the world, they inhabit it and in so doing – in threading their own paths through the meshwork – they contribute to its ever evolving weave'.

Norman took pride in designing all his tweeds. In his draughty shed, by his iron loom held together with leather straps, he talked of the global popularity of Harris Tweed: the Japanese craze for Harris Tweed mobile-phone covers, Nike's trainers in Harris Tweed, the growth of the Chinese market and the collapse in the North American market when fashions changed. Business was booming, but only a few years ago the tweed industry was in crisis. It required swift sure-footedness for this craft to survive the volatility of the global fashion industry.

Harris Tweed reached its peak in 1966, when 7.6 million metres of cloth were produced a year. It was the gold standard of tweed, a staple of school-uniform blazers, coats and, above all, men's clothing. For several decades in the middle of the last century it was a symbol of British masculinity used by school teachers and country aristocrats alike. It started as outdoor clothing for country gentlemen but, like the track suit, it crept into everyday life. Warm and relatively elastic, it provided comfort and some protection against rain. Its muted greens, browns and yellows combine colour and pattern, and yet still offer sober conventionality.

'When I came back from Glasgow, I remembered the knowledge I needed from when I had watched my uncle. It had lain dormant for fifty years. Now I weave every day and it's a way of honouring the past. As a child, I was fascinated by my uncle, and I watched him for years, and how he coped with all the hitches. We were very close.'

The shuttle flashed back and forth, and there was something almost magical as the cloth slowly appeared. I watched Norman's hands smooth, pluck, knot and pull stray threads; it was a labour of touch, his fingertips sensitized to feel for every knot and unevenness. The fragile filaments bound together in spun thread, and then woven into a dense fabric with strength, utility and beauty. In the shed amid its distinctive smells of peat fire and wool, Norman's beautiful cloth reflected not just the colours of the moor, but the history of these townships and how they have survived against all the odds.

8

Endpoint: St Kilda

Drunk with spaciousness, he turned every way,
gazing with wide open mouth and eyes, as light
created colours, clouds, distances and solid,
graspable things close at hand.

ALASDAIR GRAY, *LANARK*

I

I am now close to the end of the journey. From the windy cliffs of Mangursta on Lewis, the archipelago of St Kilda is just visible, forty miles away, beyond this ragged west coast, battered by the heaving sea. This is the edge of the edge. It is usually not the outline of land which is visible on the horizon so much as the small clouds which gather above St Kilda when the rain-laden winds – which have swept across thousands of miles of ocean from Newfoundland – hit the islands' peak of Conachair.

I scan the line where the grey sea meets the grey sky, looking for a variation in the cloud that marks the famous islands, near, and yet still far, because the water which lies between the Long Island and St Kilda is infamous for its unpredictability and fierce weather. One moment all is calm, the next there are steep waves and a driving gale, and all boats to St Kilda are cancelled for days and visitors are left stranded at Leverburgh in Harris, one of the ports for the 55-mile voyage to the islands.

I grew fond of Leverburgh, the south Harris harbour, as a staging post for various arrivals and departures on my journeys between islands. It does not get much of a billing in guide books, and the scattering of warehouses, boats, ruins and houses is not exactly scenic, but that is the point. Leverburgh is a place full of projects, some unfinished, some abandoned and some pursued with great vigour, as evidenced in the community shop, where the produce of a furiously energetic knitter was piled high: huge volumes of socks, large jumpers, hats and scarves in a distinctive, heavy, rough wool. Lord Leverhulme's wild ambitions still loom over the town, which was renamed in his honour, and over a wide area are spread the ruins of his fish-canning factories, warehouses and water tower amongst more recent warehouses, fishing paraphernalia and industrial units. One of the most prominent buildings in the port was built by Lord Leverhulme – a teetotaller – as a temperance hotel. It is abandoned, the hallway full of weeds, the glass long since smashed, and sheep shelter in the porch. It is testimony to Leverhulme's ambition, but also to a very Hebridean accommodation with ruins. They are left to crumble in their own time. In part, perhaps, due to the lack of investment available on the mainland, where ruins are rebuilt or demolished to make way for new projects. Here, land is plentiful and money is not, so the preference has been to start again rather than renovate or convert. Many homes have their predecessor sitting alongside. For much of the British Isles, in the churn of redevelopment, the slow disintegration of buildings is rare. The islands' weather ages some ruins beautifully; I loved the corrugated-iron roofs which turn a vivid orange rust like a flame on the side of a hill. When corrosion crumbles the roof's edge it can look as if it is dripping with molten metal. In Leverburgh, flowers such as irises and field geraniums have grown up amongst the stones and broken machinery.

I had encountered multiple types of loss on my journey: of land, language, country and nation. Now, at the journey's conclusion in the summer of 2015, I was heading towards the most iconic Hebridean ruin of all: St Kilda. In 1930 the last thirty-six islanders asked to be evacuated, and the street of abandoned houses in Village Bay has become one of Scotland's most famous images. In the years immediately after the evacuation, visitors described seeing the cottages still furnished, an open Bible left on the table in one; all that was missing was the animating presence of the people who had lived there. Souvenir and trophy hunters have since picked the place clean, the roof timbers have long gone and grass has grown up inside the crumbling stone walls.

Back in Leverburgh, John Maher recycles VW camper-van engines in a workshop by the pier. A former musician with the 1970s punk band the Buzzcocks, he moved to Harris from Manchester in 2002, and part of his fascination with the place was its ruins. Just before I turned up at his workshop, he had completed a photography project on the Long Island's ruins. His still lifes of abandoned crofts have a glamour akin to Caravaggio. Two-metres square, rich colours emerge from deep shadow in these images of derelict domestic interiors. The tattered 1960s wallpaper and rotting armchairs speak of the depopulation and emigration still in process, too recent and raw to prompt nostalgia. In one, a dead bird lies rotting on the sitting-room floor along with the sheep droppings. Viewing his work in Leverburgh in the souvenir shop amongst the piles of knitting, above the supermarket, brought to mind the comment of the French revolutionary thinker Louis Saint-Just: 'the present order is the disorder of the future'. Our most proud and intimate homemaking is destined to be dismembered, disintegrate and fall apart.

In the months before and after I visited St Kilda, any reference to the islands prompted keen interest. Some people make huge journeys expressly to visit the islands, the most remote part of the British Isles ever to be inhabited, and after nearly two centuries of visitors, there is no sign of the fascination with St Kilda abating. To his astonishment, Maher once bumped into both the novelist Will Self and the sculptor Antony Gormley in Leverburgh's famous butty bus – it has room for half a dozen customers – who were about to set out for the islands. As I waited on the pier in Leverburgh one morning, I listened to the banter of the crew preparing the boats which now take passengers out for day trips. It was part of a prosaic routine for them; in response to a question, one boathand cried, 'St Kilda, same old shit.' Despite its exotic reputation, the path through Leverburgh is now well worn.

By 7.30 a.m. on the day I was booked for the trip to St Kilda, a group of people were waiting on the pier in the cool grey morning. I had planned two trips, a one-day visit followed a few weeks later by a longer camp. The boat headed out of the harbour, past the island of Pabbay in the Sound of Harris, and I looked back to the beaches of south Harris with an exhilarating realization that I was finally on my way, after years of talking and reading about St Kilda. Even so, I was cautious; the wind only had to move to the south-easterly direction and the boat would not be able to land. Some trips reached St Kilda only to have to turn back without ever docking. All the passengers had been warned of the risk of cancellation; Leverburgh was often the place for waiting, disappointed and frustrated pilgrims, defeated at the final hurdle, the last barrier of the capricious Atlantic. But this was part of the point, commented local historian Bill Lawson wisely. Despite the advances in seafaring technology, St Kilda could live up to its old reputation. Its inaccessibility added a frisson of novelty in a carefully managed world where travel has been smoothed into the predictability of the playground roundabout. St Kilda is one trip you can never be sure of.

On the Harris coast I could see ruins on a promontory of machair scattered with daisies, overlooking a beautiful white beach. It is known as the Temple of Ceapabhal. Eighteen years before, on a holiday with my then tiny daughter, I had sat in the ruins and dreamed of writing about this north-west coast. Now I was in its final chapter.

A two-and-half-hour boat journey lay ahead, and as we moved out of the Sound of Harris the swell increased and my landlubber's fear of seasickness loomed. I sat outside in the rain, showered by salty spray, my gaze parked on the horizon. Looking across the grey choppy Atlantic, I could see two other scarlet boats heading to St Kilda; we formed a brave little flotilla. As we turned west, the catamaran began to tip and heave in the rough sea as it cut through the tops of the waves, churning up a bustle of frothing white water which spread behind us like a bridal train. Every now and then we smacked down hard from a wave, and the wind lashed water flat into my face.

To steady my queasiness, I stared through my binoculars, using them to frame a part of the water. I focused, as Vija Celmins the artist had done, on finding the patterns and shapes of the surface of the sea, and imagined how this rapidly changing detail was multiplied billions of times across the spread of the Atlantic. It made me dizzy, but it staved off seasickness. My fellow passengers had succumbed, turning shades of grey and yellow. The boat lurched from side to side and we were instructed to hold on tight; I later learned that there had already been three incidents of broken bones and sprains on the boat that month alone. The determination of the more elderly passengers was testimony to the compelling appeal of St Kilda.

A fellow passenger began to point out the birds. I could hardly explain that I was looking at waves. I began to appreciate his way of looking: sharp-eyed, he spotted the distant birds skimming just above the waves well before me. He noticed differences in form and wing movement which I struggled to see. The streaks of white slipping past separated out into gannets, guillemots and shearwaters in his organizing mind.

Stuart was slight and short, with a shock of white hair and deep-set eyes. He reminded me of the birds he had studied all his life. Born in Aberdeen, he joined the merchant marine as a teenager, working on tankers, and began watching birds on his long sea voyages. As I came to discover, his pattern of life had a restlessness which echoed the migrating patterns of the birds he watched. He moved between Perthshire and the wide open spaces of the Atlantic, Arctic Sea and North Sea, never settling anywhere for too long. One thing was constant: his consuming fascination with birds, seabirds in particular. He had spent decades trying to imagine himself into the way birds – especially gannets – might experience the world: how they scanned these patterned surfaces of slate grey ocean in the swell and lift of Atlantic waves; how they used the direction, temperature and force of the wind to navigate; how they found their way back to the same ledge of rock in a cliff amongst thousands of others to breed and raise their young;

how they ordered life in their teeming colonies, which, like vertically stacked cities, were intensely sociable; how they conducted their courtships, squabbles and raised their young; how new neighbourhoods emerged or old ones made room for newcomers on densely crowded outcrops and stacks. During the winter when travelling was difficult, Stuart pored over aerial photographs to count thousands of birds, trying to establish long-term population trends; the birds' heads were like tiny grains of rice against dark rock.

Along with this deep knowledge came Stuart's sense of adventure. He had scaled cliffs, braved bumpy landings and slept rough for weeks on distant islands in pursuit of his birds; it was clear why he had been roped into fieldwork for ornithology studies across an arc of northern seas for several decades, including several stints on St Kilda. For the rest of the day, I was engrossed in a stream of stories which ranged from the breeding habits of gannets to accounts of wild human life on St Kilda.

'The Ministry of Defence have been out there since 1957 and the radars operate only when the range is firing, and that's a rare event these days. So it's not much of a day's work to go and switch them on. The most demanding part is driving the 300 metres up Mullach Mòr to do it and then back down again in time for lunch. The busiest person on the base is the cook.'

What *had* kept the army busy on St Kilda, confided Stuart over the roar of the boat's engine and the spray, was the Puff Inn. The escapades and rituals around alcohol became legendary. The islands' inhabitants were an awkward combination of archaeologists and nature conservationists, many of them students, and soldiers, and they were often forced into each other's company for weeks at a time on St Kilda. What they had in common was a drinking culture. Sometime later I was shown a spoof report on the strange mores and rituals of this culture compiled by some inventive archaeologists with time on their hands. It involved large amounts of alcohol, dressing up, dares and a system of penalties paid in rounds of more drinks.

When the Ministry of Defence base on St Kilda was privatized, the defence contractor Qinetiq took over and the Puff Inn was closed. It was not easy to tell whether Stuart (who barely drank) regretted its closure. The periodic crises requiring helicopters to be scrambled from Stornoway or Benbecula to take casualties to hospital had come to an end, but so also had camaraderie between very different professions.

The only group of people to earn as much opprobrium as the soldiers were the media, in Stuart's opinion; television camera crews were the worst. They arrived with their bonhomie and presents of whisky, and then disappeared to concoct fanciful films which bore little relation to what they had seen. Stuart had experienced many journalists come and go, making up stories about the mysteries of St Kilda and claiming discovery of long-hidden secrets. One exception to this trail of impatient, demanding egotists was a Japanese camera crew. They were making a series of films about the two dozen places awarded the status of World Heritage Site twice over by UNESCO, designated for both their natural and their historical significance. They had flown to Spain to film the Alhambra, before moving on to Stornoway and embarking on a small yacht. By the time they reached St Kilda they were suffering from seasickness and were very confused as to where they were. They were absolutely charming but couldn't speak a word of English, and no one on the island could speak Japanese, so all communication was done by gesture. They had brought food from Tokyo in tiny packets, and invited everyone to join them. Stuart had sat down, cross-legged on the floor, to eat an excellent Japanese meal on St Kilda.

By the time we glimpsed the grey outlines of St Kilda on the horizon, it had been vividly painted in my mind as a place of comedy. Large quantities of visitors; a conservation scheme which had rebuilt some of the ruins into something approaching a film set; even a members club, with its own tie, for those who had visited. Stuart had great respect for some of the archaeologists (one in particular, whose meticulous research had largely been conducted in her own time while working as a cook). But for all his scepticism, Stuart was coming back, and when I asked why, his answer was uncharacteristically brief: 'Wait until you have seen St Kilda's stacks and the island of Boraraigh. I'll take any trip to come back for them.'

The steep cliffs of Hiort (the Gaelic name for the main island of the small archipelago) were now looming up in the grey mists. The boat swung round the headland into the relative shelter of Village Bay. Four islands make up St Kilda: Dùn, Soaigh, Boraraigh and Hiort, and only the last was continuously inhabited until the evacuation. Ahead of us rose the steep slopes of Mullach Mòr and Conachair. On our left lay the sharp jagged ridge which led out to the island of Dùn. At this point in midsummer the islands were cloaked in deep green, an improbable contrast to the grey of sky and seas. The scattering of stone ruins and old field enclosures, bare of trees or even scrub, spread out above the pebble shore. The gentle domesticity of this horseshoe-shaped bay was deceptive; on the other side of Conachair's peak lay nothing but sheer cliff plunging into the Atlantic, as if a side of the island had sheared away.

At various points along the west European seaboard the continent stops abruptly in cliffs that stand high above the ocean; of all the cliff faces of Norway, Faroe, west Ireland and Galicia, Hiort's Conachair is amongst the tallest. At 430 metres, its cliffs are the highest in Britain, more than three times the height of

Yorkshire's Flamborough Head or twice the height of Sussex's Beachy Head. From Conachair, one can see the island of Soaigh, less than half a mile to the north-west, with cliffs of 378 metres. Four miles over to the north-east is Boraraigh, slightly higher at 384 metres, and in between lies the vast outcropping of rock, the sea stacks of Stac an Armin, Stac Levenish and Stac Lee, the highest stacks in Britain.

The boat was anchored and we climbed into a dinghy for the final leg of the journey to the short jetty. We had arrived.

II

Few islands have exerted such a pull as St Kilda. Since the late seventeenth century visitors have been writing up their impressions of the islands for fascinated readers; there have been more than seven hundred books and still counting. Academic papers, surveys and research reports have rapidly accumulated in the last few decades. This is a place written about by visitors rather than inhabitants, and has become as much a place of the imagination as a physical reality. Even the name St Kilda was imposed by outsiders; probably derived from Skilder, the name of another island which had drifted on early maps across the Atlantic, its derivation suggests an ancient holy past. For three centuries St Kilda has offered a story in microcosm of Britain's fascination with the societies it was infiltrating, re-ordering and often ultimately destroying throughout its empire. St Kilda has been the archetypal lost country. Many empires have been best known through their ruins; St Kilda and its ruins chart how increasing contact over a century eroded the way of life of these island people and triggered the collapse of their community.

Details of life on St Kilda have been assiduously gathered by successive generations. If Lewis has suffered from British forgetfulness, St Kilda has suffered from the opposite. No aspect of the islanders' lives has been left unexplored. Ever since Victorian times, writers and artists have used St Kilda's fame for their own varied purposes and ideals. In 1878 in his book on St Kilda George Seton quoted an earlier author, John MacCulloch: 'he who had no other means of reaching the temple of fame had only to find his way to St Kilda in order to be recorded in its archives'.

I visited several exhibitions about St Kilda on the Long Island, and a new visitor centre is being planned in Lewis on the cliffs at Mangursta. There are St Kilda computer games, a St Kilda opera has toured Europe, and there are films, plays, poetry, novels and art. The story of the island, with its echoes of communal self-reliance, metropolitan appropriation and government indifference, has become iconic for the modern nation of Scotland. Like the statue of Peter Pan in Hyde Park, whose dark bronze has been polished to shining gold in one place by the passage of fond hands, St Kilda's history has been told and retold. The twenty-first century has a lust for knowing what it has lost, and projecting onto it all manner of myth.

One thing St Kilda has never enjoyed is the privilege of being perceived as ordinary, ever since the first account of a visit in 1697 by Martin Martin from Skye. No place in the British Isles has more perfectly expressed Edmund Burke's definition of the sublime, given its isolation in the vast ocean and its dramatic topography. As the minister John Macdonald of Ferintosh wrote on arriving in 1822, 'At last I caught sight of the island, a sight I had longed to see, and my heart swelled with gladness as I looked. But who could look on that island, standing erect out of the sea, with its rugged, craggy rocks, and its waste, unlovely mountains, its rough, green shore, the rude proud billows of the sea indenting all its sides as they dash against it with furious onsets, while it stands unyielding to the surf that is raging all around it, though its brow is bare and hoary with the waste and spray of the waves; who could see it thus, and unbidden venture to approach it?'

The difficulty of the journey seems to have ensured the peculiar intensity of visitors' accounts, and their tendency to embroider descriptions with lavish superlatives. There is the moment they declare themselves 'lost for words'. These are islands, like Staffa, for which language has not been sufficient. Martin Martin's early account, published in 1698, set the tone after he nearly drowned on a terrible journey to reach the islands. The fact that he had arrived on dry land probably partially accounted for his ecstatic experience of the place: 'The inhabitants of St Kilda are much happier than the generality of mankind, as being almost the only people in the world who feel the sweetness of true liberty: what the condition of the people in the Golden Age is feign'd by the poets to be, that theirs really is, I mean, in innocence and simplicity, purity, mutual love and cordial friendship, free from solicitous cares, and anxious covetousness; from envy, deceit, and dissimulation; from ambition and pride, and the consequences that attend them.'

Martin went on to declare that 'There is only this wanting to make them the happiest people in the habitable globe – namely that they themselves do not know how happy they are, and how much they are above the avarice and slavery of the rest of mankind.' Martin described the Hiortaich (as the people of Hiort were known) as 'governed by the dictates of reason and Christianity'. His account came to be seen in the course of the following century as the perfect illustration of the idea of a 'noble savage' living in nature, uncorrupted by civilization, and elements of this 'purer and more ancient Scotland' have persisted in one form or another ever since. St Kilda represented an ancient way of life, heroic and self-reliant in its harsh natural environment. In 1824 John MacCulloch asked, 'If this island is not the Utopia so long sought, where will it be found. Where is the land which has neither arms, money, law, physic, politics nor taxes ...'

Visitors saw what they wanted to see on St Kilda; MacCulloch may have been right that in his time the Hiortaich had no money or arms, but they were paying rent to their clan chief and, contrary to many accounts, there was crime. The clumsy wooden keys they made to secure their cottages are in a museum in South Uist. Different aspects of Hiortach life were singled out by different writers, reflecting their preoccupations: in the nineteenth century there was a particular interest in their moral behaviour, with plenty of comment on their low rates of illegitimacy and alcoholism; in the twentieth century praise was lavished on the St Kilda parliament, a gathering of the island's men to agree on daily tasks. It was seen as a form of early communism, 'to each according to his need, from each according to his abilities'. In 1972 Charles Maclean described St Kilda in his bestselling book *Island on the Edge of the World*, with more than a touch of romantic melodrama, as 'an ideal society' and portrayed its history as a great tragedy and as a warning: it was the prototype to which Western civilization would have to turn in response to eco-catastrophe. 'In the event of technological breakdown, widespread chaos, famine and disease the small community formed out of necessity ... may well be the basic unit of survival for those who wish to maintain freedom and stay alive.' Will Self continued in a similar vein, writing in 2013 that the islands were 'synecdoches of the human condition. Standing apart from the main, they are more legible, so perhaps not only provide the narrative of what happens to us, but how it will all end.'

What many writers chose to disregard was how much Hiort

shared with the neighbouring Long Island. The Victorian visitors arrived by cruise ship from Glasgow, and often had little knowledge of the Outer Hebrides. What they believed to be unique was commonplace on other islands: Gaelic, the love of poetry, the intense Free Church religiosity; and the St Kilda parliament was similar to the community meetings common in the Hebrides at the time (and still evident in the form of grazing committees).

Just as St Kilda could prompt idealization, it could provoke the opposite: the perception of the inhabitants as savages in urgent need of civilization. 'Nothing in Captain Cook's voyages came half so low. The natives are savage in due proportion. The air is infected by a stench almost unsupportable – a compound of rotten fish, filth of all sorts and sea fowl,' wrote Lord Brougham after his visit in 1799. In 1887 the *Glasgow Herald* journalist Robert Connell repeatedly used analogies of wild animals in his descriptions of the islanders: Gaelic worship was like the 'baying of a pack of hyenas', and one woman's gait was compared to that of a rhinoceros as he seized upon 'numerous proofs of semi savagery from which St Kildans [sic] have yet to be reclaimed'. Their Gaelic was condemned as a curse by some nineteenth-century commentators. They were ridiculed and mocked for their naivety as stories were repeated of islanders bewildered by the sight of trees or astonished by wheels when visiting the mainland. One story recounted how a Hiortach lost his way at sea and landed by the Scalpay lighthouse on Harris. Dazzled by the light, bewildered by this unknown structure, he climbed the spiral staircase, believing he must have died and gone to heaven. When he arrived at the top, he found the lighthouse keeper reading his newspaper. 'Are you God?' the Hiortach supposedly asked, to which the lighthouse keeper replied, 'Yes, and who the devil are you?'

Victorian steamer trips to St Kilda were advertised under the slogan 'Come and See Britain's Modern Primitives'. Britain was establishing its imperial mission to bring the benefits of civilization and progress, and here was an instance in its own backyard of the 'primitive' lives it was attempting to 'improve' around the world. This was the past close at hand, or so the Victorians imagined. It prompted oscillating extremes of idealization and contempt, as mainstream British culture projected onto this remote periphery its fantasies, fears and dreams.

For the Hiortaich themselves, their survival depended on a harsh subsistence economy much like that of other Hebridean islands, and the islanders' endurance and resilience were remarkable. The fierce Atlantic storms battered the cliffs, sending spray hundreds of feet into the air and drenching the small fields with salt. Grazing for the sheep was meagre and hunger was a frequent occurrence even in the twentieth century. But there was one reliable source of protein, and they developed great skills in climbing in order to harvest thousands of seabirds and their eggs. It was dangerous and there were tragedies: friends, brothers, fathers and sons were roped together and if one fell, they could pull the others to their deaths on the rocks below. Equally perilous was the sea, and the Hiortaich did not swim; even within a few feet of the rocks, men and boys drowned. When Donald John Gillies wrote his childhood memories in his eighties (he left the island as a twenty-three-year-old in 1924), his account was dominated by a series of tragedies on the cliffs and in boats, and the terrible grief that attended the loss of these men's lives. The community's survival was dependent on male labour, and every time a life was lost, the man's dependants fell back on the overstretched community for support, another characteristic St Kilda shared with neighbouring islands.

Winters were ferocious, and the islanders were usually cut off

for several months from any outside help. Fuel was always scarce
and a blazing fire was an unknown luxury, remembers Gillies.
Rather the turfs smouldered. The cold and wet were a constant
feature of life; Gillies vividly recalls how cold the schoolroom
was. Shoes were an expensive rarity, even in the twentieth
century, and most children went barefoot. Survival required an
enormous amount of work. The labour of weaving and knitting
went on into the small hours of the morning, according to the
Victorian writer George Seton. Without any pack animals, both
sexes had to carry large loads on their backs – of turfs, peat,
birds' feathers, food and wool – from the hills down to the
village. All four islands are pockmarked by hundreds of cleits,
the low domed stone structures built for storage, which were
double-walled to keep the wet out and to allow air to dry peat,
turf and occasionally birds. One and a half metres high by two
metres long, they resemble the beehive cells once used by Celtic
monks. There are cleits in even the most precipitous, near inaccessible places, high up in the cliffs. On the sheer rock cliffs of
Stac an Armin alone, there are seventy-eight cleits. They are an
extraordinary feature of the island subsistence culture, built over
centuries, representing generations of human effort.

One of the most tragic aspects of life on St Kilda was the high
rate of infant mortality. It was known as the 'sickness of eight
days' as newborns quickly succumbed to disease and exhausted
their strength, struggling to breathe. Forty-one out of the sixty-
four deaths recorded between 1855 and 1876 were infants; only
fifteen babies survived in that period. The disease struck boys
in particular, fatally weakening the community. The deaths
have now been attributed to tetanus, common on the Western
Isles, and often carried in the old blankets in which newborns
were wrapped. Seton was horrified by the rate of infant mortality (although if he had cared to enquire, he would have found

the rate was even worse in Glasgow). A minister on the island finally resolved to learn midwifery skills in Glasgow and brought them back to Hiort, and the final infant death from tetanus was recorded in 1891. Without a nurse or doctor, illness was always a danger. Increasing contact with outsiders brought new diseases, and islanders unused to common coughs and colds were afflicted. A nurse was only finally appointed a few years before the evacuation in 1930; the only chance of reaching a doctor was if a passing boat could take the invalid to Harris. One of the last recorded tragedies was that of a pregnant woman with appendicitis, who died after the long journey to hospital.

St Kilda provoked pity, an experience recommended by the eighteenth-century philosopher Edmund Burke as a comparable pleasure alongside the sublime: 'For terror is a passion which always produces delight when it does not press too close, and pity is a passion accompanied by much pleasure because it arises from love and social affection.' While the British government was noticeably reluctant to provide support for St Kilda – despite repeated requests for a regular mailboat and a jetty – individuals keenly felt a responsibility to bring the so-called benefits of civilization to the island. Two things troubled visitors in the nineteenth century: the state of the islanders' homes and the state of their souls. Visitors were offended that British citizens lived in what they described as 'hovels'; they failed to notice that the buildings were well adapted for the difficult environment. The early-nineteenth-century buildings crouched low along the ground, with walls more than two metres thick and doorways only ninety centimetres high. The habit of building up the floor over the course of the winter with ash and dung meant that by spring it was not possible to stand up inside, only crawl. It was enough to prompt one passing English yachtsman, Sir Thomas Dyke Acland, to offer a £20 prize in 1834 to the first person to rebuild their home; after the new homes were built by the islanders, they shared out the prize money to buy window glass, crockery and furniture. A few decades later, another donation prompted a second round of building, only this time it was imposed on the islanders. These new crofts were built to look like a row of English country cottages, facing out to sea, a window on either side of the doorway. They were ill-adapted for the fierce Atlantic gales, and the wind tore through the doors and windows, leaving the islanders shivering with cold. The zinc roofs let in the rain and within a short period of time they had been blown away, leaving islanders worse off than before, without the means for repairs. At least the thick rounded walls of their old dwellings had given them some protection from the ocean's roar and the winter storms.

Looking down from Mullach Sgar onto Village Bay, the scattering of stone ruins records the stages of this history. High above the shore on the slopes of Conachair are the old blackhouse ruins, lower down is the Street, formed by the line of the new blackhouses built at right angles to the shore. Interspersed between them are the draughty crofts which have come to form the iconic image of St Kilda.

The cruise ships brought other philanthropic gifts. In 1890 a ship arrived full of wedding gifts, donated by a public appeal in Sunderland, for a marriage on the island, including novelties such as a white bridal gown and an organ. The bride's father was horrified, describing the organ as the 'instrument of the devil', and insisted that the ship left immediately with all its contents. In 1913 reports of famine on the island prompted the *Daily Mail* to mount a national rescue mission, and Sir Thomas Lipton donated quantities of tea and a portrait of himself. The *Daily Mail* then carried prominent articles on the magnanimous rescue they had mounted, although they had arrived well after a government relief boat.

Outsiders were also concerned at the state of the Hiortaich's souls. Early in the nineteenth century Presbyterian missionaries arrived and preached at intense meetings which led to dramatic conversions. Along with Lewis and Harris, the Hiortaich became devoutly Free Church, and strict sabbatarians. Visitors could be personally admonished from the pulpit; in a bold inversion, the Hiortaich offered moral tutelage to their visitors for their ungodliness. By the twentieth century commentators had switched their criticisms from too little religion to too much. The oppressive weight of strict Presbyterianism had crushed the people's spirit, it was argued; in the bestselling books of the 1970s, the Free Church had become part of the tragedy in which the island's history and culture had been destroyed. Only recently has there been recognition that their faith was one of the ways in which the Hiortaich negotiated modernity. 'Religion was the vital integrating force of community life,' argues historian John Randall.

The regular arrival of cruise ships by the late nineteenth century had a distorting impact on the islands. Visitors wanted to see the sights, and they paid islanders to put on displays climbing the cliffs. They bought souvenirs of feathers, knitted gloves and eggs, and tourism became a major source of income. The visits became more and more intrusive; in 1900 Norman Heathcote wrote in his book *St Kilda*: 'I do not wonder that they dislike foreigners, so many tourists treat them as if they were wild animals at the zoo They throw sweets at them, openly mock them and I have seen them standing at the church door during service, laughing and talking and staring in as if at an entertainment got up for their amusement.' Film footage from the early twentieth century shows women knitting or spinning by their doorways who leap to their feet when they see the camera, scattering their work on the ground, hiding their faces and retreating into their homes. The camera shamelessly recorded their embarrassment and discomfort, even following the backs of the retreating figures.

The end of the St Kilda community has been as deeply contested as the rest of its history. When Seton visited in 1876 it was already clear to him that its days were numbered. He was deeply concerned that turfs from Village Bay were being used for fuel, exposing bare rock where once there had been soil to cultivate. The population had hovered between seventy and eighty inhabitants through most of the nineteenth century, but in the aftermath of the First World War, in common with other Hebridean islands, there was a rapid surge in emigration. Between 1921 and 1928 the population fell from seventy-three to thirty-seven. The community was no longer viable, and in 1930 the last thirty-six islanders petitioned the government to evacuate them. After thousands of years of human habitation, St Kilda was to be abandoned – apart from annual summer work parties. The Hiortaich asked to go to the mainland, and said they did not want to be settled together. The government rehoused many of them in Morvern on Scotland's west coast, and offered the men work. Ironically, for islanders who had never seen a tree, their new jobs were with the Forestry Commission.

Was the evacuation of St Kilda an instance of government neglect or the inevitable end to a fragile community? There have been plenty who have argued the former. The Hiortaich appear to have been divided over the evacuation decision; some later declared themselves satisfied by their new lives, but complaint was unfamiliar to their island tradition of stoicism and the reality was complex. If the infrastructure, investment and support had been available, no doubt some would have chosen to stay. But Gillies describes in his account how he and many others in the 1920s left to find a better life; he became a minister and emigrated to Canada. The irony is that within a quarter of a century habitation resumed on Hiort, with the building of an army base in 1957, and has been continuous ever since. Finally the long-needed infrastructure of regular communication and transport, along with the presence of a nurse, was put in place and has supported the army base on St Kilda for the last sixty years.

The evacuation was a hurried, painful affair. Baggage was limited and many belongings were left behind. Dogs had to be abandoned (they were tied into sacks with stones and thrown off the jetty). National interest was intense, but reporting of the evacuation was banned by the government, allegedly out of respect for the islanders' privacy. Unlike other Hebridean islands such as Mingulay, south of Barra, which was abandoned in 1911 with little comment, St Kilda became a symbol of imperial malaise and retreat. The island community's final years were the subject of the first film by the young British director Michael Powell in 1938. 'The slow shadow of Death is falling upon the Outer Isles of Scotland ... They are doomed and it is Civilisation that is killing them,' runs the film's soundtrack. Powell's *The Edge of the World* captured the islanders' dilemma in the story of two young men, one intent on leaving, the other on staying. In a challenge climbing the cliffs the latter is killed, and the remaining young man leaves to take work as a boathand on a glamorous couple's yacht, later returning to the island. The ghosts drift past him. It is a poignant elegy for a nation attempting to navigate a future dominated by American wealth and bracing itself for war, and its own imperial demise.

The month in which St Kilda was evacuated, August 1930, was marked by two events, and they captured the febrile inter-war anxiety of Britain's overstretched empire, and the sense of a civilization on the point of disintegration, the source of such revulsion to Orwell's generation of writers. Three weeks before St Kilda's evacuation, British unemployment passed the two million mark – it was set to rise much higher over the next few years. Two weeks before the evacuation, the first ever British Empire games opened in Ontario, Canada, in a brief moment of triumphalism in the face of the persistent crisis in India over independence. A few months later, in November 1930, London hosted the first Round Table Conference in a vain attempt to orchestrate a peaceful solution to the future of India. The empire was in retreat.

III

The view from the jetty in Village Bay was of the military base, a cluster of dark green prefabricated huts. A few men in army fatigues wandered back and forth. This was the radar-tracking base run by the private security multinational Qinetiq (their corporate slogan, 'People who know how to help you achieve the impossible'). The generator for the base, a large incongruous warehouse, crouched on the foreshore; fledgling birds, attracted by its warmth, got trapped in its cavernous interior. Alongside stood a row of fuel tanks and an area of hardstanding for the metal shipping containers and piled-up rubbish waiting to be taken off the island. All around was the usual detritus of a harbour, with brightly coloured plastic barrels, big bins and rubble. Stunning panoramic photographs and film footage shot on Hiort never show this. The images of Village Bay and its distinctive ruins are carefully angled to exclude the dominant feature of the place. They also exclude the concrete road which snakes up to the top of Conachair, prickly with metal masts. More military equipment stands on the lower peak of Mullach Sgar. I had been sold a pup. All these years of planning and reading to arrive at a shabby barracks which I could have found in Catterick in North Yorkshire, or on the Salisbury Plain.

Bemused, I followed Stuart, who had set off at a brisk pace straight up the hill on the rough grass; on a point of principle he never used the concrete road. Stuck into his small backpack were two bamboo sticks topped with red flags as protection against the skuas. There were several dozen pairs on Hiort and they bullied anyone daring to walk on the hills, swooping low, and on occasion slamming their webbed feet into the side of one's head. Stuart had suffered a ruptured eardrum on one encounter and he had no wish to repeat the experience.

As we clambered up the steep slope in the drizzle, we heard the whirr of a helicopter arriving on the island. A jeep drove the 200 metres from the base to the helipad to meet it. When we looked back down at the bay, a cruise ship had anchored offshore. Down amongst the ruins, fifty or so day trippers were picking their way through the low stone walls and cleits, and slowly starting the ascent of Conachair. Hiort was a busy place, all the more so after the emptiness of many mountainsides in Harris, Lewis and North Uist, its nearest neighbours.

After a couple of hours walking round Gleann Mòr, we returned to sit down on the top of Mullach Sgar, surveying the serrated edge of Dùn to the south and Gleann Mòr to the north. Stuart pointed out important places for me to visit when I returned in a few weeks' time, and recounted adventures he had had on St Kilda; on one occasion he and several others were trapped by bad weather for two weeks. In the end one of the party, a senior archaeologist, negotiated seats on the MoD helicopter. St Kilda sorely tests the devotion of those who fall under her spell.

Back down on the shore, we wandered past the old containers, the helipad and the fuel tanks to the jetty, where a group of very cold visitors were standing in the rain, waiting for the boat. The only shelter was the National Trust shop, which was probably good for sales. On our arrival the first comment of the eager warden had been to inform us of the shop's opening times. As we climbed into the dinghy to rejoin the boat, a lady was carrying her recent purchases in a large paper bag emblazoned with the National Trust's slogan, 'The Place to Shop'. I felt it was an incongruous final comment on St Kilda, although I checked myself, remembering that the island had been selling souvenirs for more than a century. Perhaps when I returned in a few weeks I could make more sense of this confusing jumble of histories, military and mythical, folk and scientific.

We headed on in the rain to the stacks and the island of Boraraigh. Nothing had prepared me for these sheer eruptions of rock out of the ocean. It was only when we were bobbing in the sea at their foot in our small boat that their improbable enormity bore down on me. Craning my neck, I looked up at the dark rock, piled high, and the gigantic slabs of gabbro tilted into the water. These massed volumes expressed the violence and chaotic force of their creation, millions of years ago.

Angus Campbell, our skipper, later showed me a 3D model of the topography of the ocean floor around St Kilda on his boat's navigation computer, built up from the depth readings he had taken. On the small screen I could see how the dramatic Stac an Armin, Boraraigh and Stac Lee have their underwater counterparts. The seabed is a scape of extraordinary peaks and plunging ravines, valleys and plateaux, the remains of that string of volcanoes along the western seaboard of Scotland sixty million years ago. Deep in the earth, rocks burst through cracks in the earth's crust, creating the dramatic landscape of St Kilda, parts of the Hebrides and even out to Rockall. The volcanoes eroded many millions of years ago and their magma cores bequeathed us these island mountains. Iceland's volcanoes are the last remnant of this long Atlantic history of ash, fire and molten rock.

I found it hard to grasp the digital images or the geological accounts, the scale of time and space was too vast to comprehend. But on a boat in an Atlantic smirr, staring at the heights of Boraraigh, I caught a tiny glimpse of these massive events and how they created the landforms on which we hang our myths.

Rock had been a constant presence during my journey, from the standing stones of Machrie in Arran to Calanais in Lewis, from the caves of St Molaise on Holy Isle to Staffa, from the cuillins of Rum to the east-coast bays of Harris. Its textures and shapes were a compressed history. Our planet is made of ungiving rock, while fertile earth has been a fragile ecological miracle; lending its name to the planet exposes our gratitude and perhaps our complacency.

The stacks' jagged cliffs offer narrow ledges crowded with the staggering 320,000 breeding pairs of seventeen species of seabird which use the St Kilda archipelago to nest and raise their young – a tenth of the entire seabird population of the British Isles. The stacks were frosted pale grey with their droppings and there was a pungent smell of ammonia mixed with the sea's rich smell of salt and minerals. As the birds swirled high above our heads, the air was full of their cries piercing the wind and the roar of the waves in this dense avian metropolis. I stared at the rows of white gannets sitting along the crevices of the cliff face, surveying the water crashing on the rocks below, and perhaps looking at us – strange, clumsy creatures with our ungainly bodies, unable to fly, and ill at ease in water. There are more than half a million seabirds on St Kilda, one of the biggest seabird colonies in the world. Every year these gannets fly thousands of miles on annual migrations before returning; they can dive thirty metres with extraordinary force, their wings folded behind them to plummet through the air, their beaks toughened to cope with the impact of their spectacular dives.

These gannets, guillemots and puffins sustained human life on St Kilda for thousands of years. Islanders crept down the cliffs in the dead of night to surprise them on their ledges, working with deathly quiet to strangle hundreds in a few hours. They depended on the birds for everything: high-protein food; feathers to sleep on and to sell to pay the rent; fulmar oil to light their lamps; and for medicine. They used the gannets' necks as rough shoes, their bones for fastenings, and they studied their flight paths to aid their navigation. The Hiortaich were in part bird people, watching and waiting for the return every year of the migrating seafowl. Although plentiful, these wild creatures could never be husbanded, and every year their arrival was a cause for thanksgiving and celebration.

The boat lurched from side to side, and I scanned the cliffs of Stac an Armin. Midway up, on a sloping narrow terrace, was a bothy made of dry stone. It was built for the Hiortaich's annual expeditions to the stack to harvest the birds and their eggs. Below it I looked for the place at the foot of the cliff where a small boat could have landed the men amongst the pounding surf; I tried to decipher the route they might have taken up the cliff face with their ropes (which were amongst the community's most precious possessions). One famous story was of a party of eight men and young boys in the eighteenth century who went to Boraraigh for a few days to harvest the birds and ended up stranded for eight months over a winter. Smallpox had broken out on Hiort and had killed so many of the adults that there were not enough men to get the boats out to pick up the group as planned. They survived, living off birds and eggs and using feathers to fashion clothing to protect themselves from the harsh winter storms. They were separated from home by only a few miles.

As the boat finally turned east to head back to Leverburgh, my fellow passengers seemed satisfied, as was I. We had achieved our purpose, despite the vagaries of the Atlantic weather, despite the seasickness, the rain and the jolt and lurch of the boat.

Two weeks later I was due to return to St Kilda. It was a day of stunning sunshine with an extraordinary clarity to the light, so the distant mountains on the mainland were sharply clear. The sea was the most perfect calm I had seen on my journey, almost glassy. I was packing up the last items of bedding and food for a week's camp on St Kilda when I received a text. The weather forecast was bad, a storm was on its way and all boats were cancelled indefinitely. I never got back to St Kilda. It was as Constantine Cavafy wrote in his poem *Ithaka*:

> *Ithaka gave you the marvellous journey.*
> *Without her you would not have set out.*
> *She has nothing left to give you now.*
> *And if you find her poor, Ithaka won't have fooled you.*
> *Wise as you will have become, so full of experience,*
> *you will have understood by then what these Ithakas*
>   *mean.*

I rode out the storm in a hostel, hunkered down on the wild, rocky east coast of Harris in Rèinigeadal, a cluster of crofts which until the early 1980s was only accessible by path across the mountains or by boat. It was set deep in a cove, with the bulk of Harris' mountains sheltering it from the Atlantic storm. The gale roared around us for the next few days, slamming into the small croft with its thick old walls, and I woke frequently in the night to listen to its shriek and moan, and the lashing of the rain on the skylights. I imagined how its full force was hitting the slope of St Kilda's Village Bay, grateful I was not there in a tent. It was an orchestral performance of sound, exhausting just to hear. As suddenly as it had started, the rain stopped one morning when I was washing up breakfast. I left and drove through a land veined with watercourses hurtling down hillsides. Waterfalls cascaded over cliffs and streams which had sprung briefly to life made their way to feed the churning fury of the swollen rivers. A kind of mad, dangerous energy was abroad, furious in its impatience.

A few days later the sun returned and I was camping on south Harris. The brilliance of the early morning dared me to brave the glassy-green chill of the sea. It was so cold I felt as if the air was sucked out of me, and I splashed wildly in the surf to keep some warmth in my limbs. As I recovered with a bowl of hot porridge, I saw the scarlet boats setting out for St Kilda. I felt a sharp stab of regret that I was not on board with my camping gear; I had missed the experience of being out on those rocks in the ocean. To hear its roar in the small hours; to wake early on a rough grey morning knowing there would be no boats; to walk the island's edges. Those red boats on the horizon were teaching me one of St Kilda's oldest truths, its inaccessibility, which my day trip had masked. Surrounded by so many wonders, it seemed greedy to hanker after one missed. St Kilda, it turned out, had given me the journey. She had nothing left to give, but she hadn't fooled me.

IV

I had reached my journey's end, but I had no sense of completion. Something intriguing but unsettling had set in during the five hours I had spent on the ocean, travelling to and from St Kilda. Staring at those dark grey seas, with rain and spray in my face, the journey had opened my mind to something unfamiliar. As I sat beside the skipper, Angus, I had seen the ocean in a different way. Any land map reduces the sea to little more than a border, a space between, but on the bank of computer screens in front of Angus, this was reversed, and the mainland receded to the edge. Centre stage were the swirls of different shades of blue between the isobaths – the lines indicating the depth of the sea – stretching to the eastern coast of Canada, up to Greenland in the north-west and over in the north-east to the Shetlands, Faroes and beyond to Norway, Svalbard and the Arctic.

This was not abstract cartography to Angus. He used these seas every day; they were his motorway, as familiar to him as the

M1 might be to a truck driver. He had just been out to Rockall, 200 miles west of Harris, to drop off a chartered surveyor from Edinburgh afflicted with an extreme form of islomania, intent on breaking the record for the longest stay on the rock (he succeeded, although the storm which cancelled our camp did a lot of damage to his equipment). Angus talked of other islands scattered across these spaces of ocean. He had recently taken two ornithologists out to the Flannan Isles, twenty miles north-west of Lewis, for a week's study of the bird colonies there. Beyond that lay Rona, forty-four miles north-east of the Butt of Lewis, the home of the rare Leach's petrels. There are ruins of a few houses and a monk's cell on the island and a carved Celtic cross was found there. A north-west opened up in my mind's eye much bigger than anything I could ever have imagined at my desk in London.

This north-western expanse explained why the Ministry of Defence was on St Kilda. While our geographical imaginations shrink to the size of our lives, defence strategists analyse maps and charts to assess land masses and sea lanes, and how they accommodate ships, submarines and the range of artillery. Their geography is a vast battleground, and this north-west has been a crucial theatre of war for the last century. St Kilda may be mythologized for its isolation and remoteness, but for much of the twentieth century it has had a ringside seat on war. The Hiortach Donald John Gillies had a vivid memory of a German submarine shelling St Kilda on 18 May 1918. The villagers fled to the hills to hide, except for the poor minister's wife, who had just had a baby. Luckily, the shells fell around the young mother and her baby, and neither was harmed. The Hiortaich had nervously witnessed German submarine activity around the island through 1915 and 1916, and several merchant ships were sunk in the vicinity. The Cold War brought the attention of Whitehall defence strategists back to St Kilda, and one of the reasons for their new interest was the space: 'One of the joys of that area of sea is that it is not on a major shipping route, and there isn't a high density of transiting merchantmen. You need vast expanses of clear water and air for the kind of testing done in South Uist and St Kilda. It's not a major air route either. Of the 500–600 aircraft in the air over the Atlantic at any moment, there is a gap in this area,' Admiral Lord West, former Chief of the Naval Staff, explained to me. 'You need 50,000-foot clearance for high-sea firings of warships to make sure they work. It's a major clearance operation to ensure no fishing boats are in the area.'

The base built on St Kilda tracks the missiles fired from the South Uist range. Here, the first guided British/US nuclear weapon, the Corporal missile, was tested, later replaced by the Sergeant and Lance tactical nuclear missiles, and in due course by the Skua and Petrel high-altitude missiles. The South Uist range still tests Rapier missiles and Unmanned Air Vehicles (more commonly known as drones). Miles of the long Atlantic beaches of South Uist, its machair and nearby sea are labelled on the map in pink capital letters, DANGER AREA.

'It's an attractive thing to have, a very useful facility. The only other place to test is in the Mediterranean,' said Lord West.

There are other major defence installations along the west Scottish seaboard, the most important being the Trident nuclear base at Faslane in the Clyde. This militarization stretches to Rockall, an uninhabitable rock in the middle of the Atlantic which was pressed into service in 1955, when it became the last imperial annexation by the British to pre-empt use by the Soviets. Closer to the mainland, between the Isle of Raasay off Skye and the Applecross peninsula, there is an underwater torpedo testing range known as BUTEC, the British Underwater Test and Evaluation Centre.

'You can deploy into open water through hidden routes between the islands where there are deepwater channels. It's very hard to pick up submarines because the islands block the sonar,' said Lord West.

The North Atlantic was a key strategic priority at the height of the threat from the USSR during the Cold War. The Soviet naval fleet was in Murmansk, then the biggest nuclear naval base in the world, and its ships only had access to the Atlantic around the top of Norway and down between Scotland and Greenland. This access point became known by the acronym GIUK: the Greenland Iceland United Kingdom Gap. Much of British imperial defence strategy was built on defending gaps; Gibraltar, Malta, Suez, Aden, Oman and Singapore were all colonies built to defend key shipping lanes and to protect British interests. The North Atlantic was one of the most sensitive gaps of all. The First and Second World Wars had demonstrated the dependence of the UK on Atlantic shipping for food, as well as reinforcements of arms and men. The area was acutely vulnerable to enemy submarines. The merchant-navy losses in the Second World War were colossal; bodies of seamen were washed up on Hebridean beaches throughout the war. In the Cold War the Soviet Union's vast superiority on land in Europe could not be matched, so it was imperative for European security to protect the Atlantic shipping lanes which could provide US reinforcements.

Admiral Lord West maintained that it was in this area of the North Atlantic that the Cold War was won: 'In the early 1980s President Reagan and the US defence chiefs wanted to move the NATO fleet to operate north of the GIUK to suppress Russian submarine activity. What followed were big exercises around north Norway, such as Ocean Safari in 1985 and Northern Wedding in 1986. It was a key moment when the Soviet Union realized it couldn't keep up. The Chief of Soviet Defence Staff argued for more investment in military research or faced being outstripped by the US. 'The UK was involved in the exercises with helicopters, Harrier jets and small aircraft carriers, and our role was to keep the submarines down – the US found that very helpful. I once kept three Russian submarines down for seventy-two hours.' His excitement was audible.

'Looking to the future, this area could become significant again. Already, Norway and Russia are squabbling about the seabed. These northern approaches to Europe could be very important. There was a huge NATO early-warning site on the Faroe Islands. The radar on Benbecula and Uist are part of the UK air-defence systems.'

Across this part of the Atlantic a vast network of listening devices has been strung under the water on the seabed, a Sound Surveillance System known as SOSUS. It has the power to pick up sounds carried hundreds of miles. In this seabed battleground, submarines have been designed to become ever quieter to avoid detection. Conflict at sea has huge destructive capabilities; that little of this potential is visible makes the masts and anonymous buildings on the hills of Hiort and sixty miles away on South Uist all the more sinister.

There is another North Atlantic geography which is vital to human survival. Indeed, we owe every second intake of sweet life-giving oxygen to its sustaining power. The Atlantic current known as the Gulf Stream, stretching from Florida up to the north-west of Europe, is the most important in the northern hemisphere. It has given the Hebrides its comparatively warm and wet climate, and brought with it a rich sea life, sustaining the islands' human habitation for millennia. The Gulf Stream brings volumes of water across the Atlantic, which is more salty than the Arctic sea. A couple of thousand miles due north from

St Kilda, past Iceland and the east coast of Greenland, is the 'North Atlantic pump', where this salty water sinks, sucking in surface water from the Arctic sea, which drives the Gulf Stream. The pump, known as the Atlantic conveyor belt, is part of the global ocean conveyor, which makes currents move around the globe in connected loops in a single system. The conveyor draws up water from the deep and replaces surface water. Waters can take 1,500 years to resurface in this cycle. The speed and volume of water moving down to the deep sea at the North Atlantic pump is the equivalent of twelve times the flow of all the world's rivers, writes oceanographer Callum Roberts. There are only two other points where sea water sinks in such volumes, both in Antarctica. Together these three pumps ensure the constant movement of volumes of water around the world. 'It turns out that the oceans are made up of many parcels of water in constant motion, driven by wind and density differences, and their origins and movements around ocean basins can be tracked,' concludes Roberts.

These pumps could become tipping points for dramatic climate change. There are levels beyond which the water temperature and density must not pass if the currents are to remain stable. If the pump collapses and currents in the global ocean conveyor weaken, it would disrupt established weather patterns and climate across the globe. The weakening of the pump would also undermine the oceans' capacity to transfer carbon dioxide from the atmosphere down into the deep sea, and at the same time inject the freshly oxygenated water at those depths which sustains life there.

I had read Roberts as I crossed the Minch to Barra, sitting on deck in the sunshine, and his words came back to me as I stood alongside Angus in the boat heading back from St Kilda to Leverburgh, the window wipers swinging back and forth to clear the beating rain. These heavy grey seas were driving huge volumes of water around the globe in a process on which Britain's mild and damp climate depended. A graphic representation of the world's currents I had seen in a museum in Oban made the oceans' currents look like a seething mass of spaghetti, whirling round the globe's wet surface.

Across these vast waters, thousands of gannets, guillemots, puffins and shearwater hunt, live and migrate, following routes north and south, east and west. This is their home, and for thousands of years they have been largely left to it, save for some harvesting by humans along the rocky edges of their oceanic world. In this scape, land is insignificant; it was a complete inversion of my landlubber's geography. I was an ingénue, stumbling upon the seafaring geography of the North Atlantic, familiar to a skipper like Angus and an ornithologist like Stuart. This ocean dwarfed my histories of place and journey. I glimpsed why the Celtic hermits perched on the cliffs and in the caves of this seaboard might have chosen silence in the presence of these great, raging, wet, wordless forces of air and water. I felt like one of the Borrowers when the roof of their tiny world was ripped off. We depend on the oxygen produced by the ocean's plankton, and half of all the carbon dioxide we emit is dissolved in these friendly oceans. The Gaelic understanding that the sea is a blessed place reveals more truth than anyone had suspected until twentieth-century science explained it to us.

V

Stuart had an idea that I should take one last journey north, and he arranged my passage with Angus. I was hungry for more time out in that big ocean. Angus agreed to my joining him on his trip back to the Flannan Isles to pick up the two ornithologists.

The night before we were to set off, I camped among the dunes at Horgabost on the west coast of Harris. The beach there is reputed to have the whitest sand of all Harris' famous beaches, with a shell content of over 90 per cent. As I put up the tent, the sunlight caught the brilliance of the white sand through the shallow water in the big bay, turning swathes of water to rich turquoise. I woke around 2 a.m. and beyond the Harris hills to the north the sky was red and pale yellow: sunset and sunrise mingling in a midsummer sky no darker than dusk. The wind was light; it was a moment already pregnant with possibility for the day and its journey, forty miles north-west of this beach. I could not sleep with the wonder of it all, and listened to the orderly waves gently breaking a few feet away.

At 5.30 a.m. the sun was already bright and warm. Its early light cast the machair as soft velvet along the west Harris coast. The green was glowing, sprinkled with yellow buttercups, as I headed the few miles to Leverburgh. Within an hour I was on the boat, looking through binoculars back at the same shore as we headed north, ploughing across a calm sea. The cliffs of the islands of Taransay and Scarp and north Harris were sharply defined, cracked with crevices and outcrops. We continued close to this wild shore, where the villages and roads peter out and for thirty miles before Mealasta, in Lewis, there is no sign of human habitation. Of all the Western Isles, this area is one of the least accessible and its silent stillness travelled across the water. The rocky islands, skerries and stacks, with deep inlets into moorland and bog, finally softened into the sandy beaches of Uig in Lewis.

Then the coast began to swing away to the east, shrinking to a smooth dark mass as it levelled out in the great moors of north Lewis. As we came out of the lee of Gallan Head, we hit the swell of open sea. The catamaran pitched as it hit the rise

of water, side on. Water came crashing over the deck in sheets
of spray and fine mist. My waterproofs were quickly drenched.
The powerful boat thumped down one moment, and was tossed
high the next, and then shoved to the side by the bullying swell.
The sky overhead was a sharp clear blue and from a way off the
seven Flannan Isles appeared on the horizon, slowly becoming
more distinct, their rounded pudding shapes slowly colouring
pale green. As we neared, we could pick out how the slope of
the main island, Eilean Mòr, was splashed with pink and white.
It sat on the blue sea like a gigantic cup cake, lavishly iced.
The white lighthouse on its summit was the birthday candle. It
was implausibly pretty, and strangely domestic, quite unlike its
sinister reputation.

On Lewis I had chatted to Cathy, an auxiliary at the hospital in Stornoway, and she had shivered with horror at the
mention of my imminent trip to the Flannan Isles. Didn't the
ornithologists staying there find it creepy? she asked. Cathy
had grown up on the west coast of Lewis, so the outline of the
Flannans on the horizon was familiar, but she had never been.
She didn't like being on the sea, nor did she like the idea of the
Flannans. In 1900, a year after the lighthouse had been opened,
a passing boat, concerned that the light had gone out, landed
to investigate and discovered that all three lighthouse men had
disappeared. Everything was in order – bar one overturned chair
in the kitchen – but there was no sign of the men. A subsequent
investigation concluded that the men had gone out in bad storms
to secure the landing ropes thirty-four metres above sea level,
and had been washed away in a freak wave. But questions persisted as to why the three men, against regulations, had left the
lighthouse at the same time and without their oilskins. Victorian
England was fascinated by the mysterious tragedy. A ballad by
Wilfrid Wilson Gibson in 1912 embellished the tale with his own

detail – he added that a meal had been left untouched on the table – and made the incident even more famous. Ever since, it has cropped up in films, novels and pop songs as a powerful and mysterious image of loss.

Various maritime mysteries have been attributed to freak waves, but there was doubt that these sudden, exceptionally large movements of water existed; some regarded them as the stuff of myth, or a delusion of the sailor's imagination. But records on an oil platform in the North Sea in 1995 finally established that millennia of sailors' stories had a basis in fact. Research since has shown that rogue waves can reach heights of twenty-five metres – more than three times the height of the average British terraced house. They can emerge suddenly in open sea, with no warning. In 2000 a British oceanographic research vessel sailing in the Rockall trough encountered twenty-nine-metre waves, the biggest ever recorded by scientific instruments in the open ocean. Perhaps a freak wave of thirty-four metres was possible on the Flannans after all. One suggestion was that the last lighthouse keeper to leave the light (against strict lighthouse regulations) hurried to warn the other two of the wall of water approaching the island. It would explain his haste – the overturned chair, the oilskins left behind – but it does not explain the carefully closed door and gate. Wilder speculations have been of murder, abduction and even kidnap by a giant bird. The mystery has never been solved.

As we approached Eilean Mòr, the thought of this terrifying wall of water lingered in my mind. The cliffs and stacks of the seven Flannan Isles showed their age, battered by thousands of years of savage Atlantic winters. Their weathered precipices belied the prettiness of the flowery island on this summer day. We anchored the catamaran under cliffs which rose sheer above us, and climbed down into a small rubber dinghy to approach the landing stage built by the Victorians for the lighthouse. The swell rose two metres or so against the seaweed-covered rocks and then fell back. Angus gently nudged the boat, heavy with the six of us, into the swell; everyone was alert. This short moment was fraught with danger. He had to manoeuvre the dingy close enough for a person to jump onto the landing stage with a rope, but not so close as to puncture the boat on the barnacles. Once the first person landed, the next crouched in the bows to wait for Angus' sharp instruction to jump. For each landing, Angus moved the boat to the right point on the rising water. Timing was everything. I was last; twice I was told to jump, only for the instruction to be retracted seconds later as the water surged onto the rocks. Hands reached out to pull me ashore, and hands behind pushed. The next moment I was gripping the seaweed and the rocks. I was on the Flannans.

From the small landing stage, steps led straight up the vertiginous cliffs. As we climbed, there was a point of bare rock where the steps had been washed away, and only the iron pegs were left behind to offer a footing. Angus had marvelled at the men who had chiselled out by hand the holes for those pegs, hundreds of them up the cliff face; now I saw what he meant. The construction of this landing stage and steps was an extraordinary achievement of Victorian engineering. I couldn't bring myself to look down until I reached the top of the steps; from there, I could see the dinghy below, tossing in the sea. It was absurdly small. A steep path led to the narrow-gauge railway built to transport building materials for the lighthouse.

Up here on the slope of the island I could see the source of the delicate drifts of pink and white. On one side was a swathe of deep pink thrift, and on the other was a huge spread of white sea campion. We waded through the springy bushes, up to our knees in the delicate white flowers, the air heavy with their sweet scent. All around us the sea was glittering in the bright sunlight, and above our heads the sky was full of puffins. On the summit I sat down at the cairn, perched on a promontory of cliff, astonished by everything around me. I was in the middle of a puffin colony, full of the sound of their whirring wings and their chortling cries. They were indifferent to this visitor. It was like being in the middle of a busy motorway intersection. Puffins were barrelling through the sky in every direction, their wings beating furiously. Their flight was curiously ungainly. They can beat their wings up to four hundred times a minute; the enormous effort gave them a panicked appearance, as if they might fall out of the sky. Later when I suggested this to Stuart, he swiftly retorted that they had a unique mobility in both air and water, diving as deep as sixty metres.

I sat and watched these companions all around me. They had an air of purposefulness, flying at a huge pace like commuters trying to catch the 5.30 train. Then suddenly they would veer off, equally intent, in another direction. The sky was full of these birds and yet in this three-dimensional maze of movement, there were no collisions. The puffins had an astonishing awareness of space and movement, their own and everyone else's.

I've already applied several anthropomorphic attributes to these birds, and I'm not the first to do so. The puffin's genus name, Fratercula, derived from the Latin, means 'little brother'. Their smart black and white plumage resembles monastic robes. We like seeing our human characteristics reflected back at us in an animal species, and for that, puffins are popular birds. They have other attributes uncannily reminiscent of humans. They stand, chest puffed out, gazing out to sea like a proud sea captain with a hint of the pompous and self-satisfied. With good reason, Stuart might have added. They are remarkably adapted to their environment; their hinged beaks can carry dozens of sand eels and small fish (the record is sixty-seven) on their long flights to catch food, saving on return trips to the burrow.

Through binoculars, I studied the birds two metres away, the detail and striations of their red-orange beaks – the tips looked slightly dirty and battered, as if worn by the hard work of burrow digging and diving for food. Their bulging cheeks were a shiny satin, the colour of a caffè latte, with eyes set into a dark triangle. Their eyes can swivel 180 degrees, enabling them to see to the side and behind. That explained how they could navigate the busy skies above Eilean Mòr. We are very clumsy creatures in comparison, with limited sight, which means that we can only see what is in front of our eyes, only compensated for by the flexibility of our necks.

Walking down from the cairn, I picked my way through the cushions of pink thrift. Close to, the flowers' colour ranged from vivid pink to rust, and finally to pale coffee when dead. The ground under foot was sprung like a mattress, riddled with puffin burrows several feet deep. I worried that I had disturbed pufflings or their parents with my meandering. I was heading towards the stone structure attributed to the monk who had given his name, Flannan, to the isles. Like St Ronan, who stayed on Rona, further north, these remarkable Celtic islophiles have left their names as a persistent legacy. Martin Martin reported in 1697 that there were regular pilgrimages to the Flannans from the Western Isles to honour the monk's memory.

The ruins of Flannan's cell were stones balanced precariously in a domed structure. Gaps between the rocks, heavily coated in brilliant yellow lichen, showed glimpses of the dark blue of the sea below where the boat was anchored, a tiny spot of red. I sat on a rock at the doorway, puffins flying above and below me, breathing a heady mixture of smells: flower scent and the ammonia of bird shit and the salty air. The cries of gannets

broke through the hubbub of puffins as they headed over the sea towards the gannetry on the neighbouring island. It was a mesmerizing moment. From here, some ninety metres above sea level, the six other Flannan Isles and their many outcrops were laid before me in the expanse of sea. Below the water's comparatively shallow surface lay the seabed that had made the Flannans a single mass of land when the sea level was lower at the end of the last Ice Age. For the Celtic hermit who built this cell, the view was part of the extreme ascetic practice, comparable to the early Christian stylites who lived on pillars in the Near East in the fifth century CE. Flannan looked out to the horizon where he believed the world ended. He did not know what that end looked like, nor did he need to find out. He lived with it as a mystery he had no need to resolve. These Celtic monks were travellers without being explorers. They did not share our imperative to know and explain. Their quest was for a different kind of comprehension, into the nature of God and his salvation. For that, living in this harsh environment was entirely apposite, experiencing at close hand life's mystery and danger. What mystifies us, in contrast, is the belief which made men live lives of such deprivation on these lonely, weatherbeaten rocks.

The path back to the boat disappeared over the edge of the cliff. With eyes averted from the dizzying blue of sea and sky and fixed on each step, I made it across the sloping rock face, balancing on the iron pegs. From the landing stage it was an easy jump into the dinghy. The two ornithologists, both young women, seemed remarkably relaxed after their week tagging puffins; scientists like these were much too sensible to be daunted by the Flannans' reputation.

Before leaving Eilean Mòr, we swung into a deep cave, balancing in the dinghy as the waves swept us into the shade. The sunlight bounced off the cave's roof and pierced the clear water, turning it the colour of pale green opals. Looking down, I could see thousands of tiny jellyfish glinting with flecks of brilliant green and trailing delicate tendrils. The water slapped at the cave's sides and the boom of the swell sounded like a bellowing from the heart of the island.

Back on the catamaran, we circled around the westernmost islands and their stacks. It was a wild place, where waves crashed on the shattered rocks and where hundreds of seals basked in the sun, their fur a bleached brown. They seemed astonished at our arrival and, one by one, rolled their cumbersome weight into the sea. From there, they viewed us suspiciously, bobbing up and down to watch our progress. We were outlandish interlopers in their world. The gannets, kittiwakes and cormorants whirled around our heads, in skies thick with the inhabitants of the stacks' colonies. This outpost of Europe was intense with life.

Later in the afternoon, back on Harris, I was still rising and falling with the swell of the boat. Getting into a car to drive over a smooth road surface put my body into another plane of motion. It was not just the movement that had left me disorientated; it was a day of such vastness that it seemed to have hollowed me out. The Scottish writer Nan Shepherd said of the Cairngorm mountains she walked: 'the mind cannot carry away all that it [the mountain] has to give nor does it always believe possible what it has carried away'.

I had had a conversation a few days before with a photographer living in Harris, who explained her interest in edges. Horizons were a matter of our perception, she pointed out; the edges I had been witnessing all day – of land, of sea, of sky – were no more than tricks of the eye, yet we lean so heavily on the line of a hill or the outline of an island to give shape and form. At the edge of the pictures by the artist Vija Celmins, the texture of the medium is exposed, and the grains of charcoal or pastel are clear, so that the edge becomes a place of exposure. Perhaps the Celtic monks understood this: that at the edge certain illusions wear thin and something fundamental about the stuff of life becomes evident.

It was partly the sheer indifference of the natural elements to human endeavour. Our projects and preoccupations shrink against their huge scale. But there was something else which now gave the visit to the Flannan Isles a hallucinatory quality: the delicate abundance of an island of flowers which, for a few weeks and on a few days, takes on an unearthly radiance at odds with all the months when it was lashed by fierce storms, and turfs are ripped from the rock and boulders thrown against the cliffs.

Later, driving back to my tent in the dunes at Horgabost on Harris, I pulled over and walked across a field to lie down on the rocks by the sea, to try and ground this dizzy euphoria. The rock was warm from the heat of the sun, and above me the oystercatchers and terns were circling, shrieking with alarm at my presence. The sun caught the white wings of the elegant tern as it swooped and dived. Deep into that blue sky I thought of two of my children, who were crossing the Atlantic high in the air above to attend a wedding. I thought of them sitting in their cramped airline seats, watching films, eating their little containers of airline food, perhaps catching a brief glimpse of the ocean below, not giving it a thought. I have done it myself many times, but in our flattening and shrinking of the world we have short-changed ourselves, and reduced our capacity for wonder rather than cultivated it. I was struck by the power of that urge to share, out of which both children were created, and out of which they were now finding their own lives. I was acutely aware that their wellbeing and safety was entirely dependent on thousands of people whose names I would never know, on the millions of small decisions and interactions of millions of other human beings. At this particular moment, their lives rested on the actions of ordinary people going about their day's work: baggage handlers, airport security, air-traffic control, cooks, cleaners, taxi drivers. We live in the trust of others. 'On the pilgrimage route, as in life, all we can do is trust,' wrote the American philosopher

William James. I was overwhelmed by the sheer wonder of it all, and grateful for the astonishing moment of benediction.

A few months later I returned to Lewis and headed beyond Uig to explore that rugged south-west coastline where the mountains come down to the sea and have been smashed into pieces – scattered stacks and rocks – by the rough tides. The Scottish referendum had come and gone, the Labour hold on Scotland had crumbled ignominiously in the 2015 general election, and the Scottish National Party was poised for further electoral triumph in 2016. These islands were still part of Britain, but there was no sense of resolution; a second referendum seemed only a matter of time. The ground was still shifting. I camped on the cliffs above Mangursta and fell asleep to the sound of waves crashing on the stacks below. I breakfasted with gannets, watching their spectacular dives, one after another, as they plummeted into the sea, and in the evening I dodged clouds of midges to marvel at the blazing sun setting behind the Flannans. The slightest breeze brought instant relief from their sharp bites; as an islander commented with a wry smile, 'We don't know where they all come from and we don't know where they all go.'

The following day the rain closed in while I climbed Mealaisbhal ('Njall's Mountain' in Norse), which overlooks Uig's sands. As I clambered up the grey rocks and reached the top, the curtains of rain parted and I glimpsed St Kilda rearing improbably large on the horizon to the west. From the mountain's summit the curve of the earth was negated, and the majesty of the extraordinary cliffs and stacks was revealed in silhouette against the sheen of the sea in the weak sun. Just to the north lay the more modest, rounded forms of the Flannans. To the south lay the journey I had travelled over the last few years. In the far distance the white beaches of Berneray and North Uist gleamed. The view was exhilarating, demanding so much of the imagination and offering a pregnant sense of the possibilities of life. As the rain drifted past, islands and mountains appeared and disappeared; the mist wrapped around me as I ducked down between wet boulders to wait for another clearing before the descent.

It had indeed proved to be a pilgrimage. I had arrived at the north-west, and it had had much to tell. Of empires, of appropriation and resistance, and how, within these politics, we may inherit or make a home, and (if we are lucky) a narrative of belonging and loyalty. This spread of Hebridean islands was not my home, but in the phrase of the Irish Gaelic poet Liam Ó Muirthile, they had proved to be a 'soul territory', speaking of histories in which, for good and ill, I stand. These histories have formed the dense weave of attachments across the British archipelago from which we now search for new definitions of nation to express and inspire human solidarity. On this edge, I see that where the weave of relationship and story frays, the filaments are exposed as fragile, whisper-thin.

Notes

I am deeply indebted to a rich literature and in these notes indicate sources for further reading.

1 Taking bearings

p. 7   '*The North was where...*' John Buchan's comment is cited in *The Idea of North* by Peter Davidson, a richly thought-provoking book (Davidson kindly explored some further points in a subsequent email correspondence). Many cultures attach huge cosmic significance to directions; curator Joanne Pilsbury of the Metropolitan Museum of Art in New York explained to me how the Aztecs saw the four directions as gods; the north was ruled by the god of fate, destiny and night.

p. 7   '*One must have a proper moral sense...*' W. H. Auden's comment is from the American edition of *Vogue*, 1954.

p. 8   '*Years before I ever went there...*' is from an article in *House and Garden*, 1947, cited in *W. H. Auden: Pennine Poet* by Alan Myers and Robert Forsythe. The latter gives an account of Auden's teenage visit to Rookhope in the North Pennines and its life-long impact on him; he had a map of it on the wall of his later home in America and wrote in his poem *Amor Loci* of how he could draw its map.

p. 13   '*The clue to many contrasts ...*' Halford Mackinder's comment is cited in Christopher Harvie's stimulating exploration of the subject, *A Floating Commonwealth*.

p. 14   '*Tradition divides Britain diagonally* . . .' Many have speculated on this north/west and south/east division but my favourite theory is that of my A-Level English teacher, Mr J. Smithies. He maintained that matches had blue heads or pink heads depending on which side of Britain's traditional divide (between the north-west and the south-east) you bought them. For most of one memorable lesson he explained how he tried to plot the boundary. At one shop which straddled the boundary, the counter ran north-west to south-east. To his immense satisfaction, one end of the counter had the blue-headed matches and the other had the pink.

p. 14   '*Celtic was the term* . . .' 'Celtic' is a notoriously vague term which has been used throughout European history to denote the uncivilized 'other'. The Greeks used it of their northern neighbours in central Europe; the Romans used it for a tribe in Gaul. The term is always used for a purpose, claims Neil MacGregor in his introduction to the British Museum's catalogue for their 2015 exhibition *The Celts*. It was the Welshman Edward Lhuyd who first applied the term to this Atlantic seaboard when he described as 'Celtic' two related families of languages, the Brythonic (Welsh, Manx and Cornish) and the Goidelic (Scottish and Irish Gaelic), in his *Archaeologia Britannica: An Account of the Languages, Histories and Customs of Great Britain*, published in 1707, the same year as the Act of Union; his work did much to shape the imagined geography of the new nation.

p. 14   '*It was "imprecise"* . . .' Murray Pittock, *Celtic Identity and the British Image*.

p. 14   '*a projection, a construct* . . .' Malcolm Chapman, *The Gaelic Vision in Scottish Culture*.

p. 15   '*Britishness – as an idea* . . .' Stephen Marche, the *Guardian*, 18 September 2014.

p. 15   '*The new and spurious* . . .' John MacCormick, *The Flag in the Wind*.

p. 16   '*The aim of knowledge* . . .' Cited in *Hegel's Grand Synthesis: A Study of Being, Thought and History* by Daniel Berthold-Bond, 1989, State of New York University Press.

p. 18   '*I never felt* ...' From an unpublished speech Saul Bellow delivered on 10 June 1984 in Lachine, Quebec, now at the Regenstein Library at the University of Chicago.

p. 19   '*imagined communities* ...' From Benedict Anderson, *Imagined Communities: Reflections on the Origins and Spread of Nationalism.*

p. 20   '*Beneath that lay* ...' From *Britons: Forging the Nation 1707–1837* by Linda Colley.

p. 22   '*the Scottish nationalist* ...' Tom Nairn, *After Britain: New Labour and the Return of Scotland.*

p. 22   '"*The West of Ireland*" ...' From Louis MacNeice's *The Strings are False.*

p. 23   '*I went to the Hebrides* ...', '*I am very sorry* ...' and '*I thought* ...' From *I Crossed the Minch* by Louis MacNeice.

p. 26   '*It is ironic* ...' Hugh MacDiarmid, *The Islands of Scotland.*

2 Jura

p. 36   '*The writer Kathleen Jamie* ...' Cited in *The Spirit of Jura.*

p. 36   '*270 named islands* ...' There are many different ways to count islands and measure coastlines. These figures are from J. M. Boyd's *A Habitable Land.* See also *The Scottish Islands* by Hamish Haswell-Smith.

p. 39   '*Greg Coffey* ...' See the *Observer,* 21 October 2012.

p. 40   '*he is not even the first millionaire* ...' Author and campaigner Andy Wightman keeps a close eye on the buying and selling of land in the Highlands and Islands on his *Land Matters* blog at www.andywightman.com.

p. 41   '*Orwell was enraptured* ...' From *The Collected Essays, Journalism and Letters of George Orwell.*

p. 42   '*As one clergyman* ...' Cited in Linda Colley's *Britons.*

p. 42   '*It inspired his riposte* ...' David Cameron's statement is quoted by Patrick Wintour in the *Guardian,* 6 September 2013: 'Britain is an island that has helped clear the European continent of fascism and was resolute in doing that throughout the Second World War. Britain is an island that helped abolish slavery that has invented most of the things worth inventing, including every sport currently played around the world, that still today is responsible for art, literature and music that delights the entire world. We are very proud of everything we do as a small island – a small island that has the sixth largest economy, the fourth best funded military, some of the most effective diplomats, the proudest history, one of the best records for art and literature and contribution to philosophy and world civilization.' Cameron then adds the comment quoted.

p. 43   *'Such are the tangles ... our politicians'* It is not just politicians and authors who get muddled; for a fascinating discussion of the nomenclature of Great Britain see the introduction (pp. xxviii–xxxvii) to Norman Davies' history *The Isles* (Macmillan, 1999). He points out the confusion of the library cataloguing systems of both Britain and the USA, whereby a search under 'the UK' brings up no works of history, but under 'Great Britain' brings up 641; a search under 'England' cross references back to 'Great Britain' and shows exactly the same tally of 641.

p. 43   *'John Donne warned ...'* Meditation XVII, *Devotions Upon Emergent Occasions.*

p. 44   *'Literary critic Peter Conrad ...'* For further discussion of the island theme in British history see Conrad's stimulating book, *Islands.*

p. 46   *'Islands we beheld in plenty ...'* From Robert Louis Stevenson, *Collected Memoirs, Travel Sketches and Island Literature,* e-artnow, 2015.

p. 46   *'The claiming of Rockall ... 1982'* See Andy Wightman's *The Poor Had No Lawyers* for the extraordinary account.

p. 49   *'Mackenzie was part of an exodus ...'* This is well described by Paul Fussell in *Abroad: British Literary Traveling Between the Wars.*

p. 51   *'The islands inspired a wealth of books ...'* One of the most influential is Neil Gunn's *Off in a Boat* (1938). Others include: *Across Hebridean Seas* (1937), *Hebridean Lore and Romance* (1937), *The Islands of Scotland* (1939), *Hebridean Journey* (1929), *The Book of Barra* (1936).

p. 53   *'writers turned their travels ... '* Sam Hynes is cited by Paul Fussell in *Abroad*.

p. 53   *'these places are symbols of freedom ...'* From Gavin Maxwell's foreword to *Ring of Bright Water*.

p. 53   *'His record as an environmentalist ...'* Contrary to his reputation as a conservationist, Maxwell's first venture in the Hebrides was a brutal whaling business on the island of Soay. It failed. See a vivid account of a troubled man's life in Douglas Botting's *The Saga of Ring of Bright Water*.

p. 54   *'I have two copies ...'* Cited in Douglas Botting, *The Saga of Ring of Bright Water*.

p. 54   *'A new generation of writers ...'* This includes Adam Nicolson, who wrote about the Shiants, the islands he inherited, which had once been owned by Compton Mackenzie, in *Sea Room*, a book brimming with Britain's island tradition, with nods to Crusoe and Maxwell among many others.

p. 54   *'I like islands ...'* Will Self, 'Inching Along the Edge of the World', *New York Times*, 27 November 2000.

p. 54   *'there remains a part of me ...'* 'Will Self on Charles Maclean's *St Kilda*', *New Statesman*, 27 November 2000

p. 55   *'For Kathleen Jamie and Robert Macfarlane ...'* Kathleen Jamie has written two superb collections of essays which include several on the Hebrides, *Sightlines* and *Findings*. Robert Macfarlane's work on the Western Isles in *Wild Places* and *The Old Ways: A Journey on Foot* has justifiably received great acclaim.

p. 57   *'This was where we stopped ...'* For details of Orwell's stay on Jura, see Gordon Bowker's biography, *George Orwell*, and *George Orwell: A Life in Letters*.

p. 66   *'The poet Robin Robertson ...'* 'Corryvreckan' is in Robertson's collection *Hill of Doors*, Picador, 2013.

3 Iona

p. 71   *'A thin place ...'* Cited by Ron Ferguson in his biography, *George MacLeod: Founder of the Iona Community*.

p. 77   *'Scientists have described ...'* See J. M. Boyd, *A Habitable Land*.

p. 77   '*The Atlantic had been richly mythologized* ...' See Barry Cunliffe's magnificent *Facing the Ocean*, which cites Hesiod, Al Idrisi and Pindar.

p. 79   '*The Christian monks arrived on Iona* ...' See Ian Bradley, *Columba: Pilgrim and Penitent*, and Adomnán, *Life of St Columba*.

p. 84   '*This rock was used to build* ...' See www.buildingconservation. com/articles/rockofages/rockofages.htm (retrieved 11/11/15).

p. 85   '*the inimitable seaside brightness* ...' From 'Memoirs of an Islet' in *Memories and Portraits, The Complete Works of Robert Louis Stevenson*, Delphi Classics, 2015.

p. 86   '*The most powerful evidence* ...' See Bernard Meehan, *The Book of Kells*, a stunning tribute to this extraordinary work of art.

p. 90   '*Various books in the genre* ...' The well-stocked Iona Community bookshop gives a taste of the varied contemporary interpretations of Celtic Christianity, which include work by the Irish poet and writer John O'Donohue (*Anam Cara* was an international bestseller), among many others. One author, the theologian Ian Bradley, acknowledged in a telephone conversation that his own understanding of Celtic Christianity had been greatly challenged and subsequently influenced by the critique of Donald Meek.

p. 90   '*The romantic repossession* ...' See Donald Meek, *The Quest for Celtic Christianity*.

p. 92   '*More than anyone, George MacLeod* ...' Ron Ferguson's biography is an engrossing study of a complex man.

p. 94   '*A small copy of one of the great Iona crosses* ...' People often attribute the start of an association with Iona to an object carved with Celtic designs: the gift of a cross, piece of jewellery or a picture. My Scottish family holidays as a child owed their origin to the Celtic memorial cross my father, a sculptor, carved and installed in the Croick graveyard. He was partly paid in free holidays for the family on the estate's croft.

p. 98   '*In an important speech* ...' John Smith's speech is available online at www.johnsmithmemorialtrust.org/media/63970/ Reclaiming-the-Ground.pdf (retrieved 11/11/15).

4 Staffa

p. 105   *'We saw, but surely …'* Wordsworth, Sonnet XXVI, 'Cave of Staffa'.

p. 107   *'One early traveller reported …'* L. A. Necker de Saussure in his *Travels in Scotland* (1821).

p. 108   *'Compared to this …'* Joseph Banks, *Journal of a Voyage* (1772).

p. 111   *'Macpherson's work provoked fierce controversy …'* There is a vast literature on the Ossianic controversy. A turning point was the publication of Derick S. Thomson's *The Gaelic Sources of Macpherson's 'Ossian'* in 1952. Fiona Stafford's *Sublime Savage* (1988) is widely respected for its balanced assessment of Macpherson, but the debate goes on, as evidenced in the recent publication of *Samuel Johnson, the Ossian Fraud and the Celtic Revival in Great Britain and Ireland* by Thomas M. Curley. James Mulholland in the *Journal of Oral Tradition*, 24 February 2009, pp. 393–414, explores how as print became dominant in the eighteenth century, it distinguished itself from the oral tradition in a binary linked to other binaries such as civilized/uncivilized. See also discussions of the controversy in James Hunter's *The Other Side of Sorrow* and Murray Pittock's *Celtic Identity and the British Image*.

p. 112   *'Caves have long been …'* Ted Nield has written evocatively on caves in the Western imagination in *Underlands*.

p. 116   *'It was oddly enfeebling …'* Malcolm Andrews made the comment in a conversation; see also his fascinating book, *In Search of the Picturesque*.

p. 116   *'Cliffs of darkness …'* From 'Lines Addressed to Ranald Macdonald, Esq., of Staffa' in *The Poetical Works of Sir Walter Scott*, Vol. 10 (Oxford, 1913).

p. 117   *'It was impossible to describe it …'* From *Keats: Selected Poems and Letters*, edited by Robert Gittings (Heinemann, 1995). See also Andrew Motion's biography, *Keats*, for a vivid account of his visit.

p. 118   *'Thomas Gray recommended …'* Cited in Malcolm Andrews, *In Search of the Picturesque*.

p. 119   *'Britain was not alone in projecting …'* Neal Ascherson explores this idea in his history, *The Black Sea: Coasts and Conquests* (Vintage, 2007).

p. 119 '*The most animating and lofty ideas ...*' Cited in Malcolm Andrews, *In Search of the Picturesque.*

p. 120 '*The artist who captured ...*' In 2014 a major exhibition, *Turner and the Sea*, at London's National Maritime Museum included *Staffa, Fingal's Cave* on loan from Yale, which enabled me to study the painting closely for my interpretation.

p. 121 '*In order to make you understand ...*' Mendelssohn's letter to his family is quoted in *Mendelssohn: Essays* by R. Larry Todd (Routledge, 2007). Fingal's Cave is widely credited with inspiring Mendelssohn but Todd suggests that it was more generally his visit to the Hebrides. (See www.mendelssohninscotland. com for wonderful background on the composer's visit to Staffa, including a copy of the vivid letter written by his travelling companion, Karl Klingemann.)

p. 123 'Staffa *was bought, unseen ...*' For the impact of the painting in the US, see Christine Riding and Richard Johns, *Turner and the Sea*.

p. 125 '*This was an imaginative construction ...*' For a discussion of Romanticism, see Jonathan Bate, *The Song of the Earth*; for how this applied in Scotland, see James Hunter, *The Other Side of Sorrow*, Malcolm Chapman, *The Gaelic Vision in Scottish Culture*, and Peter Womack, *Improvement and Romance*. Womack argues that capitalism is a geographical phenomenon and entails a 'hierarchisation of space'; in the case of Britain, that hierarchy ensured a peripheralization of the Highlands as a myth which combined themes such as imagination, superstition, vision, poetry and holiday. 'Even those who seek to uphold its interests ... found that they were doing so in the glowing and reverent language which ratifies its oppression.' Womack highlights the preoccupation with trees and how they came to represent the 'landlord's signature on the land'.

p. 125 '*One traveller to the Highlands, John Dalrymple ...*' *An Essay on Landscape Gardening* (Greenwich, 1823).

p. 126 '*some of Gaelic's most eminent poets ...*' The most prominent example would be Alasdair mac Mhaighstir Alasdair

(1698–1770), who is regarded as the finest Gaelic poet of the eighteenth century. He was also Gaelic tutor to Charles Stuart. A collection of his poetry was published as *The Resurrection of the Ancient Scottish Language* in 1751.

p. 127 '*The Scottish Gael* ...' Malcolm Chapman, *The Gaelic Vision in Scottish Culture.*

p. 127 '*Britain exported* ...' See T. M. Devine, *The Scottish Nation 1700–2007.*

5 Rum

p. 131 '*we think place is about space* ...' From Rebecca Solnit, *The Faraway Nearby*. Her writing has been a huge influence; see also *A Book of Migrations* and *Wanderlust*, Granta, 2014.

p. 135 '*There is a great deal* ...' John MacCulloch was a pioneering geologist and wrote *A Description of the Western Islands of Scotland, Including the Isle of Man* (1819).

p. 141 '*Rum is the site* ...' For more on the prehistory of the Hebrides, see one archaeologist's account of his fascination with the region, *To the Islands*, by Steven Mithen (Two Ravens Press, 2010).

p. 142 '*The long history* ...' John Love, a former warden on the island, has written the definitive history: *Rum: A Landscape Without Figures*. See also Magnus Magnusson, *Rum: Nature's Island.*

p. 143 '*This painful conclusion* ...' There is a large literature on the Clearances, including T. M. Devine's *The Scottish Nation 1700–2007* and *Clanship to Crofters' War*; James Hunter's *The Making of the Crofting Community* and *The Other Side of Sorrow.*

p. 148 '*essential belief* ...' Andro Linklater's fascinating book *Owning the Earth* was published posthumously after he fell ill on a visit to Eigg.

p. 149 '*These ideas also transformed rural England* ...' English enclosure was the subject of lamentation in the poetry of Northamptonshire-born John Clare.

p. 154 '*He bought Rum* ...' Alastair Scott's *Eccentric Wealth* offers rich detail on this strange chapter in Rum's history.

p. 161 '*Accrington's working classes* ...' Accrington, now part of

Hyndburn, is twenty-eighth out of 326 districts in England in the *English Indices of Deprivation 2015*.

p. 161   *'On a walk early ...'* Since my visit there have been improvements thanks to donations from the Pilgrim Trust, amongst others. It is now called the Tigh Iain Dhonnchaidh, Cleadale Crofting Museum at Croft No. 6.

p. 164   *'Our practical comprehensive knowledge ...'* Yet there were no predators of deer on Rum, so the research experiment made little sense from the start.

p. 165   *'the castle has become ...'* In 2003 Rum was the subject of an episode of the BBC television series *Restoration*.

p. 165   *'Tons of this soft wet moss ...'* There is a wonderful account of the gathering of sphagnum, first in Scotland and then in uplands throughout Britain in the First World War at www.rbg-web2, thanks to the initiative of an Edinburgh-based surgeon. Sphagnum absorbs twenty times its own volume in liquid and promotes antisepsis. These islands and uplands are literally salvific.

p. 166   *'the most stupendous succession ...'* Sir Archibald Geikie, *The Ancient Volcanoes of Great Britain*, Vol. 2 (Macmillan, 1897).

p. 167   *'At night they return ...'* A recording of the shearwater can be found on the British Library Sound Archive, www.sounds.bl.uk.

6 Eriskay

p. 175   *'The most imposing ...'* Our Lady of the Isles was carved by Scottish sculptor Hew Lorimer, to whom Peter Davidson first drew my attention. He also did the carvings on the façade of the National Library of Scotland.

p. 179   *'Below spread a magnificent stretch ...'* There is a large literature on the Jacobite rebellion. T. M. Devine's *The Scottish Nation 1700–2007* is a good starting point. I drew on Christopher Duffy's *The '45*; essays by Allan MacInnes and Hugh Cheape in *Jacobitism and the '45*, edited by Michael Lynch; and Murray Pittock's *Jacobitism*.

p. 182   *'George MacLeod, the founder ...'* See Ron Ferguson, *George MacLeod: Founder of the Iona Community*.

p. 183   '*one of the historians of the period* ...' Hugh Cheape in *Jacobitism and the '45*, edited by Michael Lynch.

p. 186   '*the great English historian* ...' G. M. Trevelyan, *History of England* (1926). In *G. M. Trevelyan: A Life in History* (1992) David Cannadine writes, 'For fifty years, Trevelyan acted as a public moralist, public teacher and public benefactor, wielding unchallenged cultural authority.'

p. 190   '*One of the first to gather* ...' See Campbell's introduction to his collection, *Popular Tales of the West Highlands by J. F. Campbell of Islay* (1860–62).

p. 191   '*Busy and prosperous island fishing* ...' See James Hunter, *The Other Side of Sorrow*; Peter Womack, *Improvement and Romance*.

p. 191   '*This renewed fascination* ...' See Ernest Renan, *What is a Nation?* Also Matthew Arnold, *On the Study of Celtic Literature*.

p. 192   '*The projection onto the distant north-west* ...' Malcolm Chapman, *The Gaelic Vision in Scottish Culture*.

p. 192   '*A handsome, charismatic* ...' Roger Hutchinson has written a detailed biography of this remarkable man, *Father Allan*. See also *Strange Things* by John Campbell and Trevor Hall.

p. 192   '*A bird with a terrible* ...' From Father Allan's notes, reprinted in *Strange Things*.

p. 194   '*In 1895 Goodrich-Freer* ...' In a further curious twist the Society for Psychical Research had a close relationship with the beginnings of the Fabian Society. Several dedicated researchers for the society, such as Frank Podmore (an associate of Freer), were instrumental in setting up the latter. At this early stage of incubation, an interest in the paranormal and an interest in planning industrial society to achieve greater welfare seem to have been connected.

p. 197   '*John Lorne Campbell reflected* ...' Cited in Malcolm Chapman, *The Gaelic Vision in Scottish Culture*.

p. 197   Womack's conclusion to his book *Improvement and Romance* succinctly captures the dilemma of those who study the Highlands and Islands, 'seeing the myth's implicit colonialism, its cooption by militarism ... the vulgarities and duplicity of its products ... we reach for the hatchet of the demystifier ... yet we pause for the possibility which the myth cherishes and deforms ... that we can discover an authentic way of living'.

7 Lewis

p. 205   '*In Lochmaddy's art centre* ...' For more information on Vija Celmins' work, see www.tate.org.uk/art/artists/ vija-celmins–2731.

p. 209   '*Yet a harsh history has left its legacy* ...' The shockingly high rates of fuel poverty are rising (70 per cent of households in 2013/14) due to a combination of low incomes, poorly insulated homes and high fuel costs. See www.cne-siar.gov.uk (reprot of 6 June 2014, retrieved October 2015).

p. 209   '*It has some of the highest rates of church going* ...' Donald Trump, the American property developer and US presidential candidate in 2016, is the son of a Leòdhasach mother; in talking about his background, he summed up the island as 'serious Scotland'.

p. 209   '*dominated by a number of strict Presbyterian* ...' The Free Church (pejoratively referred to as the Wee Frees) emerged from a remarkable episode in Scottish history, the Great Disruption of 1843, when a significant proportion of the clergy of the Church of Scotland walked out of the Kirk's General Assembly, losing their homes and churches, in protest at the power of landed patronage in church appointments.

p. 210   '*his poetry and prose informed by* ...' See Matthew McGuire's introduction to Iain Crichton Smith's *New Collected Poems*. A couple of early readers questioned my emphasis on the work of Crichton Smith rather than the widely admired Raasay-born Sorley MacLean, or other respected Leòdhasaich poets such as Derick Thomson or Donald MacAulay, who were more sympathetic to the island. I suspect the appeal lies in part in that sense of displacement in Crichton Smith's work and in the recognition that, while he was very critical of the Presbyterian Christianity with which he was brought up, it 'has been internalized in me ... and its dilemmas will always be with me'. The poet Edwin Morgan writes, 'things that restrict and stifle have always been Smith's target,' in his essay in *ScotLit*, 23, Winter 2000.

p. 210   *'On the shore at Timsgearraidh ...'* My thanks to Malkie Maclean for his account of the graveyard story on a snowy winter walk.

p. 211   *'Arthur Ransome ...'* He is believed to have set the last of the twelve-volume *Swallows and Amazons* series, *The Great Northern?* (1947), in Uig.

p. 211   *'Historians have pieced ...'* See *The Lewis Chessmen* by James Robinson (British Museum Press, 2004) and *The Lewis Chessmen Unmasked* by David H. Caldwell, Mark A. Hall and Caroline M. Wilkinson (National Museums Scotland, 2010). Also *The Vikings in Lewis* by Brittany Schorn and Judy Quinn, available online from the Centre for the Study of the Viking Age, Nottingham University www.nottingham.ac.uk/research/groups/csva/documents/lmfpublications/lmf2-isleoflewis,the-vikingsinlewis.pdf.

p. 212   *'The Norse (also known as Vikings) ...'* In 1156 this multi-ethnic culture of Gael and Norse led to Somerled's powerful Kingdom of the Isles, which ruled the Hebrides and much of Scotland's west coast, including Ardnamurchan and Kintyre, until its effective demise in 1493. Its power lay in its seamanship (evoked in the beautiful carvings of galleys on the tomb in Rodel church in south Harris). Somerled's dynasty, based in Islay, instituted the Council of the Isles. The title Lord of the Isles is now held by Prince Charles, as male heir to the British throne.

p. 214   *'an assemblage of elves or gnomes ...'* From Daniel Wilson, *The Archaeology and Prehistoric Annals of Scotland* (1851).

p. 215   *'Matters became even more complicated ...'* On Iceland's claim to the chessmen, see 'The Enigma of the Lewis Chessmen' at www.en.chessbase.com/post/the-enigma-of-the-lewis-chemen (retrieved 11 November 2015); for the Norwegian response, see www.en.chessbase.com. Also see the *Daily Telegraph*, www.telegraph.co.uk/culture/culturenews/7994966/Iceland-now-claim-they-made-Lewis-Chessmen.html.

p. 219   *'In this reading of Scotland's record ...'* Malkie Maclean's point was echoed in some of the reservations I heard expressed by islanders towards independence. The No vote won in the Western Isles, but by 53 per cent to 47 per cent, a narrower margin than the national vote.

p. 220   *'Crichton Smith describes growing up ...'* The quotes are from his collection of essays, *Towards the Human.*

p. 223   *'Gaelic scholar Michael Newton ...'* From *Warriors of the Word.* See also *At the Edge* by Joseph Murphy; A. Fiona D. Mackenzie, 'The Cheviot, The Stag ... and The White, White Rock?: Community, Identity and the Environmental Threat on the Isle of Harris', in *Environment and Planning D: Society and Space*, 1998, Vol. 16, pp. 509–32; A. Fiona D. Mackenzie, 'Reclaiming Place', pp. 535–60. Another helpful perspective from Ireland is John Tomaney, 'Parish and Universe: Patrick Kavanagh's Poetics of the Local', *Environment and Planning D: Society and Space*, 2010, Vol. 28, No 2.

p. 224   *'Gaelic's attentiveness to place ...'* See John Murray, *Reading the Gaelic Landscape: Leughadh Aghaidh na Tìre.*

p. 224   *'The ideal is to maintain ...'* The striking South Uist saying, 'Eat bread ...', comes from *The Silent Weaver: The Extraordinary Life and Work of Angus MacPhee* by Roger Hutchinson (Birlinn, 2011), the remarkable account of an islander traumatized by enlisting in the Second World War, who spent his life in an asylum in Inverness and turned to weaving a variety of found materials such as grass. There are examples of his work in the Kildonan Museum, South Uist.

p. 226   *'Crichton Smith points to the word* cliù *...'* Iain Crichton Smith, *Towards the Human.*

p. 227   *'Lewis had the highest proportion ...'* There is further information on several local history websites, including www. HebrideanConnections.com and www.ceats.org.uk, the West Side Historical Society (Comann Eachdraidh an Taobh). The anniversary of the First World War was marked in 2014 by a major exhibition in Stornoway.

p. 229   *'A ship heavily packed ...'* See John Macleod, *When I Heard the Bell: The Loss of the Iolaire.*

p. 231   *'The islander ...'* See Crichton Smith, *Towards the Human.*

p. 231   *'forty million people …'* This figure is cited in *Road to Independence* by Murray Pittock. See also T. M. Devine, *To the Ends of the Earth: Scotland's Global Diaspora 1750–2010*. For an account of the impact on the Hebrides see *Island Emigrants*, published by the Islands Book Trust.

p. 237   *'It is a remarkable epitaph …'* For more on Matheson, see *Opium and Empire* by Richard J. Grace. Also, an intriguing history on the company's website, www.jardines.com/the-group/history. html.

p. 238   *'Of all the eccentrics …'* See two fascinating accounts: *The Soap Man: Lewis, Harris and Lord Leverhulme* by Roger Hutchinson, and *So Clean: Lord Leverhulme, Soap and Civilisation* by Brian Lewis.

p. 243   *'wild land map of Scotland …'* Scottish Natural Heritage, June 2014, www.snh.gov.uk.

p. 243   'William Harcourt …' The Home Secretary helped persuade Gladstone to set up the Napier Commission, which gathered evidence from across the Highlands and Islands of the people's experience of the Clearances. The influential report was published in 1884.

p. 243   *'At Baile Ailein …'* The distinguished Scottish artist Will Maclean has designed all four of the monuments on Lewis (the other three are at Suileachan, Aignish and Griais), and they were built by stonemason Jim Crawford. See www.art-first.co.uk/will_maclean/installations.html. For more on the Crofters' War see T. M. Devine, *Clanship to Crofters' War*, and, more specifically, *The Lewis Land Struggle* by Joni Buchanan.

p. 245   *'Two thirds of Hebrideans …'* For more on community ownership, see Community Land Scotland, www.community-landscotland.org.uk, and Andy Wightman's blog, *Land Matters*, www.andywightman.com.

p. 246   *'For Agnes, language …'* Joseph Murphy explores this issue in *At the Edge: Walking the Atlantic Coast of Ireland and Scotland*.

p. 246   *'sustainable rural development …'* See Frank Rennie, 'Human Ecology and Concepts of Sustainable Development in a Crofting Township', *Folk Life* (*Journal of Ethnology*), 2008, Vol. 46.

p. 247   'In a dramatic example …' Robert Macfarlane has written in detail of the islanders' relationship with the moor, in *Landmarks* (Hamish Hamilton, 2015) and *The Old Ways*.

p. 248 *'The response to the Lewis wind-farm project...'* See A. Fiona D. Mackenzie, 'The Cheviot, The Stag... and The White, White Rock?: Community, Identity and the Environmental Threat on the Isle of Harris', in *Environment and Planning D: Society and Space*, 1998, Vol. 16; Alastair McIntosh's rousing *Soil and Soul*; and 'Gifted Places: The Inalienable Nature of Belonging in Place' by Julia Bennett.

p. 249 *'geography which struggled...'* From Edward Said, *Culture and Imperialism* (Alfred A. Knopf, 1993). See also Jane Jacobs' *The Edge of Empire* (Psychology Press, 1996), which cites Said's comment that empires could not have been 'without important philosophical and imaginative processes at work in the production... acquisition, subordination and settlement of space'.

p. 249 *'In their campaign to rally...'* The Gaelic word *còraichean* in the *Essential Gaelic Dictionary* carries ethical associations of what is right, and a sense of obligation, privilege and claim as well as 'rights'.

p. 249 *'More battles lie head...'* See Joseph Murphy, 'Understanding Transition-Periphery Dynamics: Renewable Energy in the Highlands and Islands of Scotland', *Environment and Planning A*, 2013, Vol. 45, pp. 691–709.

p. 250 *'That conflict is perfectly illustrated...'* For more on GIS, see www.engineerlive.com/content/22779.

p. 250 *'This is the placelessness...'* See Arturo Escobar, 'Culture Sits in Places: Reflections on Globalism and Subaltern Strategies of Localization', *Political Geography*, 2001, Vol. 20, pp. 139–74.

p. 250 *'elites are cosmopolitan...'* Manuel Castells, *The Rise of the Network Society*, (Blackwell, 1996).

p. 251 *'The historic role of capitalism itself...'* John Berger, *Pig Earth* (Writers and Readers, 1987).

p. 251 *'I see in Britain...'* From Crichton Smith, *Towards the Human*.

p. 253 *'this tangle is the texture...'* From Tim Ingold, *Being Alive* (Routledge, 2011).

8 St Kilda

p. 259   *'Back in Leverburgh ...'* Some of John Maher's photographs can be seen (and bought) at www.theflyingmonk.co.uk.

p. 260   *'the present order ...'* These words have been carved into rocks placed on a hill at Little Sparta, the garden of the artist Ian Hamilton Finlay in the Pentlands, near Edinburgh.

p. 261   *'Looking across the grey choppy Atlantic ...'* Angus Campbell has won the affection and admiration of many of those who take his boat out to St Kilda, www.kildacruises.co.uk.

p. 267   *'George Seton quoted ...'* Of the hundreds of books on St Kilda, George Seton's *St Kilda* is still one of the most comprehensive.

p. 267   *'I visited several ...'* There are exhibitions at Lochmaddy in North Uist, an extensive collection of documents and videos at Seallam!, in Harris, and some artefacts in Kildonan, South Uist. Progress on the new centre at Mangursta, Ionad Hiort, can be found at www.ionadhiort.org.uk.

p. 267   *'At last I caught sight ...'* Quoted in J. Kennedy, *The Apostle of the North: The Life and Labours of the Rev Dr Macdonald* (Nelson, 1866). John Macdonald was known as the 'Apostle of the North' for his passionate preaching.

p. 268   *'Martin Martin's early account ...'* A Late Voyage to St Kilda.

p. 269   *'If this island is not the Utopia ...'* John MacCulloch, *The Highlands and Western Islands.* Also useful is *Rewriting St Kilda: New Views on Old Ideas*, edited by Bob Chambers.

p. 269   *'synecdoches of the human condition ...'* Esquire magazine, 2013.

p. 270   *'Nothing in Captain Cook's voyages ...'* Lord Brougham is cited in *Rewriting St Kilda.*

p. 270   *'analogies of wild animals ...'* Robert Connell, *St Kilda and the St Kildians* (1888).

p. 271   *'a harsh subsistence economy ...'* Donald John Gillies' *The Truth about St Kilda* is an enthralling description; most of what has been written about St Kilda is by outsiders, while this is the work of a Hiortach.

p. 273   *'For terror is a passion ...'* Edmund Burke, *The Works of the Right Honourable Edmund Burke*, Vol. I (1801).

p. 273   *'It was enough to prompt ...'* Sir Thomas Dyke Acland later named his yacht *St Kilda*, and by a strange quirk it bequeathed its name to a beach in Melbourne, Australia. Internet searches for St Kilda bring up this popular resort: 'Prepare to play in St Kilda, where you can kick up your heels by the seashore, by the stage at live music venues or on the whirligigs at Luna Park.'

p. 276   '*Religion was the vital* . . .' From the introduction to the Islands Book Trust's *The Decline and Fall of St Kilda*.

p. 276   '*Film footage from the early* . . .' Seallam!, Harris, has an excellent collection of audiovisual material, including this footage and the queen's visit to the island with a young Prince Edward.

p. 281   '*Deep in the earth* . . .' See a summary in *The Outer Hebrides: A Landscape Fashioned by Geology* by Kathryn Goodenough and Jon Merritt (Scottish Natural Heritage, 2011). Also, *A Habitable Land* by J. M. Boyd.

p. 289   '*Across this part of the Atlantic* . . .' Long suspected, information about SOSUS was only declassified in 1991.

p. 289   '*The Gulf Stream brings* . . .' For more information, see Callum Roberts' riveting *The Ocean of Life*. Also worth visiting is Oban's Ocean Explorer Centre.

p. 301   '*On the pilgrimage route* . . .' William James, *The Varieties of Religious Experience*, Longman, 1902.

p. 303   '*In the phrase of* . . .' I am indebted to the Irish translator and poet Aodán Mac Póilin for a wonderful evening in Uig, in which he mentioned this lovely phrase from the poem 'Thuaidh'.

Select Bibliography

Adomnán, *Life of St Columba*, 1995, Penguin

Anderson, Benedict, *Imagined Communities: Reflections on the Origins and Spread of Nationalism*, 2006, Verso

Andrews, Malcolm, *In Search of the Picturesque*, 1989, Stanford University Press

Arnold, Matthew, *On the Study of Celtic Literature*, 1866

Ascherson, Neal, *Stone Voices*, 2003, Granta

Bate, Jonathan, *The Song of the Earth*, 2000, Picador

Bennett, Julia, 'Gifted Places: The Inalienable Nature of Belonging in Place', *Environment and Planning D: Society and Space*, 2014, Vol. 32, no. 4

Boswell, James, *The Journal of a Tour to the Hebrides*, 1785; Penguin, 1984

Botting, Douglas, *The Saga of Ring of Bright Water: The Enigma of Gavin Maxwell*, 2004, Neil Wilson Publishing

Bowker, Gordon, *George Orwell*, 2003, Little Brown

Boyd J. M. and Boyd I. L., *A Habitable Land*, 1996, Birlinn

Bradley, Ian, *Celtic Christianity: Making Myths and Chasing Dreams*, 1999, Edinburgh University Press

Bradley, Ian, *Columba: Pilgrim and Penitent*, 1996, Wild Goose Publications

Buchanan, Joni, *The Lewis Land Struggle: Na Gaisgich*, 1996, Acair

Burke, Edmund, *A Philosophical Enquiry into the Origin of Our Ideas of the Sublime and Beautiful*, 1757

Campbell, John L., and Hall, Trevor H., *Strange Things*, 1968, Routledge & Kegan Paul

Carmichael, Alexander, *Carmina Gadelica*, Vols I and II, 2007, Forgotten Books

Carruthers, Gerard, ed. *English Romanticism and the Celtic World*, 2010, Cambridge University Press

Chambers, Bob, ed., *Rewriting St Kilda*, 2010, Islands Book Trust

Chapman, Malcolm, *The Gaelic Vision in Scottish Culture*, 1978, Croom Helm

Colley Linda, *Britons: Forging the Nation: 1707–1837*, 1992, Yale University Press

Colley, Linda, *Acts of Union and Disunion*, 2014, Profile

Colls, Robert, *Orwell: English Radical*, 2013, Oxford University Press

Conrad, Peter, *Islands: A Trip Through Time and Space*, 2009, Thames & Hudson

Cooper, Derek, *Hebridean Connection*, 1991, Fontana

Cooper, Derek, *The Road to the Isles*, 1979, Chambers

Crichton Smith, Iain, *New Collected Poems*, 2011, Carcanet

Crichton Smith, Iain, *Towards the Human*, 1986, Saltire Society

Cunliffe, Barry, *Facing the Ocean: The Atlantic and Its Peoples 8000 BC to AD 1500*, 2001, Oxford University Press

Curley, Thomas M., *Samuel Johnson, the Ossian Fraud and the Celtic Revival in Great Britain and Ireland*, 2014, Cambridge University Press

Davidson, Peter, *The Idea of North*, 2005, Reaktion

Defoe, Daniel, *A Tour Thro' the Whole Island of Great Britain*, 1724–7

Devine, T. M., *Clanship to Crofters' War: The Social Transformation of the Scottish Highlands*, 2013, Manchester University Press

Devine, T. M., *The Scottish Nation: 1700–2007*, 2006, Penguin

Devine, T. M., *To the Ends of the Earth: Scotland's Global Diaspora, 1750–2010*, 2011, Penguin

Duffy, Christopher, *The '45: Bonnie Prince Charlie and the Untold Story of the Jacobite Rising*, 2007, Weidenfeld and Nicolson

Evans, Gareth, and Robson, Di, ed., *Towards Re-Enchantment*, 2010, Artevents

Ferguson, Ron, *George MacLeod: Founder of the Iona Community*, 2004, Wild Goose Publications

Fraser Darling, Frank, *Island Years, Island Farm*, 2011, Little Toller Books

Fussell, Paul, *Abroad: British Literary Traveling Between the Wars*, 1982, Oxford University Press

Gillies, Donald John, *The Truth about St Kilda: An Islander's Memoir*, 2010, John Donald

Gordon Cummings, C. F., *In the Hebrides*, 1883

Grace, Richard J., *Opium and Empire: The Lives and Careers of William Jardine and James Matheson*, 2014, McGill-Queens University Press

Harrison, David, *When Languages Die*, Oxford University Press, 2007

Harvie, Christopher, *A Floating Commonwealth*, 2008, Oxford University Press

Hassan, Gerry, *Caledonia Dreaming: The Quest for a Different Scotland*, Luath Press, 2014

Haswell-Smith, Hamish, *The Scottish Islands*, 1996, Canongate

Hunter, James, 'Rights-Based Land Reform in Scotland: Making the Case in Light of International Experience', discussion paper for Community Land Scotland, February 2014

Hunter, James, *The Making of the Crofting Community*, 2000, John Donald Publishers

Hunter, James, *The Other Side of Sorrow*, 2014, Birlinn

Hutchinson, Roger, *Father Allan: The Life and Legacy of a Hebridean Priest*, 2010, Birlinn

Hutchinson, Roger, *The Soap Man: Lewis, Harris and Lord Leverhulme*, Birlinn, 2003

Islands Book Trust, *Island Emigrants*, 2010, Islands Book Trust

Islands Book Trust, *The Decline and Fall of St Kilda*, 2006, Islands Book Trust

Jamie, Kathleen, *Findings*, 2005, Sort of Books

Jamie, Kathleen, *Sightlines*, 2012, Sort of Books

Johnson, Samuel, *A Journey to the Western Islands of Scotland*, 1775; Penguin, 1984

Kearney, Hugh, *The British Isles: A History of Four Nations*, 2012, Cambridge University Press

Kenny, Colum, *Molaise: Abbot of Leighlin and Hermit of Holy Island*, 1998, Morrigan

Kenny, Michael, *The Politics of English Nationhood*, 2014, Oxford University Press

Lawrence, D. H., *The Man Who Loved Islands*, available free at http://riverbendnelligen.com/themanwholovedislands.html

Lewis, Brian, *So Clean: Lord Leverhulme, Soap and Civilization*, 2008, Manchester University Press

Linklater, Andro, *Compton Mackenzie: A Life*, 1987, Chatto & Windus

Linklater, Andro, *Owning the Earth: The Transforming History of Land Ownership*, 2014, Bloomsbury

Lippard, Lucy, *The Lure of the Local: Sense of Place in a Multi-centered Society*, 2007, The New Press

Lorne Campbell, John, *A Very Civil People: Hebridean Folk, History and Tradition*, 2014, Birlinn

Love, John A., *Rum: A Landscape Without Figures*, 2001, Birlinn

Lynch, Michael, ed., *Jacobitism and the '45*, 1995, Historical Association Committee for Scotland and the Historical Association

MacCormick, John, *The Flag in the Wind*, 1955; Birlinn, 2008

MacCulloch, John, *The Highlands and Western Islands*, 1824

MacDiarmid, Hugh, *The Islands of Scotland*, 1939, Batsford

Macdonald, Fiona, *Island Voices*, 1992, Canongate

Macdonald, Fraser, 'St Kilda and the Sublime', *Cultural Geographies*, 2001, Vol. 8

Macfarlane, Robert, *The Old Ways: A Journey on Foot*, 2013, Penguin

Macfarlane, Robert, *Wild Places*, 2008, Granta

Mackenzie, A. Fiona D., 'Re-claiming Place: The Millennium Forest, Borgie, North Sutherland, Scotland', *Environment and Planning D: Society and Space*, 2001, Vol. 20, no. 5

Mackenzie, Compton, *Whisky Galore*, 1947, Penguin

Maclean, Charlie, *Islands on the Edge of the World*, 1972; Canongate, 1992

MacLean, Malcolm, and Carrell, Christopher, ed., *As an Fhearann: From the Land*, 1986, Mainstream Publishing

Macleod, John, *When I Heard the Bell: The Loss of the Iolaire*, 2010, Birlinn

MacNeice, Louis, *I Crossed the Minch*, 2007, Polygon

Macpherson, James, *Fragments of Ancient Poetry Collected in the Highlands of Scotland and Translated from the Gaelic or Erse Language*, 1760

Macpherson, James, *The Works of Ossian*, 1765

Magnusson, Magnus, *Rum: Nature's Island*, 1997, Luath Press

Marr, Andrew, *The Battle for Scotland*, 2013, Penguin

Martin, Martin, *A Late Voyage to St Kilda*, 1698

Maxwell, Gavin, *Ring of Bright Water*, 1960; Little Toller Books, 2009

McIntosh, Alastair, *Soil and Soul: People Versus Corporate Power*, 2009, Aurum Press

Meehan, Bernard, *The Book of Kells: An Illustrated Introduction to the Manuscript in Trinity College Dublin*, 2012, Thames & Hudson

Meek, Donald, *The Quest for Celtic Christianity*, 2000, Handsel Press

Monod, Paul; Pittock, Murray; Szechi, Daniel, ed., *Loyalty and Identity: Jacobitism at Home and Abroad*, 2010, Palgrave Macmillan

Motion, Andrew, *Keats*, 1997, Faber & Faber

Murphy, Joseph, 'From Place to Exile', *Transactions of the Institute of British Geographers*, 2011

Murphy, Joseph, *At the Edge: Walking the Atlantic Coast of Ireland and Scotland*, 2009, Sandstone Press

Murray, John, *Reading the Gaelic Landscape: Leughadh Aghaidh na Tìre*, 2014, Whittles Publishing

Myers, Alan, and Forsythe, Robert, *W. H. Auden: Pennine Poet*, 1999, North Pennines Heritage Trust

Newton, Malcolm, *Warriors of the Word*, 2009, Birlinn

Nicolson, Adam, *Sea Room: An Island Life*, 2001, HarperCollins

Nield, Ted, *Underlands: A Journey Through Britain's Lost Landscape*, 2014, Granta

Oppenheim, Janet, *The Other World: Spiritualism and Psychical Research: 1850–1914*, 1988, Cambridge University Press

Orwell, George, *George Orwell: A Life in Letters*, 2011, Penguin Classics

Orwell, George, *Nineteen Eighty-Four*, 1949; Penguin, 2004

Orwell, George, *The Collected Essays: Journalism and Letters of George Orwell*, ed. Sonia Orwell and Ian Angus, Vol. 4, *In Front of Your Nose: 1945–50*, 1970, Penguin

Pittock, Murray, *Celtic Identity and the British Image*, 1999, Manchester University Press

Pittock, Murray, *Jacobitism*, 1998, Palgrave Macmillan

Pittock, Murray, *The Myth of the Jacobite Clans*, 2009, Edinburgh University Press

Pittock, Murray, *The Road to Independence: Scotland in the Balance*, 2014, Reaktion

Prebble, John, *The Highland Clearances*, 1963, Penguin

Renan, Ernest, *Qu'est-ce qu'une nation?* (*What is a Nation?*), 1882; Presses-Pocket, 1992

Richards, Eric, *Debating the Clearances*, 2007, Edinburgh University Press

Riding, Christine, and Johns, Richard, *Turner and the Sea*, 2014, Thames & Hudson

Roberts, Callum, *The Ocean of Life: The Fate of Man and the Sea*, 2013, Allen Lane

Said, Edward, *Culture and Imperialism*, 1993, Alfred A. Knopf

Scott, Alastair, *Eccentric Wealth: The Bulloughs of Rum*, 2011, Birlinn

Scottish Book Trust, ed., *The Spirit of Jura*, 2009, Polygon

Seton, George, *St Kilda*, 1878; Birlinn, 2012

Solnit, Rebecca, *A Book of Migrations*, 2011, Verso

Solnit, Rebecca, *The Faraway Nearby*, 2013, Granta

Stafford, Fiona, *Sublime Savage: James Macpherson and the Poems of Ossian*, 1988, Edinburgh University Press

Steel, Tom, *The Life and Death of St Kilda*, 1975; Harper Press, 2011

Thomson, Derick S., *The Gaelic Sources of Macpherson's 'Ossian'*, 1952, Aberdeen University Studies Series, No. 130

Trevor Roper, Hugh, *The Invention of Scotland: Myth and History*, 2008, Yale University Press

Wightman, Andy, *The Poor Had No Lawyers: Who Owns Scotland (And How They Got It)*, 2013, Birlinn

Womack, Peter, *Improvement and Romance: Constructing the Myth of the Highlands*, 1989, Macmillan

Acknowledgements

This is a hybrid book, part curation, part investigation; it weaves together narratives which are personal, those which are very particular to the Hebrides, and those at the centre of political life in London and Edinburgh. Inevitably, the journeying has been complex, heading into many byways. A friend aptly advised early in the process that I see Michael Powell's film *I Know Where I'm Going!* While I could never match the elegance and glamour of Wendy Hiller as she set out on the night train from London in her satin nightgown, on damp nights in my tent the comparison brought a wry smile. The truth of course is that I didn't know where I was going (apart from north-west), and that was the point.

I set myself a route and then stumbled over the stories which helped me make sense of the place and its place in the history of our nations. At every turn, my gratitude is to the guides I found who generously offered their knowledge, time, insight and humour, despite on occasions being uncertain as to where I was heading. In particular they include Stuart Murray, Malkie Maclean, Agnes and Frank Rennie. All of them offered warm hospitality and long conversations. Finlay and Norma Macleod, John Randall and Bill Lawson kindly helped with enquiries.

Amongst many other things, they helped me navigate the difficulties of Gaelic spelling (beware the Ordnance Survey). I owe Angus Campbell a great deal for kindly allowing me to join him on the trip to the Flannan Isles and for answering questions; and thanks to Ruari Beaton for a bone-shaking tour of the Sound of Harris in a rib. In addition, there were helpful conversations with Neil Buchanan, Joanna Anderson, Molly and John Harvey, John Macleod, Brian and Joan Wilson, the Harris Tweed Association, and early in my research Pat Kane, Richard Holloway and Gerry Hassan, among others, offered some vital pointers to the extraordinary story that is Scotland's history in the Union.

The photographer Murdo Macleod I met as a colleague for the *Guardian* in 1996 while following a story on Holy Isle. When I asked for help twelve years later, he emailed a long list of contacts. He also kindly let me use two of his wonderful photos. I owe him a big debt. I am grateful to Alastair McIntosh and his wife Varene for their hospitality and conversation.

I am grateful to those I shared suppers with in hostels, those I chatted to in the campsites, those I met on the road. Sometimes I knew their names, sometimes not, but we shared a love of these landscapes. Thanks to my kayaking instructor, who hauled me back to Castlebay in a brisk wind after a blissful day floating around seaweed towards Vatersay. Thanks to the elderly gentleman who gave me a dance at the ceilidh in Castlebay's hotel.

I owe great thanks to my mother for two things: a birthday gift which helped ease the cost of the research, and managing to endure all my childhood holidays in the Highlands with such fortitude. I am more than aware of the struggle it must have entailed to keep us all fed and dry in that tiny croft, and my memories are all of her humour and imagination in keeping us entertained. My father left me this legacy of a compass point, north-west, an heiress to an old tradition. I am also grateful to my four brothers and sisters for the adventures we once shared in Amat.

This book owes much to friendship; in particular Brigit Connolly, Professor John Tomaney, James Mariott and Mark Vernon, all of whom spurred me on with suggestions of books, ideas and encouragement. John Tomaney's thought-provoking seminar at UCL in July 2014 on local belonging brought together a wonderful range of thinkers and led me to Joseph Murphy, another geographer (University of Glasgow), who has shared the fascination – he walked 1,200 miles along the Irish and Scottish Atlantic coasts – and generously suggested useful articles. Tomaney, Marriott and Murphy kindly found the time for a very careful reading of the draft.

I owe a great debt to my aunt, Barbara Bender, the distinguished archaeologist and anthropologist, whose understanding of landscape and place have always been a great inspiration to me. Both she and her partner John Torrance commented on a draft, with many insightful points and vital corrections.

I am grateful for very useful conversations: with Robert Crawford Smith on Hegel; with Ted Nield on geology; with Ian Jack on Scottish history (which delightfully culminated in an email exchange as to which were our preferred weapons in 1746, broadswords or muskets); with Gerry Hassan for arranging some wonderfully interesting conversations in Glasgow and Ullapool in the exciting autumn of 2014, with, among others, Fintan O'Toole, David Torrance, Adam Tompkin, Kathleen Jamie, Susan Stewart, James Hunter and Douglas and Isabel Fraser. Good friends Libby Brooks and Rinchen Khandro have on occasions offered a bed for the night, cups of tea and a chat. My thanks to James Hunter for coming into Inverness one wintry morning to talk; to Malcolm Andrews for discussing Turner,

Romanticism and travel; to Ian Bradley for discussing Celtic Christianity; to Guðmantur Thórarinsson for discussions on the Lewis chessmen; to my former *Guardian* colleague Richard Norton Taylor for introducing me to Admiral Lord West; to Irving Finkel for introducing me to the Lewis chessmen; to Neil MacGregor for his encouragement and enthusiasm; to Richard Tomlin for his photo of Holy Isle; to Rob Humphrey (author of the excellent *Rough Guide to the Highlands and Islands*), who lent copious books, maps and pamphlets, and over tea in the British Library would offer ideas, suggestions and interrogate half-baked theories. Few interlocutors have been as wise and thoughtful as David McKie, a former *Guardian* colleague.

In the Hebrides I appreciated many of the ways in which history is remembered and honoured, but two instances stand out. The Gatliff Trust runs three hostels in South Uist, Berneray and Harris. In all three I found a bed, a well-equipped kitchen, a warm stove and an honesty box for the modest payment; all are old crofts beautifully restored in extraordinary places. The second was the Cleadale Crofting Museum at Croft No. 6 on Eigg described in Chapter 5. A share of the royalties goes to both. (Donations are welcomed by the Gatliff Hebridean Hostels Trust, 30 Francis Street, Stornoway, Western Isles, HS1 2ND; the Cleadale Crofting Museum, Commun Eachdraidh Eige, Eigg Primary School, Isle of Eigg PH42 4RL.)

Book writing is a lonely business, which makes the support of an agent and editor invaluable. I have been very lucky in my former agent Natasha Fairweather and my present agent Sarah Chalfant; their expertise and wise advice has been immensely appreciated. My editor at Granta, Bella Lacey, has been a delight to work with and full of enthusiasm for the book she inherited from her predecessor, the wonderful Sara Holloway. I am indebted to a keen-eyed copyeditor, Daphne Tagg.

Many of the journeys I took alone, but on some of them I had excellent company. My son Matt joined me in Iona, Eigg and Rum; the family joined me on Islay and Jura; Jock, Charlotte, Helena and Jamie were with us on Arran's Holy Isle; Brigit managed to get away for two days to Barra, and Fran Panetta joined me for a week in Lewis. My daughter Ellie joined me on the journey back to London. With many of them I shared noodles, cocoa and, with a few of them, the odd tipple of whisky. Lastly my thanks to Luke for his unwavering faith in me and to Simon, who sent me on my way with the warmest sleeping bag ever invented and whose vicarious pleasure in the texts and photos recording my astonishingly beautiful journeys is testimony to his great generosity of heart.

On my travels and since, I have often been asked where I stand on Scottish independence. 'Torn' would be the only way to describe my sympathy for a nation deciding its own destiny and finding in the quest for nationhood a solidarity, sense of purpose and political engagement which has eluded Britain over much of the last generation. Yet at the same time I am, for better or worse, British, and believe that identity would be impoverished in countless ways by Scottish independence – this book is a bid to surface this issue. The real challenge that lies ahead is for England, to reimagine itself and to move finally beyond its histories of empire and domination of Celtic neighbours, to develop new political structures to share this multinational archipelago.

At night, as I settle into bed with the hum of London's traffic, a memory sometimes comes to me of the stacks of St Kilda and Flannan and the roar of the Atlantic swell crashing on the rocks. The scream of the gannets as they circle in the air overhead. The long swift glide of the Manx shearwater over the grey water as they slowly dip and raise their slim, elegant wings. On the shore at Calanais on Lewis, a distant dog barks and the tide laps against the seaweed-covered rocks. 'The random glitter of the sun and the wind', in the words of the poet Iain Crichton Smith. My world has become more spacious and enchanted than I could ever have imagined.

Permissions

All possible care has been taken to trace the rights holders and secure permission for the texts quoted in this book. If there are any omissions, credits can be added in future editions following a request in writing to the publisher. Grateful acknowledgement is made for permission to reproduce lines of poetry or prose excerpts.

Quotation from 1984 Quebec speech by Saul Bellow. Copyright © Saul Bellow 1984, by kind permission of The Wylie Agency (UK) Limited

Lines from 'Aberdeen' by Iain Crichton Smith, from *New Collected Poems* (Carcanet, 2011); extracts from *Towards the Human* by Iain Crichton Smith, (Saltire Society, 1986). By kind permission of Carcanet Press Limited.

Excerpt from *Lanark: A Life in Four Books* by Alasdair Gray, first published in Great Britain by Canongate Books Ltd, 14 High Street, Edinburgh, EH1 1TE

Excerpts from *The Strings are False: An Unfinished Autobiography* by Louis MacNeice (Faber and Faber, 1965); *I Crossed the Minch* by Louis MacNeice (Reprinted by Birlinn, 2007) and lines from 'The Hebrides' from *Collected Poems*, (Faber & Faber, 2007).

Copyright © The Estate of Louis MacNeice, by kind permission of David Higham Associates.

Excerpt from *Ring of Bright Water* by Gavin Maxwell (reprinted by Little Toller Books, 2009) by kind permission of The Marsh Agency on behalf of Gavin Maxwell Enterprises Ltd.

Excerpts from *The Quest for Celtic Christianity* by Donald E. Meek, (Handsel Press, 2000) by kind permission of the publishers.

Excerpts from *George Orwell: A Life in Letters*. Copyright © George Orwell. Compilation copyright © The Estate of the late Sonia Maxwell Orwell 2010. Introduction and Notes copyright © Peter Davison 2010. All rights reserved.

Excerpts from *Nineteen Eighty-Four* by George Orwell. Copyright © George Orwell, 1948. Reprinted by permission of Bill Hamilton as the Literary Executor of the Estate of the Late Sonia Brownell Orwell. For permission in the US, copyright ©1949 by Houghton Mifflin Harcourt Publishing Company, renewed 1977 by Sonia Brownell Orwell. Reprinted by permission of Houghton Mifflin Harcourt Publishing Company. All rights reserved.

Excerpts from *The Collected Essays, Journalism and Letters of George Orwell, Volume IV: In Front of Your Nose, 1945–50*. Copyright © 1968 by Sonia Brownell Orwell and renewed 1996 by Mark Hamilton. Reprinted by permission of Houghton Mifflin Harcourt Publishing Company. All rights reserved.

Illustration Credits

Thanks to Richard Tomlin for his image of Holy Isle; to Murdo Macleod for his images of Barnhill and St Kilda. The image of George Orwell and Richard Blair is by Vernon Richards; the Burmese crucifixion is from the album of George Bullough. The Queen, Lewis chesspiece © National Museums of Scotland.

All remaining photographs are by the author.

Index

Numbers in *italics* refer to illustrations.